International African Library 22
General Editors: J. D. Y. Peel, David Parkin and Colin Murray

SONGS OF THE WOMEN MIGRANTS

The *International African Library* is a major monograph series from the International African Institute and complements its quarterly periodical *Africa*, the premier journal in the field of African studies. Theoretically informed ethnographies, studies of social relations 'on the ground' which are sensitive to local cultural forms, have long been central to the Institute's publications programme. The *IAL* maintains this strength but extends it into new areas of contemporary concern, both practical and intellectual. It includes works focused on problems of development, especially on the linkages between the local and national levels of society; studies along the interface between the social and environmental sciences; and historical studies, especially those of a social, cultural or interdisciplinary character.

International African Library

General Editors

J. D. Y. Peel, David Parkin *and* Colin Murray

SONGS OF THE WOMEN MIGRANTS
PERFORMANCE AND IDENTITY IN SOUTH AFRICA

DEBORAH JAMES

EDINBURGH UNIVERSITY PRESS
for the International African Institute, London

To Patrick, Ben and Caitlin.
And in fond memory of Philip Mnisi.

© Deborah James, 1999

Edinburgh University Press Ltd
22 George Square, Edinburgh

Typeset in Plantin
by Koinonia, Bury, and
printed and bound in Great Britain

A CIP record for this book is available
from the British Library

ISBN 0 7486 1304 8 (paperback)

CONTENTS

LIST OF MAPS, TABLES AND FIGURES

Maps

Tables

Figures

ACKNOWLEDGEMENTS

My interest in African music was first kindled by Andrew Tracey, whose Steel Band I joined in 1976. During a brief sojourn in Durban in 1982, I met and began to play music with Kevin Volans, whose friendship and influence have also been inspirational. My enthusiasm for African music was further kindled by contact with members of the small and supportive community of ethnomusicologists in South Africa, who would meet at the annual Ethnomusicology Symposium: Chris Ballantine, Veit Erlmann, David Coplan, Jonathan Clegg, Sibongile Khumalo, Motsumi Makhene. Subsequently I have met and benefited from the friendship and support of other students and researchers in the field, including Angela Impey, Louise Meintjies and Carol Muller.

From the anthropological side, my sources of inspiration have been, in particular, Professor David Hammond-Tooke, David Webster and Patrick Pearson; all members of the Witwatersrand University Anthropology Department when I became a student there and when I later joined the staff. In more recent years Adam Kuper gave me encouragement and support with this research. He has given generously of his time, and has combined encouraging words with astute criticism in his comments on the various drafts which lay behind the production of this final one. I cannot thank him enough for his help.

I gratefully acknowledge the financial support of various grants from the University of the Witwatersrand; the University Research Committee, the Council Grant for Human and Social Sciences, and the Mellon fund. The University's African Studies Institute, and in particular its director, Professor Charles van Onselen, offered valuable help and support. It was, indeed, two people working at the African Studies Institute who first introduced me to urban *kiba* performance: Santu Mofokeng, photographer, and Emmanuel Kgomo, researcher, who at the time were documenting this music. Thomas Nkadimeng of the Institute later worked as my interpreter. And the office space which I was loaned at the Institute enabled me during my sabbatical and during a subsequent period of leave to hide away from the responsibilities of normal life, and concentrate on the serious business of writing.

Thanks are due to Santu Mofokeng of the African Studies Institute for the use of his excellent photographic material. Laura Cloete lent me her considerable skills as a film-maker and gave up a Sunday afternoon to help me capture some of the pyrotechnics of *kiba* on video.

The librarians in the Government Publications, Church of the Province, Africana, and Geography sections of the Witwatersrand University library were extremely helpful in providing me with materials, and in showing me where to look for what I needed. The staff of the Witwatersrand University Computer Centre gave me valuable assistance in printing out various drafts. Mr Stickler of the Cartography Unit, and Mr Naidoo of Central Graphics, helped to produce some of the graphic materials.

Rob Allingham and Albert Ramaluli of Gallo Africa gave up hours of their time to have discussions with me about the South African record and popular music industry in general, and about northern Sotho music in particular. Lucky Monama of Gallo also discussed these matters with me. I am grateful to Rob for the evenings he spent recording examples of *kiba* and *harepa* music for me from his own private record collection.

I presented drafts of chapters at the following seminars and conferences, and am thankful to the people who offered comments and criticisms at these: the African Studies Institute Seminar of Witwatersrand University; the History Workshop of Witwatersrand University; the Anthropology Department Seminar of Witwatersrand University; the African Studies Seminar of Natal University, Durban; the Association for Anthropology in South Africa conference held at Rand Afrikaans University in 1991 and at University of Durban-Westville in 1992; and the Ethnomusicology Symposia held at Rhodes University in 1991 and at Natal University, Durban, in 1993. The following people read and commented on earlier drafts of chapters: Belinda Bozzoli, Peter Delius, Jim Kiernan, John Argyle, Leslie Bank, Jonathan Stadler, Sakkie Niehaus, Isabel Hofmeyr, Liz Gunner, Patrick Pearson. Particular thanks to Patrick Pearson and Isabel Hofmeyr for their many insightful suggestions and criticisms, and for undertaking the thankless task of reading the entire manuscript at the end.

I am grateful to those who did interpreting and translating work for me: Anna Madihlaba, Neo Phakathi, Kgomotso Masemola, Thomas Nkadimeng, Philip Mbiba, and Sam Nchabeleng. In particular, I owe Philip Mnisi a debt of gratitude I can never repay. He did not act simply as an interpreter. His empathetic and appealing manner endeared people to him in a quite remarkable way. Without him, I could never have made the kind of meaningful contact which made this project possible. He was murdered on 4 July 1992; yet another victim of the senseless violence which afflicts the lives of black people in South Africa. His killers have never been found or brought to justice. Although Philip's death makes the debt I owe truly unrepayable, I hope that the completion of this book with which he helped me will stand as some kind of testimony to his abilities.

I wish to thank a number of people for their hospitality to me during the period of my fieldwork: the staff and those I met and talked to at Jane Furse hospital, where I stayed during 1989, and in particular Belinda and Johann Rissik; the Franciscan sisters Eilish and Rena at Apel, Sekhukhune, for their hospitality and kindness in having me to stay during my fieldwork in 1991; and the next-door clinic sister Winnie who put me up for the night.

One of my major debts is, of course, the one I owe to the informants who participated with such enthusiasm in teaching me what I know about *kiba*. I hope that, in eventually publicising this knowledge beyond the confines of academe, I will in some way be able to fulfil my obligations to the men and women of *kiba*.

Far greater than any of those listed above, but perhaps less easily quantifiable, is my indebtedness to family members – consanguines, affines, and those included in the domestic sphere by virtue of 'fictive kinship'. Margaret Tembo, as well as being a trusted employee who has looked after my children Ben and Caitlin, has been like a family member to me (and I am aware of all the caveats which direct one away from such a characterisation). As a perennial student who eventually began to make something like a living out of academic life, I am grateful to my parents, David and Jenepher James, for financial and moral support and, in more recent years, for extensive help with child-care while I was doing research or writing. My parents-in-law, Norman and Lynette Pearson, have also given generously of their support and of their time as babysitters. But greatest of all is the debt I owe to my husband, Patrick Pearson, who followed up the initial enthusiasm he imparted to me about studying anthropology in the first place by supporting me wholeheartedly during the researching and writing of this book. His backing of the project went far beyond the moral and the emotional. While I spent large chunks of every weekend attending Sunday performances in Alexandra or Tembisa, or interviewing men and women in their rooms in suburban backyards or in their township shacks; while I travelled to Lebowa for periods of fieldwork lasting for weeks at a time; or later when I used days of what should have been family leisure time to write up my research; Patrick was holding the proverbial fort and putting in hours of child-care.

It remains for me to make the usual disclaimer: while all of the people named above are to be thanked for their help, encouragement and support, none beside myself can be held responsible for the opinions expressed or conclusions arrived at.

INTRODUCTION

On Sunday 17 March 1990, as on other Sundays, the piece of open ground adjoining the Number 1 Men's Hostel in Alexandra township near Johannesburg was a focus of intense musical activity. It began in a fairly desultory way during the late morning, but gradually built up to a fever pitch of excitement by the late afternoon. Sometime around midday, a shrill whistle sounded. Individual men dressed in everyday clothes dislodged themselves from groups of drinkers sitting around in makeshift bars on tins under tattered plastic shading, and grouped themselves on one side of the drummers who began to play a set of hide-covered drums. In a rhythmical sequence, each man started to blow a note on a single aluminium pipe hanging around his neck from a piece of thong. The tune produced by these combined pipe-sounds was the regimental song *monti*, used on this occasion as on most others to provide an introduction to the day's dancing. Still continuing to blow their pipes, the men danced outwards from their grouped position to form a circle around the drummers. These men were the *dinaka* (pipes/pipe-players) of the group *SK Alex*.

As the drumming and dancing progressed through a series of different rhythms, a small crowd gathered. At the end of the first performance, the men retreated into the hostel to change into their full dancing gear, consisting of authentic Scottish kilts, white boxer shorts, white tennis shoes, white lounge shirts, seedpod leg-rattles and headdresses with ostrich feathers and goats' horns. During their next performance the crowd gathering to watch increased substantially in size and in enthusiasm until it was pressing inwards, threatening to engulf the dancers in its midst. It was kept at bay, with difficulty, by group members called 'policemen' wielding whips.

After the final dance in this session, the men danced a formal retreat from the makeshift arena, leaving only their three drummers in place. They were replaced by a group of about ten women who danced the circle back into shape and began to sing *o tla loiwa ke batho* (people will bewitch you). The women's clothing was more eye-catching and colourful than the Scottish-style garb of their male counterparts, although their dancing was somewhat more sedate. Strikingly uniform in colour and style, their dress consisted of layers of cloths tied around the waist, and Victorian-style cotton smocks

Figure I.1 Men's *kiba*: The regimental song *Monti*. Alexandra township (Photo: Santu Mofokeng)

with copious gathers and elaborate embroidery. Beaded bands adorned their waists, necks and arms, and around their ankles they wore leg-rattles made of plastic milk-bottle containers.

In a different part of the open ground, the sound of drumming announced the onset of dancing by a different set of *dinaka*: that of *Maaparankwe SK Land* (those of the royal leopard-skin clothing, Sekhukhuneland). It attracted a new audience, which later swelled to include some of the spectators of the first dance session. These dancers, too, were replaced in due course by their female partners wearing brightly and distinctively coloured uniforms.

Each of these groups of *dinaka* with its female partner *koša* group represented a particular home area in the Northern Province[1] whose inhab-itants were currently residing in a specific area of the Reef. *SK Alex*, for example, consisted of dancers from the rural region of *Sekhukhune* residing in Alexandra township, and equivalent groups in Alexandra represented the regions of *Matlala*, *Moletši*, *Molepo* and others: areas of rural origin which were announced to the township audience by names painted on the side of each group's drums.

The dances of *dinaka* and *koša* are the men's and women's versions respectively of a broader musical style or genre known as *kiba* (*go kiba*, to

Figure I.2 Women's *kiba*: *ditšhweu tša malebogo* performing at Funda Centre, Soweto (Photo: Santu Mofokeng)

beat time, to stamp) which is played widely on the Reef and in surrounding areas of industrial and domestic employment. In the compounds of mines, power stations and factories, fostered by management as a form of competitive recreation, it has been an exclusively male genre since the onset of male labour migration to the Reef. It was only in the last two decades, and in the less restrictive environment of the townships, that it acquired a female version. Women's *kiba* developed its polished form among female migrants in the towns, and is a transformation of originally rural songs. It has subsequently spread back to rural villages of the Northern Province, where it is known mostly as *lebowa*.

In its rural guise, as *lebowa*, the women's genre was pressed into service by local elites and politicians to glorify the black homeland of the same name. The homeland, officially established to house all speakers of northern Sotho or sePedi, and endowed with self-governing status in fulfilment of *apartheid* policy, had its own parliament, 'chief minister', and a series of ministries staffed by platoons of local bureaucrats. When I was conducting fieldwork in the Nebo district of Lebowa during 1983, it was commonplace that on state-sponsored occasions, from the opening of the Lebowa parliament right down to local events like the welcoming of a new headmaster, the presence of suited bureaucrats was always matched by that of *kiba* groups of women singers in their brightly coloured smocks and headscarves, often adorned with pink plastic pot-scourers or with costume jewellery. Images of these singers were also to be found in published form: both in the popular press and adorning the front pages of magazines of local or national government propaganda. I myself was made an honorary member of *Dipalela tlala* (defeaters of hunger), the local *lebowa* dance group in the village where I was staying, and attired in their distinctive uniform I accompanied them to perform at several singing engagements.

As a rurally based researcher, it was apparent to me that the only male equivalent to this widespread and popular female activity was football. This equivalence was confirmed for me when I went into a young woman's house and saw displayed on the wall two team photographs, in uniform. One showed her together with her dance team, and the other depicted her brother together with his football team. Older men, absent as migrants for most of the year and returning only at weekends, were active neither in sporting nor in musical events.

Some of my older co-singers in Nebo indicated, however, that their husbands and brothers had been involved in weekend performances of *kiba* during the period before they had moved to the Lebowa homeland in the 1950s–1960s, when they were working and living as labour tenants on surrounding white-owned farms. They explained that the new women's fashion *lebowa* which they had learned by imitation from women's groups in the neighbouring magisterial district of Sekhukhune, and which they were currently performing alongside some older women's styles, was distinct from these older styles in being the women's equivalent of *kiba*, formerly the preserve of men.

But men's *kiba* was nowhere to be seen in the countryside. It was only later, in 1990, that I saw it being performed in the context in which it had long become naturalised: on the dusty wastegrounds of Reef townships, played and danced by male migrants from a variety of areas in the Northern Province. It was at this stage, also on a township dancing-ground, that I had my first sight of the *kiba* singing and dancing of migrant women. During the whole of 1990, I became a habitual visitor at the weekly Sunday practices in Alexandra, and at many weekend performances both in Alexandra and at rural venues. Accompanied by Malete Thomas Nkadimeng, who helped with interviewing and translation, I spent long hours on Saturday mornings or afternoons having conversations with men and women about their lives and their music. Our discussions with men took place in Alexandra or Tembisa: in the open space near the hostel where some were living, or seated outside the shacks where others resided. Speaking to women, on the other hand, entailed visiting them in the 'servants' rooms' where most stayed in the back yards of their white employers' homes.

In March of the following year, 1991, there was an invasion of hostels in a number of Reef townships, including Alexandra, by 'the Zulus' or 'Inkatha'. More accurately, the invaders were co-ordinated groups of unemployed Zulu youths from outside the township, whose motives have not to this day been elucidated. They drove out the hostels' previous residents, including large numbers of northern Sotho-speaking migrant men from the Northern Province: *kiba*'s natural audience in Alexandra.

This invasion and occupation had the effect of sending *kiba* into a temporary exile. Dancers from Alexandra, as from other townships such as those adjoining Springs and Germiston, deprived of their informal arena beside the hostels, sought refuge by joining other groups in less strife-torn areas, or simply stopped singing for a period. The Tembisa-based group *Maaparankwe SK Land*, for example, stopped meeting on the empty ground by the Tembisa hostel, and held their weekly practices, instead, in the road outside the Tembisa house of Jan Seašane, the group leader. The Alexandra-based group *Ditšhweu tša Malebogo* could find no alternative practice ground, and was able to meet during the later part of 1991 only for the monthly meeting of the *mohodišano* (rotating credit association) to which most of its singers belonged in parallel with their membership of the singing group.

This partial hiatus in urban performance prompted my more detailed investigation of *kiba*'s rural roots. During 1991 I visited villages in the Sekhukhune district of Lebowa, where, aided by the interviewing skills of student and local resident Philip Mnisi, I began to find out more about the rural performance of women's *kiba*. We visited women's groups in the villages of GaNkwana and Mphanama, and conducted extensive discussions with the members of the group *Dithabaneng*, in Nchabeleng village. We also discovered that there was a revival of men's *kiba* in the village, with older retired migrants teaching young men – mostly politically active 'comrades' who had previously played football in their leisure time – to play and dance. Trying to establish the broader musical context of *kiba* music, we visited the well-known *harepa* (German autoharp) player Johannes Mokgwadi at his home in GaMasha, and attended a performance by him at the wedding of Aaron Motswaledi, a prominent ANC activist in the area who by the time of writing had become ANC member of parliament in the Northern Province.

During the years between 1989, when I began the research for this book, and 1992, when I started to write it up in earnest, I developed a three-pronged methodology. One aspect of this corresponded with what anthropologists usually term 'participant observation': long hours observing *kiba* performance, and asking participants and audience about the nature and significance of various aspects of the music and dance. The second entailed discussions with – and often heated arguments between – individual performers or groups of performers about the significance of the music and lyrics. The third involved discussions, sometimes recorded and subsequently transcribed, with particular informants. These were aimed at collecting life-histories, but were focused specifically on people's lives as workers and as musicians, and on areas of overlap between these two.

While conducting discussions of this kind with numerous people within the world of Northern Province migrancy, I collected details about twenty urban-based migrant women in particular. It is on the life-histories, opinions, and lyrical compositions of these women, seen against the context of information gleaned from discussions with other musicians and audience members, that the explorations and conclusions of this book are primarily based.

The years since 1992 have seen a variety of changes in the social context of *kiba* dancing. Dancers and their audience have elected for the most part to remain distant from the hostels where many previously lived, despite the uneasy truce which has brought at least a temporary halt to the conflict between hostel-dwellers and township residents. Replacing this earlier source of shelter, several men and one or two women have managed to build or rent shacks in established Alexandra yards, or in one of the sprawling shack-settlements which have sprung up on the margins of Alexandra or Tembisa. Most female dancers, however, have had to retain their temporary and uncertain foothold in the mostly meagre backyard accommodation built for domestic servants in Johannesburg suburbs, or have exchanged one such 'servant's room' for another as they moved from employer to employer in search of better working conditions.

During this exile from the world of the hostels, *kiba* dancers have continued to find spaces and opportunities, in the townships and in the countryside, to pursue their art. But *kiba* dancing can now be enjoyed, not only in the dusty streets of Alexandra and Tembisa and of these townships' adjoining shack settlements, but also on TV and on the stages of national and international music festivals. The group *Maaparankwe SK Land*, having received and responded to several invitations to play at festivals in Europe and south-east Asia, has tentatively joined the ranks of those who perform 'world music'. A new era introduces a global audience for this local genre. But, even invited into this transcendent sphere, *kiba* singers' response remains deeply divided along gender lines because of disparities in work and living conditions. Some male singers' factory employers, for example, have funded their workers and given them extended leave, while the householders who provide unskilled domestic employment to most female singers have been unable or unwilling to do either.

THE SOCIAL CONSTITUENCY OF *KIBA*

The musical family to which *kiba* belongs, and the broader family of cultural practices and beliefs in which it is situated, is characterised as *wa sesotho* (of *sesotho*) or, more recently, *wa setšo* (of origin: traditional). Applied to the class of music *mmino wa setšo* (traditional music) of which *kiba* is considered a part, the term *setšo* has been used by promoters, elites, and presenters on the radio and television. It substitutes for the older term *mmino wa sesotho* (sotho music) which is still interchanged with it on occasion. As the term gained currency, migrant performers came to view *mmino wa setšo* as an accurate description of the performance project in which they were involved. They enter *mmino wa setšo* competitions, belong to a Lebowa *mmino wa setšo* association, and wear printed T-shirts announcing their commitment to this kind of music.

What defines this category of 'traditional' things is, in part, its presumed links to a particular social constituency: a group of people which is thought of as concerning itself with things 'of origin' or 'of tradition'. Socially defined in this way, the significance of 'origin', however, broadens itself in certain contexts to incorporate members of other, opposed social categories, and even at times the whole of a projected or imagined 'nation'.

The social categories which are of most relevance in defining music are those – paired and opposed – which refer to mission Christianity and which translate into English roughly as 'Christian/traditionalist'. Historically, these categories derive their existence from the acceptance or rejection of the Lutheran mission, with its insistence on the transfer of allegiance from chiefs to the *moruti* (mission minister) and its eschewing of tribal initiation. Particularly in a heartland district like Sekhukhune which was the site of a nineteenth-century polity, this division manifested itself in extreme form, with Christians distancing themselves physically from those remaining affiliated to the chief, moving away to farms or mission stations distant from the sites of chiefly power (Delius 1983: 160–78). But even within smaller reserve areas there were pronounced rifts. Most villages were, and some remain, physically and geographically divided between Christian and non-Christian sections (Mphahlele 1971: 4; Sansom 1991–2: 397–401).

Although the rifts thus established within rural Northern Province communities were not altogether unprecedented, since those who accepted the mission way were often those who had been marginal to society or disaffected with its leaders (Pauw 1974: 427–8; Delius 1983: 112–4), these rifts became newly conceptualised around the pivotal feature of Christianity. The resulting social categories were differently named in *sotho*[2] depending on the stance of the namer. Those proud to have affiliated themselves to the Christian way called themselves *bakriste* (Christians) and termed their opposites *baheitene* (heathens). Those aligning themselves with the chiefs called themselves *baditšhaba* (those of the nation) in opposition to the derogatorily named *majakane* or *majekane* (Christians).[3] The geographical divide in many rural communities is named in similar vein: *setšhabeng* is the place of those of the nation, and *majekaneng* is the place of the Christians. The paired terms *majekane/baditšhaba* and *bakriste/baheitene*, while orienting themselves by reference to a common dividing line, thus imply opposing moral views of the division.[4]

Although these dichotomous categories remain in current use, their rigidity as concepts is applicable more when referring to cultural practices than when used to describe individuals or social groups. *Baditšhaba*, it is universally agreed, are the people who both play and listen to *mmino wa setšo* (traditional music), while *majakane* appreciate *mmino wa kereke* (church music) and a range of associated forms. It is the clarity of the division between opposing types of music, rather than the sharpness of the social division between Christians and non-Christians, which gives *mmino wa setšo* its distinctiveness as a category of music.

But where the terms *are* used to describe individuals or groups of people, these describe not so much the Christian/traditionalist divide as the class or status-group division which originally arose out of it. The *majekane* who are said to disparage *mmino wa setšo* were often early immigrants to the cities where they formed the ranks of the urbanised work force, or have remained in the country and form part of a 'respectable' middle class self-employed in small businesses, or working in education and various branches of the civil service. The *baditšhaba* from whom they distinguish themselves, rather than necessarily being adherents of 'traditional' religion, are mostly low-paid migrant workers, with strong links to a rural base which they visit frequently, to which they intend to return upon retirement from work, and which they regard as *gae* (home).

The story of a man called Lucas Sefoka shows how the performance of *mmino wa setšo* not only provided an identity to migrants belonging to the social category of *baditšhaba*, but also gave them access to the support and succour of people sharing a common rural home. He was born in 1944, in the *setšhabeng* section of Sefoka village in Sekhukhune. He attended school up to Standard 3 but, shortly after completing the first stage of initiation, he and others of his initiation regiment ran away from home to work on white farms. While working there, they remitted a small amount of money home, and in between jobs they returned home for a period to complete the last stage of initiation. After about five years of farm work Lucas Sefoka and his paternal cousin Philip Sefoka decided to go by railway bus to Pretoria to look for better-paid jobs. Although they had not informed any of their relatives in Pretoria of their intention, and were apprehensive about arriving unawaited in a place with so many people, they were fortunate to see a man of the same age-group – and from a neighbouring village – at the station. He took them to sleep in the backyard room of an old man from Sefoka village. Soon, both men had been fixed up with jobs as gardeners and with accommodation through contacts with fellow-villagers, and had been introduced to the Mamelodi branch of the *Sekhukhune kiba* players. When, a year later, Lucas left Pretoria to work in Johannesburg in a job found for him by his maternal cousin, he was transferred to the Alexandra club, *SK Alex*. After he had been disabled in an industrial accident, some relatives who were also fellow-dancers accommodated him in a room in the yard where they lived in Alexandra, and he made a small living as a fruit vendor. At the time of writing he was the leader of the Alexandra dance club *SK Alex*.[5]

Migrants achieving upward mobility sometimes switched from one of these social categories to the other and underwent a corresponding musical conversion. Although originally socialised by peers and parents into the rudiments of *kiba* performance, they ceased their involvement as they began to mix primarily with people who considered this music socially inappropriate, and thus of no aesthetic value. Some abandoned all involvement with the music. Others, though ceasing to be direct performers of *kiba*, concerned themselves with its promotion. One was a man who moved up through the ranks of the work force at his factory to become the secretary of its recreational club. His duties included the organising of competitions between local dance teams and those representing other factories or mines. Another, Piet Makola, had achieved upward mobility through the classic 'poor-boy-made-good' means of success in sport. He founded a co-ordinating body called the *Mmino wa setšo* Association. Modelled on a football league, the aim of this body was to promote competition between, and the financial rewarding and professionalisation of, *kiba* performers. Both these men, in assuming the role of patron, were indicating their aspirations to middle-class status, their social distance from the ranks of the music's performers, and hence their remoteness from the social category of *baditshaba*.

The insistence of informants that *kiba* is 'for *baditšhaba*' indicates, then, not that this cultural form is oriented towards 'traditionalists' rather than Christians, but that it generally appeals to poor migrants rather than to people of higher status.

There is a further complexity in understanding 'origin' or 'tradition' in terms of its social constituency if one considers the differences between male and female migrant performers of this music. For male migrants, the learning of *kiba* as young men at their rural homes has either been continued into adult performance if they remained within the social and economic bracket of poor and rurally based workers, or been discontinued if they move beyond this bracket. For migrant women, however, the link between the culture of girlhood and that of working adulthood is inverted, as I will explain below.

Women who have been performing rural women's 'traditional' genres since childhood are mostly from heartland reserve areas such as *Sekhukhune*. These women do not migrate, but rely on male migrant earnings for support, as Chapter 5 will demonstrate. In contrast, the migrant women on

Figure I.3 *Kiba* championships held by the *Mmino wa setšo* Association: judges and performers (Photo: Santu Mofokeng)

the Reef who currently perform *kiba* in town mostly grew up in areas – known collectively as *Leboa* (the north) – peripheral to and north of this heartland. After girlhood, their predominant culture and songs were those of school and church, as is recounted in Chapter 6, and their present-day performance of the genre represents something of a cultural revival. For these three major constituencies of *kiba* from the Northern Province – migrant men, their stay-at-home wives, and mostly unmarried migrant women – the notion of a music which invokes or is sanctioned by 'tradition' or 'origin' is very different.

This points to some fundamental discontinuities, both stylistically and in terms of social constituency, between men's and women's urban performance. Said to have been originally imported into the northern Sotho area from further north, the genre known as *kiba* has been part of male rural and urban migrant culture for as long as men from the northern Sotho rural hinterland have been travelling to the mines and factories of the Pretoria, Witwatersrand, Vereeniging (PWV) area to work as migrants. Women's performance – both rural and urban – has in contrast been included within the definition of *kiba* only since the mid-1970s. The women's version of the genre had its roots in a series of older, rural performance styles of young women, and was not merely an imitation of its male equivalent. As I will show in Chapter 3, women's *kiba* is arguably closer in style to this female

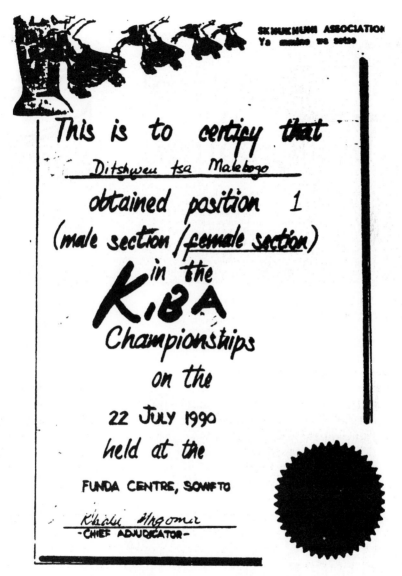

Figure I.4 *Kiba* championships: certificate awarded to members of winning group *Ditšhweu tša Malebogo*

rural culture than it is to the men's genre whose definition and whose urban performance space and context it now shares.

Whatever their differences of gender, style and social background, however, the one respect in which the performers of men's and women's *kiba* stand united also marks them off from the heterogeneous urban mass

Historical background

T he people of Lebowa are generally known as the Northern Sotho, but in reality the population consists of a variety of peoples, including some Ndebele, Tswana, Swazi, Tsonga and Venda tribes. These tribes are not related to each other and therefore have no common history.

The name Pedi or Bapedi is frequently used for the group as a whole. However, this name is not acceptable to the Northern Sotho, since Pedi refers to the Pedi kingdom, which did not include all of the Northern Sotho tribes.

Bapedi is thus not acceptable as a name for either the population or the territory. Owing to the linguistic and cultural diversity in the territory, the neutral name Lebowa was chosen, which means "the north".

The history of Lebowa can be broadly divided into the following periods:

Figure I.5 Picture of women *kiba* singers in the government-published *Informa*. (*Informa* Nov./Dec. 1989, 36 (10)

usually identified as the agents of urban musical change (Barber 1987). This is the distrust and even fear of the broader urban environment of the township or urban location and of its people which most performers and listeners claim to have. Most were careful to make clear to me the distinction between themselves and the category of fully-fledged urban residents and township-dwellers, whom they characterised as ill-mannered, drunk and violent. As part of their insistence that 'home' is in the country rather than in the socially disrupted world of the urban location, both men and women migrants performing *kiba* in town are adamant that they want their children to remain in the country, to be educated there, and if possible to find employment there.

As it emerges, the division of the social world between the categories of 'people from home' and 'people from the location', like that between *baditšhaba* and *majekane*, states things more starkly than they appear in reality. The world of the township or location – Alexandra, Tembisa, Daveyton, and others on and around the Reef (see Map 3) – in fact plays an essential role in the lives and especially in the performance schedules of these players and singers. For migrant women, living in backyard servants' rooms in white suburbia and flocking to Alexandra or Tembisa on a Sunday, these areas provide a venue for relaxation and enjoyment away from the eyes of their employers. For migrant men, the townships have provided a residential base as well as an arena for leisure. Many live in shacks, and some even in permanent township houses, in these areas, and a number resided in hostels until the violence of March 1991 drove them from these to seek refuge with relatives living in other township accommodation or with girlfriends or wives living in the backyards of white suburbia.

Being both conceptually outside of and yet physically within the township meant that social boundaries were fluid. Among the regular attenders of *kiba* performance were migrants from a wide diversity of language groups. There were also people from northern Sotho-speaking areas whose higher educational levels, economic position, and long-standing urban residence and membership of mission churches would place them firmly within the category of *majekane* and of 'people from the location'. They took a nostalgic delight in observing the performance of a genre which they once knew as children but had outgrown or moved beyond, and their frequent or occasional attendance at these weekly practices served to include them within *kiba*'s broader imagined community.

While resonating with local interpretations, an attempt to define the things and music of *setšo* by reference to a social constituency is thus more complex than it first appears. Allegedly restricted to *baditshaba* (those of the nation), *setšo* extends at times to incorporate and symbolise a nation conceived of in more modern terms, especially when used by elites both within the former homeland of Lebowa and in urban communities who identify themselves with a broader northern Sotho collectivity. In rural areas, the use of women's *kiba* by national elites within the Lebowa home-land to carry the message of a broader regional unity is clearly indicated by its other name, *lebowa*, which echoes that of the homeland itself. Official publications of the *apartheid* government made extensive use of *kiba* women's colourful uniforms to adorn and give interest to their otherwise drab appearance (see Figure I.5). In much the same way, politicians in other parts of Africa have come to identify dancing 'as a centrally important element in what they were trying to define as a new culture', perhaps even aiding in its fossilisation 'as an officially patronized part of public culture' (Vail and White 1991: 264–5).

The theme of national unity is carried through, as well, in urban performances, organised by teachers or educationalists, and associated with such events as the opening of a northern Sotho school, or the anniversary of a women's federation, in Soweto or Mamelodi.[6] Here, the 'imagined' community associated with the style not only included the population of the former homeland's eleven magisterial districts, but also extended to include an urban populace thought of as directly or indirectly associated with the rural northern Sotho-speaking areas.

The use of tradition to glorify a broader Lebowa identity, while initiated by local elites in the instances described here, cannot be understood outside the context of *apartheid*'s policy of ethnic separation. Elites within the homeland derived their position and standing in part from the existence of this policy, and their use of 'tradition' must be seen against the background of a broader manipulation, effected through many different channels, of ethnic identities by the South African *apartheid* government (Spiegel 1989).

MEDIA, URBANISATION AND MIGRANCY

To understand the significance of a music claiming to derive from 'tradition' or 'origin' within the broader context of South African society, we must then look beyond the organic links which unite performers and audience in a particular locale, and examine the interaction between the politically dispossessed and the financially or politically powerful. Unequal control over cultural expression has been evident in attempts by company management to promote the competitive performance of tribal dance as a strategy to contain the energies of a compounded labour force. It has also been manifest in the manipulation of music for financial or ideological gain by the state-controlled media and by white-owned record companies such as Gallo.

Black traditional music in South Africa, whether promoted by manage-ment, by state-owned media or by capitalist corporations, has generally been interpreted as a means of ideological control over a passive populace. Various attempts by state and capital to manipulate listeners' and audiences' tastes have been seen as a bid to deny the emergence of a permanently urbanised black population, and to promote instead the vision of a rurally rooted migrant labour force. 'Traditional', in this context, describes a variety of musics which were promoted by media and/or management during the 1950s and 1960s to bolster this vision: either syncretic forms played by rural musicians or those more thoroughly indigenous in style (Coplan 1979: 198, 206–7; Ballantine 1989: 308). The term evokes the futility of the state's pretence that black people, by the 1950s and 1960s, were still country-dwellers primarily oriented to customary ways rather than townspeople accustomed to a sophisticated city life and favouring jazz as a means of cultural expression.

From this perspective, traditional or neo-traditional music was what the state manipulated in order to implement, or at its most futile to claim an illusory success for, its policy of keeping Africans as residents of ethnic reserves rather than allowing them to become city-dwellers. But the evidence suggests that urban African identity in this period was already considerably divided, and that there was a large body of listeners – primarily migrant, domestic and industrial labourers (Coplan 1979: 207) – who did prefer to participate in rural styles, or to listen to the 'neo-traditional' instrumental and vocal jive which the media was disseminating (Hamm 1987: 354). The choice of music broadcast by the South African Broadcasting Corporation's (SABC's) ethnic radio stations was, then, at least partly dictated by the preference of listeners.[7]

This represents an acknowledgement, from an ethnomusicologist's point of view, of something to which several historians and sociologists have already drawn attention: that South African urbanisation has been an uneven rather than a relentlessly unidirectional process, and that its halting progress has been due to local and internal factors as well as to externally imposed state initiatives. It is not only the whims of *apartheid* policy, but also pre-colonial or pre-industrial cleavages within local societies, and differing degrees of internally generated resistance to proletarianisation, which have kept large sections of the work force living within the rural reserves (Bozzoli 1983: 21; Marks and Rathbone 1982b: 19; Stichter 1985: 7–16). And it was partly these uneven processes of proletarianisation and urbanisation that laid down the rudimentary outlines of the division between a class of better-off, longer-urbanised and 'respectable' people, and an underclass of poorer people, often arriving later, and sometimes from more destitute areas (Bozzoli 1991: 123).[8]

Described in the world of Northern Province migrancy in terms of religious orientation rather than in terms of length of connection with the city, this rudimentary class division corresponds roughly with the *sotho* distinction between *majekane* and *baditšhaba*. Attempts by the media to manipulate ethnicity within northern Sotho-speaking populations of the

Transvaal through the use of traditional music have targeted *baditšhaba* in particular – the more poorly-paid and rurally rooted section of the Northern Province labour force. From 1940 through to the 1960s, record companies such as Gallo and its subsidiaries, and the SABC under the guidance of Yvonne Huskisson, recorded and made largely unsuccessful attempts to disseminate *kiba* and other styles of *mmino wa setšo* (see discography). Its lack of popularity during this period is not, however, a simple indication that migrant members of the *baditšhaba* category were uninterested in *mmino wa setšo*. It points rather to the unsuitability of the genre, as a total event involving dance, music, and dramatic tableaux, to the format of recorded sound, and indicates its fittingness to a situation in which the links between performers and audience are immediate and unmediated. An individual genre, playing the same songs on a *harepa* without the dance spectacle, enjoyed greater success on record than did *kiba* itself.

By contrast, the recordings made and disseminated by Radio Lebowa and by SABC television in the late 1970s and 1980s have been more popular. This relates to the greater immediacy of television recordings, which do manage to capture something of the whole *kiba* event. It also reflects the success of the cultural revival – patronised by national and local elites as well as by the media – of which the recent emergence and development of women's *kiba* has been a part. Here, the divisiveness of apparently rigid classes or social categories is transcended in the appeal of 'traditional' music, in certain contexts, to people from both categories.

With *kiba* as with other forms of 'traditional' music played by migrants, attempts have thus been made to manipulate the genre for financial and ideological gain by a range of people, from the talent scouts and record producers of record companies, to the personnel managers of mining companies employing large numbers of Northern Province migrants and promoting the competitive performance of *kiba* as part of a strategy of control – or at least containment of the energies of – a cooped-up labour force. These interventions have left intact, in some cases even strengthened, but never diminished, the organic connection of *kiba* to its performers and audiences.

The term 'traditional', applied to music, is thus an emotive one. Critics of *apartheid*'s social engineering have used it to disparage and deny the effectiveness of state strategies in curbing the flow of urbanisation. But to those urban workers rooted in the country for whatever reason, the emotive appeal of a music which speaks of 'home' and 'origin' while enabling them to formulate an identity as migrants in town is one which cannot be denied.

The significance of Northern Province traditional music, performed in the context of migrancy, can thus be looked at in the context of debates within ethnomusicology and within studies on performance. Tradition, here, appears more flexible, less amenable to outside manipulation, and less restricted to circumscribed social groupings than some of the literature would have us believe. But tradition is invoked in very different ways by various social constituencies in the world of migrant music: by male migrants, by dependent wives, and by independent female migrants. It is the meaning of tradition for this last constituency, both within and beyond the sphere of musical performance, and the role of tradition in facilitating the construction of a specifically female migrant identity, which have been my major concern in the chapters which follow. But in order to understand the unusual way in which tradition or origin is invoked by such women, I have shown how their experience compares with that of other *kiba* performers: with migrant men on the one hand, and with the dependent wives or sisters of migrant men on the other.

The book thus begins with two chapters in which the differential exper-ience of men and women migrants is discussed, and moves on to a third in which the male and female versions of the *kiba* genre are analysed in relation to one another. Women's *kiba*, I conclude, represents a creative combin-ation of pre-existing women's and men's music: it has strong continuities with the former, but has transcended the domestic and rural preoccupations and the marginalised status of women's performance by claiming to be part of a genre which was previously the exclusive preserve of male migrants.

Migrant women's performance of this formerly male music, and their claiming of a quasi-male identity through this performance, is not an isolated instance in a life otherwise wholly female in its orientation. It is one part of a broader process of identity construction in which women use the materials of *setšo* or *sesotho*, and incorporate continuities with female rural experience, while claiming status in equivalence with men within a male-dominated world. The next four chapters explore aspects of this process, focusing particularly on migrant women's place within their rural households and families, and on the 'life-cycle' and processes of female socialisation within these families.

Perhaps flying in the face of chronological convention, the events and scenarios described in this exploration move from the present and immediate realities lived by adults, backwards to their remembered childhoods and adolescences; from their urban experiences to their rural ones. Thus, after Chapter 2 has spelt out the lives and concerns of migrant women within an urban context, Chapter 4 shows something of their sense of themselves as responsible breadwinners in the context of their rural families, acting 'as sons' ought to do. Their experiences of childhood and early socialisation, formative in the process of identity-construction but in refracted and unexpected ways, are presented only in Chapter 6. Placed here, they contrast strongly with the more orthodox and custom-bound childhood experiences of the rurally resident women singers described in Chapter 5.

I have written this account in such a way as to facilitate the continuous contrasting of one understanding of *setšo* or *sesotho* with another: the different ways in which these concepts have significance for migrant men and migrant women, and their different significances for migrant and for stay-at-home dependent women.

What Chapters 2, 4, 6 and 7 attempt to do, then, is to give some insight into the way in which the construction of identity actually proceeds. Rather than being something created 'out of thin air' or produced by an entirely random process of bricolage, the finding of a sense of self – as *sotho* – within the broader world of urban migrancy by these women is both facilitated and paralleled by their taking up of positions within a series of smaller spheres, less inclusive in breadth and span. It is as though their identifying of themselves as almost-men included within a particular ethnicity proceeded through a simultaneous claiming of quasi-male status within these nesting spheres: the household which each supports and over which each now presides, and the extended family including relatives both living and deceased from which each has inherited certain gifts and qualities, and within which many now play the major spiritual roles of divination and ancestral propitiation. As with the broader, apparently ethnic identity, none of these was automatically 'given'; all had to be actively striven for and created.

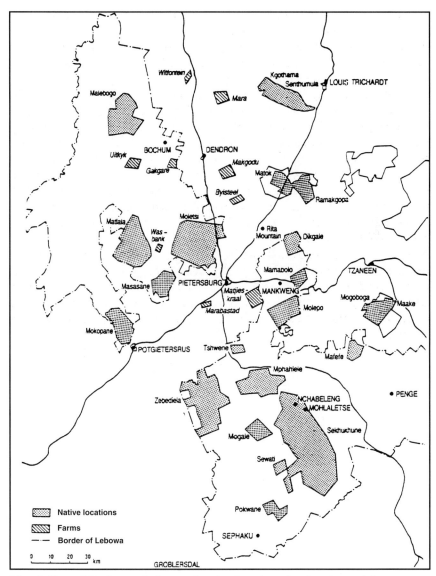

Map 1 Part of the former Lebowa, showing locations, landmarks, and farms
mentioned in the text

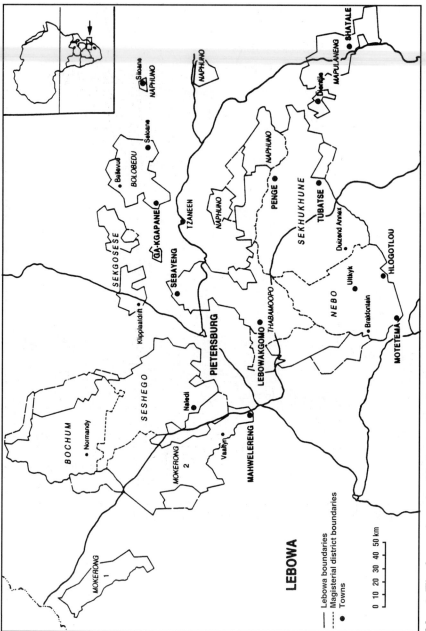

Map 2 The former homeland Lebowa, showing boundaries of pre-1994 magisterial districts

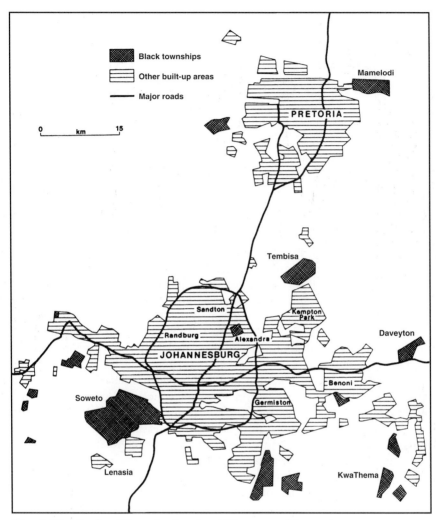

Map 3 The Reef and Pretoria, showing African townships

1

HOME BOYS, HOME DANCES:
MIGRANTS CREATE PAST AND PLACE

Watching the obvious attraction exercised by 'traditional' music and dance upon Northern Province migrants, I became aware that much of its appeal lay in its being thought of as 'music from home'. But the 'home' which evinced such feelings of emotion was not simply a place in the Northern Province of the 1990s. It was symbolised through invocations, images and symbols which made it the location of a heroic and chiefly past. As my conversations with migrants proceeded I realised that 'home' did not signify merely a geographical area in the country whose inhabitants, when in town, could share resources and provide material and social benefits for each other (a common theme in accounts of home-based migrant associations from elsewhere in Africa). It also embodied a wealth of local knowledge about the pre-colonial past, and about the significance of that past for present-day migrant experience.

But this past, and its meaning, differed between different regions in the broader Northern Province region. A major conceptual cleavage, initially hidden from me due to the stressing of *kiba* as a style of all Lebowa, divided the area south-east from that north-west of Pietersburg – *Sekhukhune* and *Leboa*[1] respectively. This divide, which neatly split the Reef-based migrant performing constituency into two and then further separated *Leboa* into a series of much smaller constituencies, was based on varying pre-colonial histories, and on varying experiences of domination and resistance in the post-colonial period. These varying experiences in turn resulted in perform-ance groups from the two areas using the heroic chiefly idiom differentially. Chiefship and its trappings are invoked with greater frequency and intensity by male migrants from *Sekhukhune*, where those from *Leboa* intersperse emblems of chiefly authority with a range of alternative, less politically charged symbols of identity.

What became evident was that this knowledge about and apprehension of the past was not pre-ordained or passively accepted. Leaders and rank-and-file dancers, through their performances themselves, played an active role in construing and reinterpreting the significance of the 'home', the past, and the traditions on whose existence the strength of their dance groupings was predicated.

MIGRANT ASSOCIATION

When I began my research in 1989, the immediate academic context was one of selective neglect. Migrant mobilisation on the basis of a shared home had for several decades been a topic virtually ignored by several generations of South African anthropologists.

The *effects* of migrancy on rural communities had certainly been well documented. These showed for example how absent migrants' wives, left to undertake agricultural duties, had become increasingly dependent on migrant remittances to sustain their farming activities (Murray 1981; Manona 1980); or demonstrated how migrants' dependents or deserted kin had evolved a series of kinship arrangements and household types distinguished by extreme fluidity and susceptibility to change and often displaying marked degrees of economic differentiation (Murray 1981; Spiegel 1980, 1987). Studies with a more cultural focus chronicled the way in which adapted rituals served to reincorporate returning migrants into their communities (McAllister 1985). Even studies focusing more specifically on aspects of life in South Africa's rural reserves or homelands – population removals, the effects of resettlement on farm labour tenants and former township dwellers, and the development of the long-distance taxi trade in 'homeland' areas – had as their backdrop the movement of country-dwellers to and from their jobs in town.

But these studies, in focusing on the rural pole of the migrant experience, had failed to take up the challenge of understanding how migrants drew on their rural origins to arrange their lives in the cities. After the Mayers' Eastern Cape study was published in 1971, this issue was largely neglected by South African anthropologists,[2] despite having received considerable attention from writers working on the Zambian Copperbelt and in West and East Africa at about the same time (Mitchell 1956; Harries-Jones 1969; Little 1967; Parkin 1969; Southall 1975a, 1975b).

What explains the reluctance of scholars in South Africa to investigate this topic? It may have been partly because of their refusal to endorse the notion that the ethnic differences reified by the *apartheid* state were experienced as real by country-dwellers or migrants. Giving credence to notions of a rural 'home' or common origin as a basis for migrant association would implicitly have endorsed the state's creation of the so-called homelands for people of particular ethnic groups. South African scholarly writing in the 'struggle' vein (Freund 1994; Gordon and Spiegel 1993) tended to emphasise how these homeland areas had been peopled and governed by means of top-down processes. Populated through the enforcement of the infamous 'influx control' and other forms of resettlement, the homelands had been subjected to agricultural 'betterment' policies, implemented partly through the offices of the new system of government called Bantu Authorities. If a homeland such as Lebowa was thought by writers of this generation to have an objective existence this was due to its physical redefinition, its repopulation and its redesignation by the planners of *apartheid*.

This reluctance to investigate home-based associations was particularly strong among anthropologists, due perhaps to their awareness that there was a disturbing similarity between the definitive cultural features stressed by their forebears and the concept of ethnic uniqueness which was used to justify the depredations of *apartheid*. Rather than anthropologists, the few writers who *did* take up the challenge of documenting the formal or informal mobilisation of migrants from particular areas on the basis of a shared home were certain social historians (Guy and Thabane 1987; Delius 1989, 1990). These writers, like the anthropologists of the Copperbelt and East and West Africa mentioned earlier, showed how home-based migrant associations provided a number of services for their members, usually centred on self-help and social welfare. Benefits ranged from the provision of clinics and schools in their home villages or helping members to save money, through to the less tangible but equally important facilities of recreation, companionship and social identity; but one of the main spurs to ethnic association was the need to repatriate the bodies of dead migrants for burial at 'home' (Southall 1975a: 272; Delius 1989).

What anthropological writers working in other parts of Africa in the 1960s and 1970s had shown, and what anthropologists working in South Africa should perhaps have realised, was that despite the emphasis on a common ancestry and home these associations were not necessarily narrow or conservative in focus. They were sources more often of advancement and progress in the urban setting than of the backward-looking traditionalism associated with the Red Xhosa of South Africa (Mayer and Mayer 1971). Starting with shared and familiar norms as a kind of 'given', many such groupings gave their members a route to urban adaptation and modernity (Little 1967, 1973: 421).

What southern African social historians added to this account was a demonstration that migrant associations were not timeless, but changed in accordance with the altered circumstances and aspirations of their constituencies. Although societies of Pedi migrants from the *Sekhukhune* area of the Northern Province originated in the need to return bodies home for burial, for example, they later spawned new groupings. These served as the basis for extensive political mobilisation in response to state attempts to interfere with land use and rural government. In turn they became the basis for ANC membership in the 1940s and 1950s (Delius 1989, 1990).[3]

Delius's work on the *Sekhukhune* area, and the work of Molepo – a writer originally from the Pietersburg district – on an area of *Leboa*, provide some insights into the strength and continuity of home-based groupings among migrant males from these two parts of the Northern Province, and thus merit further consideration here. I will show in the next chapter how this use of a home base contrasts markedly with the manner in which female migrants from the same area have organised themselves.

Based in reserves in *Sekhukhune* and *Leboa*, men began leaving home to work for wages well before the collapse of the reserve economy had made it imperative that they do so. Control over the movement of these migrants to the diamond mines of Kimberley during the period 1870–90 was exercised, with varying degrees of success, by chiefs and labour agents. Further attempts to regulate the flow of labour, and to stand between migrants and their freedom to seek their own jobs, were pursued during the twentieth century by prospective employers such as the mining houses, and by the state itself. Operating within the reserves and 'homelands' in accordance with state policy on the control of urban influx, the mine labour recruiting organisations occasionally found themselves in competition with state-initiated labour recruitment strategies (Delius 1983: 62–82, 1986, 1989: 582; Molepo 1984: 8, 18; Wilson 1972: 3, 96–7).

These attempts to channel the flow of labour were only partly successful in directing the actual movement of male migrants from the Northern Province. Workers attempting to remain free of these controls used nearby employment opportunities such as farms and local mines as stepping-stones to jobs in and around Pretoria, Johannesburg and the East Rand. By 1930 there were two major spheres of employment for Northern Province male migrants. One was compounded mine labour, mostly recruited within the reserves, and concentrated at the Premier Diamond Mine east of Pretoria and at a range of gold mines on the East Rand. The other was domestic service in the suburbs of Pretoria and Johannesburg; an option which many preferred since it was less arduous and dangerous (Delius 1989: 582–3; Molepo 1984: 28).

As wages for domestic servants fell and an expanding economy provided new opportunities, many of these migrants moved out of their previous enclaves to find a range of jobs in the service sector and in industrial and factory employment. This entailed the informal establishment of new enclaves, with men from particular areas favouring specific factories. The Iscor steel works in Pretoria became a major employer of labour from *Sekhukhune*, for example, while the Modderfontein Dynamite Factory on the northern outskirts of Johannesburg employed large numbers of men from the areas further north. In some cases, migrants from particular areas held virtual monopolies over jobs in specific factories (Delius 1989: 593; Molepo 1984: 26, 28–9, 32–4).

As these men began to avoid the recruiters of compounded labour and to move into industrial and service employment, they also started to seek accommodation in municipal hostels designed as single-sex dormitories. Between the 1930s and the 1950s male migrants from the Northern

Table 1.1 Northern Sotho speakers living in Reef districts: 1985 (RSA Population Census, 1985, 02-85-01: 256–78).

District	Northern Sotho speakers	Total African population	Northern Sotho speakers as percentage of total African population
Benoni	20 893	135 481	15.4
Kempton Park	44 248	162 581	27.2
Randburg	23 139	104 848	22.1
Johannesburg	74 933	809 255	9.3
Randfontein	4 254	53 240	7.9
Roodepoort	5 498	73 967	7.4

Province were starting to cluster in the Jeppe and Denver hostels in Johannesburg (Delius 1989: 594; Molepo 1983: 75).

In later decades, a range of new hostels were built in the black townships of the Reef and Pretoria, as part of the state's policy to disallow urban accommodation to anyone but single workers. In these, as in the hostels built earlier, Sotho-speaking migrants from the Northern Province established enclaves. Given the costliness of transport and the importance of visits to their rural-based families, it is not surprising that geographical proximity to their rural home played a part in determining in which of these hostels they chose to settle. The areas they favoured were in Alexandra to the north-east of Johannesburg (part of Randburg district), Tembisa to the north of Kempton Park, KwaThema adjoining Springs, and Daveyton adjoining Benoni. There were fewer migrants from the Northern Province, or Lebowa as it was now called, living in hostels or houses in Soweto to the south-west of Johannesburg (classified within Johannesburg district) or in the black townships of the West Rand (see Table 1.1).[4]

It was, then, around the scarce resources of jobs and accommodation that male migrants from *Sekhukhune* and the reserve areas further north in *Leboa* organised themselves. The strength of their commitment to this joint enterprise was based not only on having a shared rural home, but also on patterns of male association established during the process of initiation. Members of the same *mphato* (initiation regiment) would leave home together to look for work. In other cases, men would make contact with people from the same chiefdom or village after arriving in town, using special meeting-places in Johannesburg or Pretoria. These contacts helped people to find jobs, provided them with temporary accommodation, and gave a range of related support. Even in cases where migrant men had been living, not in close proximity with their fellows in compound or hostel accommodation, but scattered in the suburbs as domestic servants, their association as co-initiates or people from the same home area laid the basis for their coming together on Sundays in recreation (Delius 1989: 583–92; Molepo 1984: 39).[5]

The writings of social historians on which this account is based do not mention the existence of groups based on musical performance except in passing. But my own findings about migrant association during the period 1960–90 reflect broad themes very similar to those discussed by Delius and Molepo, and suggest that *kiba* groups overlapped with, and played similarly supportive roles to, the home-based associations which these writers document.

What is strikingly similar to the organisation of male migrants from the same area at an earlier time, and to that documented in other parts of Africa, is the degree of overlap between groupings at different levels of incorporation. In many cases the members of the same dance group are also family members, co-initiates, people from the same village, members of the same burial society, and inhabitants of the same Reef hostels. The situation is strongly comparable to that described by Clegg for Zulu migrant men:

> This ... became part of the home-boy structure ... the little grouping of people who come from the same district, they live in the same hostel when they go to Johannesburg. In the hostel they have a burial society, a drinking club, a savings club, a dance team. So the dance team becomes incorporated into the home-boy structure. (1982: 10)

LOCAL KNOWLEDGE, LOCAL DIVISIONS:
LEBOA AND *SEKHUKHUNE*

To resume the line of argument with which this chapter began, it would seem that South African anthropologists neglecting to investigate the significance of 'home' for rurally based migrants had fallen into the trap of using an unmitigatedly 'political economy' approach (Ortner 1984; Roseberry 1989: 12). They had allowed their emphasis on the transforming power of the capitalist metropolis to obscure the social and cultural specificities of the communities thus transformed.[6] Their documenting of the devastating effects of the *apartheid* state's projects of social engineering had assumed a uniformity among the communities on which these changes were wrought, and hence a uniformity of their effects and the way in which these were experienced.

But if the labour-sending areas were not, indeed, as homogeneous as the political economists had supposed, what exactly were the distinctive features of history, local knowledge and local experience which had made the inhabitants of *Sekhukhune* and *Leboa* think of themselves as different from each other, from the earliest days of migration until today (Delius 1989: 588, 591)? And why was it that in *kiba* performance *Sekhukhune* remained indivisible while *Leboa* was further subdivided into smaller units na   after small reserve areas in the north – *Moletši, Matlala, Malebogo* others?[7] The key to understanding this contrast between one large subsuming south-eastern home area and a splintered assortment of sn north-western homes lay in a complex interaction between 'our history' and 'their history' (Roseberry 1989: 142): between the machinations of the *apartheid* state and the reinterpreted pre-colonial experiences of those it had attempted to incorporate.

The homeland of Lebowa created by government policy-makers for all speakers of Northern Sotho obscured a complex diversity of local group-ings. Some of these had moved into the area from the west, and others from the areas to the north of the Limpopo River known as *Bokhalaka* (lit. 'the place of the Kalanga', equivalent to present-day Zimbabwe). If a degree of cultural and linguistic uniformity came to exist between these diverse people, at its geographical edges this blurred, through a variety of dialects and practices, into other languages and customs (Krige 1937; van Warmelo 1974: 72). For example, *sesotho*, as northern Sotho is mostly called by its own speakers, is thought of as changing as one moves further northwards, giving way to *setlokwa* and eventually to *setswetla*.

The later creation of homelands for separate ethnic groups was informed by the decision of which of these linguistic/cultural complexes to recognise as distinct 'languages' with their accompanying 'cultures', and which to regard merely as dialects or variants of *sesotho*. When the boundary of Lebowa was drawn it included the speakers of *setlokwa* but defined the speakers of *setswetla* as having a separate language and hence as belonging rather to the 'homeland' of Venda (see van Warmelo 1952, 1953: 3). Because of the lack of a neat correspondence between geographical area and language unit, this was to involve the forcible resettlement of large numbers of people to the areas designated appropriate to their language group. Both the relative diversity – and the overarching uniformity – of language and culture in the Northern Province area thus came to be used by government planners in the paired activities of dividing certain groups of people from each other, and combining other groups together.

Within the north-western area, *Leboa*, there were other forms of local knowledge apart from these locally recognised distinctions in dialect by means of which the inhabitants of particular areas could be identified. In the course of their migrations into and around the Northern Province area, clusters of people from diverse origins had come to centre themselves on a series of *dikgoro* (s. *kgoro*) or ruling nuclear groups (Bothma 1976: 184; Krige 1937: 328). The people clustered together in a particular *kgoro* would identify themselves through their shared symbolic allegiance to an animal – *tau* (lion), *kolobe* (pig), *noko* (porcupine) and the like.[8] But the reserve areas allocated to these groupings by the Native Locations Commissions of the nineteenth and early twentieth centuries, which later became the basis of the *apartheid* government's expanded 'homelands', were known by the names of the chiefs of these ruling families – *Matlala, Molepo, Mogoboya, Mamabolo*, and others (see Map 1).[9] This partly reflected the centrality of chiefs in the systems of control and tribal administration devised by a succession of South African governments and refined in the 1950s during the *apartheid* era.

For the members of these minor north-western polities, and for those who eventually became labour migrants from them, this provided two alternative means for invoking the idea of home. The people known as coming from the *Mogoboya* area, for example, speak of themselves in certain contexts by the use of this name, but in others as those who *bina noko* (sing/dance the porcupine); the people of *Mamabolo* as those who *bina kolobe* (sing/dance the pig); and so on.

For a migrant from *Sekhukhune* to the south-east of Pietersburg, the names and symbols used in regional identification are less varied. They refer mostly to the centralised ruling aristocracy which held sway in the region during the late eighteenth and nineteenth centuries – the Marota or Maroteng – and to the Pedi polity, consisting originally of a range of smaller groupings with diverse totemic identifications, over which it had established dominance. In the wake of conquest, they had maintained their dominance through a variety of socio-political mechanisms, including the use of court mediators, the bringing together of local youths in initiation regiments under chiefly control, and the establishment and maintenance of unequal political alliances through cousin marriage.[10]

The Pedi polity or empire enjoyed its period of greatest dominance under Thulare during the late eighteenth and early nineteenth centuries. It resumed its influence in the region under Chief Sekwati and then Chief Sekhukhune, whose name the Pedi area still bears. Even after the definitive defeat suffered by Pedi warriors at the hands of the British in 1878, this era of Pedi supremacy continued to make its influence felt, as will be seen below.[11]

The contrast between the diversity of smaller rural homes on the basis of which *Leboa* migrants constructed their associations, and the larger and more unified home of the *Sekhukhune* migrants, was thus linked to contrasts in the extent and range of the power of pre-colonial polities, and in the way these are made to appear in the present. But this contrast cannot be properly understood without reference to the more recent histories of these polities. Of especial significance are the ways in which they reacted to the impositions of state policy, and especially to attempts by the state to interfere with the use and the administration of agricultural land.

LAND: RESERVE AND 'TRUST'

In the wake of their defeat, the Pedi were allocated a reserve. The territory, *Sekhukhune*, is located between the Olifants River and the Transvaal Drakensberg range, and crossed by the Leolo mountains. Centrally situated in the reserve is Mohlaletse, the seat of the Pedi paramountcy. The term 'heartland' has been used in this and other similar contexts in South Africa to capture the idea of a territory, previously associated with a powerful and independent local polity, which despite defeat at the hands of colonial forces has seen little white settlement besides that by missionaries, doctors and state functionaries such as magistrates and Native Commissioners.

The limits of the official magisterial district of Sekhukhune were not, and are not, recognised by local conceptualisations, which extend its boundaries to all parts of the Lebowa 'homeland' south of Pietersburg, and even to much of the white farming area beyond. Bids were made to expand the officially recognised reserve area through the purchase of some of this white farmland, first by 'the tribe', and later by the state's South African Native Trust which was established expressly for this purpose. But even on those white farms which were never thought of as destined for inclusion in the 'homeland' there were people living under conditions of rent- and labour-tenancy whose sense of themselves as part of a broader polity appears to have derived from their proximity to the geographical base of the Pedi paramountcy within *Sekhukhune*.[12]

In contrast to the heartland of *Sekhukhune*, the reserves set aside for African occupation in the *Leboa* area north of Pietersburg were small and scattered, corresponding with the relatively low level of political central-isation which each chiefdom had achieved in the nineteenth century, and were interspersed with areas of white farming and settlement. Though chiefs lived on these reserves, many of their subjects were moving away to settle on neighbouring farms in the first few decades of the twentieth century. In some cases, such as that of Chief Mamabolo, these rulers were said to have little jurisdiction over their subjects because of their wide dispersal, but this was not a reason for them to wish for their people's concentration within the reserve areas: Chief Sentimula, for example, explicitly stated that he wished for those he ruled to stay on the farms since they would make a better living there.[13]

At a time when those identifying themselves with *Sekhukhune* were moving back into the reserve as their chiefs made bids to purchase more adjoining farm land for communal tenure, many people whom the state saw as denizens of the northern reserves were attempting to move or remain outside of these reserves, by grouping together and buying or renting their own land, beyond the sphere of chiefly control, for advanced agricultural use.[14]

Both northern and southern reserves were later augmented by the addition of land purchased for their inhabitants by the South African Bantu Trust. This was intended not only to accommodate the existing population of the reserves and its natural increase, but also to provide space for the settlement of the thousands of people – many of them the tenants on or owners of farms in the 'white' areas mentioned above – who were to be resettled into the homelands with the infamous 'population removals' of the

1950s and 1960s, or who were to move there on a more voluntary basis.[15] Accompanying the removals was a broader strategy of control, which included the planned imposition of Bantu Authorities, a system of government in which so-called traditional chiefs were to have their powers transformed into those of administrative middlemen. It also involved a plan for agricultural 'betterment' within the homelands themselves, in terms of which villages were replanned, their occupants moved into new residential areas, their cattle culled and their use of agricultural land 'rationalised'. Both the newly purchased areas and the enforced system of agricultural planning carried out within them came to be known in local parlance simply as 'Trust'.

This attempt to interfere in the lives of rural Africans met with differential responses in the areas south and north of Pietersburg. In the southern area of *Sekhukhune*, the government's strategy to resettle communities in 'bettered' villages and to impose its vision of appropriate chiefly authority on them sparked violent rebellion. Pedi royals, with overwhelming support from their rural and migrant followers, refused to serve as puppet chiefs within the Bantu Authorities system. The Pedi paramount was exiled, and his successors, since returned to *Sekhukhune*, have been given no special recognition privileging them above other 'Tribal Authorities' in the region. But the marginality of the Pedi chiefship within the official authority structures of the Lebowa 'homeland' as a whole has enhanced rather than reduced the chiefship's status in the eyes of many local inhabitants.[16]

In the reserves of *Leboa*, in contrast, there was a less effective expression of people's antipathy to state interference with land and government. This was at least partly because, in the North, many of the people who were to be forced into residence in the Trust areas consolidated as the northern part of the Lebowa homeland had lived most of their lives away from these areas, and lacked the strength of attachment to the land felt by their heartland counterparts in *Sekhukhune*.[17]

Based on these varying experiences of domination and resistance, inhabitants from the two areas invoke identity in different ways. For migrants from one of the small reserves in *Leboa*, the symbols used in identifying their home region may be those of region, of local chiefly authority, or of totem. A male migrant, Isaac Lelahana, for example, told me in a casual conversation that he belongs on the one hand to a *kiba* group named *Moletši* after the reserve which he calls home, and on the other to a burial society called *Kwena Moloto* which combines the totemic name of *kwena* (crocodile) with the name of the local chief, Moloto. In performance or ritual circumstances such as those in which *direto* (praises) are spoken, markers of region and political authority are abandoned in favour of the more evocative totemic name of *kwena*.

In the discourse of migrants from south of Pietersburg, in contrast, the themes and symbols used are consistently those of royalty, referring back to a heritage of centralised dominance in the region. In most contexts, including those of *kiba* and *dirata* (praise) performance, the names used are those of the former Chief Sekhukhune, the Pedi ruling group to which he belonged, and the trappings of royalty which marked his power – *mošate* (chief's kraal), *aparankwe* (royal leopard-skin clothing), and the like.[18] Based on the heritage of Pedi rule, and filtered through the experiences of insurgency and defiance, the symbolic invoking of the chiefship thus represents the past glories, not only of its dominance in the region during the nineteenth century, but also of its resistance to dominance during the twentieth.

The different degrees to which these polities were centralised in the pre-colonial era and the ways in which they then accommodated or reacted against later forms of authority thus laid the foundations for present-day migrant organisation and identity.

HOME: SHIFTS AND EMPHASES

But the invocation of these images of nineteenth century chiefdoms and twentieth century defiance in contemporary migrant organisation does not occur through the automatic structuring of the present along lines laid down by the past. Rather, it involves the inventive agency of individual migrants. In the literature on migrant organisation by anthropologists working in West, East and Central Africa, the notion of a 'regional association' implied a fixity rather than a flexibility of the 'region' on which such an association is based. Despite one claim that 'the basis of common origin is often more imaginary than real' (Little 1967: 27), much of this literature has tended to take for granted the existence of a clearly defined rural home or place of origin, which in turn provided a clear-cut basis for membership. It left little room for the possibility that the conceptualisation of this 'home' might allow for subtle shifts in emphasis, or for creative representation by individual agents.

To demonstrate this point, and to show the evocativeness of the symbols of royalty used by *kiba* performers from the *Sekhukhune* area, we can look at the story of one of the best and most professional *kiba* groups on the Reef. *Maaparankwe SK Land* (those of the royal leopard-skin clothing, Sekhukhuneland) is a *kiba* group which at the time of writing was meeting every Sunday in the backyard of the house in Tembisa belonging to its *serokolo* (leader),[19] Jan Seašane, and which practises in the road just outside the house. It has been meeting at this venue ever since the violence of 1991 caused its members to flee from the Tembisa hostel.

Like the male members of other *kiba* groups, Seašane and his fellow performers have been playing and dancing *kiba* since they were children, when as herdboys they used to practise the dance in imitation of adult men, using reeds instead of the *dinaka tša tshipi* (metal end-blown pipes) which they now play as adults. After a short stint of farm labour, and a further stint as a 'kitchen boy' in Germiston, Seašane sought work at a mine in the same area. Here, his ability to perform was seen as a special attribute marking him off from the rank and file: he and other musicians were told '*dinaka* players, stand on one side', and he describes himself as having been 'hired because of this art'. The *kiba* group with which he played and danced while working here bore the name of the mine on which its members worked: a fact which caused considerable resentment, as men felt that their skill as a group was not rewarded, and that it accrued instead to the glory and good name of their employers.[20]

As Jan Seašane and many of his cohorts moved from the mine into employment in brickworks, light industry, and the like, so a separation was established between their place of work and place of residence, with *kiba* centred more on the latter. Jan built a shack in a yard in the township of Tintela, adjoining Edenvale, in 1959, and called his wife from home to join him. Here, he and a number of his friends became *masole* (rank-and-file members, lit. 'soldiers') of a *kiba* group founded and led by a man called Mantjane. The group was now free of the institutional pressures of mine living to which many members had previously been subject. It was at this stage identified by reference to the name of its founder, but was understood as being composed of men from the broader *Sekhukhune* area.

The late 1960s saw the removal under the Group Areas Act of Africans resident on the East Rand from older to newer and more remote townships.[21] The *kiba* group moved to Tembisa with its members, where its activities centred on the single men's hostel where many members were housed.

Some years later, an influx of new members prompted a debate on what name the group should now be given:

> there were some people who joined us from Magakala, and most people thought that we are all from Magakala, and that this is the Magakala group. So we changed to *Maaparankwe* because every chief is a *leapara nkwe* [one who wears royal leopard-skin clothing]. Our group came to be known as *dinaka tša mošate* [the pipes of the chief's kraal]. It became *SK*, and everybody knows that *SK* is Sekhukhune the chief of chiefs.[22]

The favouring of this broader definition now made explicit the previously tacit understanding that the group was the musical representative, in this particular town area, of the broader *Sekhukhune* constituency. With the gradual freeing of *kiba* from the constraints of compound life, this trend in naming became current throughout all Reef areas where there were

ESKOM

TRIBAL DANCING

STANDARD BANK ARENA

5 MAY 1991

PRESENTED BY

PARTICIPATING TEAMS

#	Team	Place	No.
1	AMAZULU CHILDREN (GIRLS)	P.T. & M.	12
2	AMAPONDO CHILDREN	GROOTVLEI	13
3	AMAZULU	KENDAL	12
4	AMABACA GUMBOOTS	LETHABO	20
5	AMAXHOSA CHILDREN	DUVHA	35
6	AMASHANGAAN CHAUKE	ROSHERVILLE	30
7	AMAZULU CHILDREN (BOYS)	P T & M.	28
8	AMA-NDEBELE	KRIEL	15
9	AMABACA GUMBOOTS	KRIEL (1)	15
10	BAPEDI	KRIEL (1)	24
11	BASOTHO	HENDRINA	15
12	AMAZULU CHILDREN	LETHABO	25
13	AMABACA CHILDREN	KRIEL (1)	10
14	AMAZULU CHILDREN	P.T. & M.	20
15	AMASWAZI ZINGILI	INGAGANE	12
16	AMAPONDO	KENDAL	12
17	AMAZULU	GROOTVLEI	33
18	AMASWAZI	TUTUKA	25
19	AMAZULU	DUVHA	28
20	AMABACA GUMBOOTS	MATLA	10
21	AMAZULU CHILDREN	MAJUBA	25
22	AMABACA GUMBOOTS	KRIEL (2)	10
23	AMASWAZI	DRAKENSBERG	25
24	AMAZULU CHILDREN	ARNOT	17
25	AMABACA GUMBOOTS	MATLA	15
26	AMAZULU	KRIEL (2)	35
27	AMASWAZI	MAJUBA	25
28	BAPEDI	KRIEL	25
29	AMAZULU CHILDREN	ARNOT	20
30	AMABACA GUMBOOTS	DRAKENSBERG	14
31	AMASWAZI	DUVHA	25
32	AMAZULU CHILDREN	KENDAL	30
33	AMASWAZI ZINGILI	ARNOT	25
34	AMAZULU	MATLA	15
35	AMASWAZI	LETHABO	28
36	AMAZULU CHILDREN	KRIEL	30
37	AMASWAZI ZINGILI	COLENSO	36
38	AMAZULU	ARNOT	30
39	AMASWAZI	COLENSO	24
40	AMAZULU CHILDREN	HENDRINA	40
41	AMAZULU CHILDREN	GROOTVLEI	55
42	AMAZULU	TUTUKA	45
43	AMAZULU	DUVHA	50
44	AMAZULU	ARNOT	30
45	AMASHANGAAN AMABUNDA	KRIEL	70
		ROSHERVILLE	
		TEMBISA	

Figure 1.1 Programme of annual traditional dance festival, sponsored by the parastatal ESCOM (Electricity Supply Commission), a major employer of black labour. *Maaparankwe* appears last on the programme.

sufficient northern Sotho-speakers to support *kiba* groups, resulting in such groups as *SK Benoni, SK Alexandra, SK Mamelodi* and *SK Germiston*. The use of additional names, like *Bapedi Champions* by *SK Benoni*, or like *Maaparankwe* by the group which would otherwise have been known as *SK Tembisa*, restated the same basic allegiance to *Sekhukhune*, but did so by referring to more emotionally charged symbols and unifying identities.

In all these cases the name *SK* is paired with the name of a Reef area or township. This might be interpreted as a merging of both rural and urban sources of identity, but it should be remembered that the urban part of the name was not entirely under performers' own control. *Maaparankwe*, for example, while certainly seeing themselves as being 'from' Tembisa, were wary of attempts made by the township's new superintendent to appropriate their fame and earnings for his own kudos as a municipal official:

> what troubled us is the bad experience on the mines, where people would dance for nothing. This is because the money that was won was always taken by the mine dance organisers. ... This also happened to us in Tembisa where the superintendent took away the money. ... Martin of Tembisa asked us to be under his control in Tembisa. He said he liked this *sepedi koša* [Pedi singing]. After competing for money, he would take the money that we had won and give us two big *makoko* [tins] of beer; others would get *bogobe* [mealie meal porridge]. Most of us didn't know that we were being used.[23]

What the subdivision of the total pool of players from *Sekhukhune* between different Reef townships did provide was a league for the purposes of competition. The fiercest dance contests involve rivalry, not between men from different rural areas, but between those from the same broad rural home – sometimes even brothers or cousins – whose place of urban residence divides them geographically while working on the Reef. Despite the fierceness of competition, the boundaries between these smaller urban subdivisions of *SK* are permeable; men from *Sekhukhune* who leave one urban area to live and work in another can get an automatic 'transfer' to the appropriate *SK kiba* group.[24]

The move for men from backyard suburban rooms, through mine employment, into informal shack settlements and later to the dormitory accommodation of the new townships entailed a shifting membership for *kiba* and an accompanying change in the identity which a group's name was seen as designating. It was particularly their transcending of the controlled and restrictive environment of the mines which allowed these players a greater freedom to define their own identity. But, despite an underlying assumption about the performers' connection to the constant and unfluctuating rural base of *Sekhukhune*, this connection was not an automatic one. It was, in fact, largely in the highly charged and strongly communal

Figure 1.2 Members of the *SK Alex* partner-groups (Photo: Santu Mofokeng)

activities involved in *kiba* performance that these links to home were enunciated, dramatised and maintained. Music and dance were, and are, central in linking migrants to 'home'.

HOME: PERFORMANCE AND COMMUNITY

Given the amount of time which labour migrants have devoted to dancing and music throughout Africa, it is surprising that so little attention has been paid to the way in which these people use it to define their origins and destinies. Both the *compins* of Sierra Leone (Little 1967: 158–60) and the *gumbas* of Ouagadougou (Skinner 1974: 209–10) were organised around dancing, but this activity is seen merely as facilitating the other group undertakings more conventionally associated with tribal or migrant associations. In Sierra Leone, for example, the *compins'* dancing allowed men and women marginal to urban life a structured sense of belonging, and of participating in the life of the city,[25] while in Ouagadougou dances provided for structured and formalised interactions between youths of both sexes.

Where migrant dancing has received attention in its own right, the belief that it reiterates rurally based styles and themes has led to its being seen as conservative. The form and content of these dances are assumed by Argyle, in a recent article reassessing *kalela* and comparing it with other African genres, to mirror those of the dances from the rural areas which migrants call home (1991: 77–8). In South Africa, in particular, such dancing has been interpreted as an acquiescent response to the plans of management to keep workers content. By harnessing migrants' energies in pursuit of backward-looking traditionalism, it supposedly diverts their attention from the more pressing issues of unfair labour practice and exploitation.[26]

But migrant dances, and the contexts in which they are performed, cannot be assumed to exhibit simple continuities with rural culture.[27] According to the view of performance theorists, each apparent repetition of a ceremonial or aesthetic formula in fact involves 'critical difference', and thus newly creates rather than merely repeating it (Drewal 1991). In line with this view, *kiba* should be seen not as reiterating country practices in town but as activating a new world of experience in which the gap between country and town is bridged. Like other southern African migrant styles, it is thus 'part of the very reconstruction of the migrants' world' (Erlmann 1991: 158; see also Coplan 1987; Moodie 1991).

Home is invoked, then, not simply through repeating the actions previously executed during a rural childhood and youth. Home also involves an active reconstruction of group cohesiveness in the urban context. This is true of both men and women migrant performers. But for women, because the basis for this reconstructed identity is a more tenuous one, its creation involves a greater degree of initiative, as will be shown further on.

The *kiba* performers of *Maaparankwe* have striven for, and achieved, a unified home under the zealous leadership of their male *serokolo* (leader), Jan Seašane, and his female counterpart, Julia Lelahana. Through performance itself, and through the creative manipulation of the performance context, they have constructed a moral community with common values and experiences. The two performances described below were festive events, modelled on but imaginatively transforming the more usual weekly-practice format.

> *Mokete wa matswala a ngwana* (child's birthday party)
> Jan Seašane and a rank-and-file group member, Flora Mohlomi, arranged a birthday party for the grandson of Julia Lelahana, *Maaparankwe*'s female leader (*serokolo*). The grandson, together with his mother, were spending a few weeks in Johannesburg on a visit. Jan had previously organised a similar party for his grandson, named Maradona after the famous Argentinian footballer.
>
> The party took place at the group's normal practice venue, in the street outside Jan's house in Tembisa. To begin with, women marched into the performance space in the street from Jan's backyard, singing and dancing *Tšhukutšwane*. One carried the child, another a huge basin full of scones which had been baked for the event, and a third and a fourth carried a table on which the child's birthday presents had been placed.

After this dance was complete, and the child and objects had been set down, the organiser, Flora, opened the presents, and then spoke praises to the child, to which the group then responded in chorus. A ceremonial giving of money known as *serotwana* (lit. 'small basket') then ensued. A male group member laid down a newspaper package, placing a R5 note next to it on the table, and saying 'This R5 says that no one will open the package'. This established a betting sequence, with a succession of people approaching the table to lay down money, alternately 'to open' and 'to keep closed' the newspaper parcel. The final bet succeeded in keeping the parcel 'closed', and its contents were never revealed. The mother of the child was then asked to record the names of donors and the amounts given in a book, so that reciprocity on future occasions could be ensured.

Men and women then performed in the usual sequence for the rest of the afternoon.

Festivals of reparation

Also centring on Julia Lelahana, these festivals were set in motion to heal a rupture between her and another group member whom she had offended. Julia had made disparaging remarks in reference to the fact that some women are 'afraid of having children', and the woman had interpreted these as a direct personal criticism and statement about her own infertility. The perceived wrongs were righted, at Jan Seašane's suggestion, by holding two 'home' performances. The first was at the offended member's house in the *Mamabolo* area. During the performance Julia made apologies and reparations, and Jan announced to the audience at large why the dance was being held. A second performance was hosted by Julia at her home in the *Moletši* area, at which the offended woman gave Julia a goat 'for keeping her mouth shut'; that is, for retracting and apologising for her original criticism, and for undertaking not to be so critical in future.

On both these occasions, musical performance was used to give dramatic and visible shape to *Maaparankwe*'s striving, motivated primarily but not solely by its highly committed leaders, for a sense of solidarity and unity. The first event set up a dance-centred ceremony, related only remotely to the 'traditional' naming ceremony for a child, to incorporate into the urban-based group a home-based relative of one of its members. The second succeeded in resolving a dispute between two members regarding themselves as 'fellow-home-people' by engaging in dance and oratory at the actual homes of each of these people. The imagery of visiting, hospitality and home were all invoked here in the successful healing of a threatened rupture in the fabric of *kiba*.

This feeling of belonging to a broader moral community has been achieved, as well, through the management of the group's financial affairs on the basis of strictly maintained principles. Although priding itself on its professionalism in dance, *Maaparankwe* operates as an amateur club, whose profits never accrue to individual members but are kept in a common fund and are used only to sustain the activities of the group.[28] This fund is used to pay for the group's year-opening and year-closing parties, at which a cow or sheep is usually slaughtered and large quantities of beer and soft drink are consumed. It also provides for the group's transport to performances. Each member is expected at some point to invite the group back to his/her rural home to perform for some important function, such as a wedding or a girl's coming out from initiation. This is how each member fulfils his/her obligation to host the group at home, and – in theory – to pay fellow-dancers for their performance. But the group's rate for members is so much lower than that for non-members that it rarely covers the cost of transport. This is then subsidised, instead, by the group as a whole from its fund.[29]

Related financial transactions, too, are governed by a strong sense of moral correctness. At a performance at Ga-Selepe in *Sekhukhune*, the hostess tried to recoup some of the cost of hiring the group by erecting a makeshift amphitheatre out of sheets of plastic on a wooden frame, and by charging an entrance fee to all would-be spectators. The group's sense of outrage was so strong that they performed for the minimum possible time, and omitted their most exciting acts. They considered that a more acceptable way for her to have recouped her losses would be to have sold beer at the event, as normally occurs at a *stokvel* or rotating-credit party. But it was beyond the bounds of *kiba* performance morality to charge an entrance fee. In this as in other financial transactions, the group activates and maintains a morality of sharing, in which the maximising of profits is decried.

It is thus within the immediacies of performance itself, and in the shared moral principles which govern the contexts where performance takes place, that a sense of a new community is created by *kiba*. This occurs partly through the cohesive psycho-social effects of co-ordinated and rhythmic dancing (Radcliffe-Brown 1948: 248–52; Thompson 1974: 14–16, 27–8; Chernoff 1979: 113–14, 125–7). But the use of dance in the festive events organised by these migrants should be understood, not as expressing pre-ordained values deriving from rural society, but as actively attempting to create a sense of unity and balance in a context in which such conditions would otherwise be lacking (Fernandez 1973: 216–17; Blacking 1962). Singing, dancing and playing in these events – and controlling the values which govern them – give men and women a sense of being a part of *Maaparankwe*.

It was for the migrant women who perform *kiba* that this innovative creation of community involved particular imagination. If, for migrant men, the existence of home-based associations was not simply given, but required the imaginative intervention of individual agents, for women this identity had to be created virtually from scratch. To understand the reasons for this, we must look briefly at the kinds of rural background from which these women came. A more thorough exploration of this background will be undertaken in Chapter 6.

MEN AND WOMEN

The description of *Maaparankwe's* activities on the preceding pages indicates a keen participation by both men and women in the group's engagements and performances. But women's membership of such clubs has been a comparatively recent phenomenon. *Kiba* clubs and the genre of the same name were exclusively male in membership from the first appearance on the Reef of this type of music until the late 1970s. At around this date, *kiba* groups began to acquire female migrant members. This, together with other influences, set in motion the process through which the previously male genre acquired a female version.[30] Although, in particular groups, the alliances between male and female performers were far from stable, for reasons to be discussed below, women's *kiba* as a general phenomenon grew gradually in strength of numbers and in excellence of performance throughout the 1980s and into the 1990s. Most men's groups on the Reef now have female migrant members.

Some precise examples will demonstrate these points. The groups with which Jan Seašane had been dancing and playing since the late 1940s when he first came to the Reef to work had been exclusively male in membership. It was not until 1988 that his club, now called *Maaparankwe*, was approached for the first time by a prospective female partner-group, whose members had previously been briefly aligned with *SK Alex*. Having never before had female partners, *Maaparankwe* were hesitant, and asked for time to consider the proposal. But since committing themselves to the partnership, male and female members have expressed positive attitudes about it, in the main. Women have their own *malokwane* (leader),[31] *mogadi wa malokwane* (leader's deputy) and committee, and are careful to represent their own point of view at meetings. Although there are occasions when they feel that their representatives are not listened to, and although they are expected to assume some roles based on stereotypes deriving from husband/ wife interactions, such as preparing food at celebrations, they feel on the whole that they enjoy a greater degree of autonomy than any of them has had in other migrant clubs or societies. And there is strong commitment, by men and women alike, to the project of maintaining the group's moral principles and its professional standards.

In forming a partnership with the men of *Maaparankwe*, then, these women have become stable members of a migrant association. Their case approximates to something which has become a norm in the world of *kiba*:

that each man's group is partnered by a group of women. But this norm obscures a range of actual experiences. Preceding the admission of these women into *Maaparankwe*, they had entered into a series of fleeting relationships with male *kiba* groups. For some other female singers, such as the current female partners of *SK Alex*, this pattern of brief partnerships ending in conflict has proved more the rule than the exception. Some singers have, indeed, resolved on the basis of previous experience to remain independent of male groups altogether. The women of *Ditšhweu tša Malebogo* (the bright ones of *Malebogo*), for example, feel that the risks of doing without male protection in the harsh world of the townships are compensated for by their freedom to manage their own affairs without male interference. Whether eschewing male alliances, or fleetingly or more firmly linked to a club of male performers, what is interesting about these groups of women migrant singers is that their membership is drawn almost exclusively from the northern areas known collectively as *Leboa*. Even those clubs which have teamed together with men from *Sekhukhune* and so allegedly represent this area contain no women originating there.

When I first became aware of this disparity, obscured during the early days of fieldwork by the common symbols and identities which men and their female partners invoked, there seemed to be two possible explanations which could be explored. One was that there were more female migrants from *Leboa* than from *Sekhukhune*. The alternative was that, although comparable numbers of women migrated from both areas, only those from *Leboa* experienced the desire or need, or were able to develop the autonomy, to join migrant associations in their own right.

Investigating these possible explanations proved to be difficult. Sources, both written and oral, tend to obscure or even deny the existence of female migrancy from both regions. Women's migration is hidden, first, within communities in the labour-sending areas. A version of the 'woman's place is in the home' ideology makes both migrant men and their stay-at-home wives in these communities either condemn female migrancy as an unusual and unfortunate aberration, or deny its existence altogether, even in cases where there is independent evidence of it. Discussions with informants in the rural areas from which these women come do not yield images of group strategies pursued by female migrants comparable with those followed by generations of their male counterparts.

The existence of Northern Province women migrants in this generation tends to be hidden, too, from the archival record. This is partly because female migrancy from these areas is a very much more recent phenomenon than male migrancy. Whereas all male *kiba* players belong to a second or third generation of migrants, almost all the female *kiba* singers I know belong to the first generation of women in their families who came to work in town, and many belong to the first generation of urban labourers of any kind, male or female. Most arrived on the Reef after the middle to late 1960s.[32]

Another set of reasons why this generation of migrants is difficult to trace in published sources relates to the sphere of employment in which they work: domestic service. Obtaining employment as a domestic servant is not done through the recruiting agencies whose records are often used to yield figures on male migrancy. Recruitment to this sphere of employment is private and *ad hoc*, with women getting jobs through relatives or going from door to door to look for work. When individual women do find employment, they reside in a broad scatter of suburban areas, rather than being clustered together in specific hostels. Another reason for these women's invisibility as workers is the fact that, during the 1960s and into the 1970s when they began coming to town, the control of African movement into urban areas was very strictly enforced (Bonner 1990: 247; Gay 1980: 46). Employers often colluded with their employees in keeping their identity and whereabouts a secret from the authorities.[33]

Figures on female employment are available from the South African population census, but these are notoriously unreliable, particularly for rural areas of the country characterised by high levels of illiteracy. If the obstacles enumerated above have served to conceal the true extent of female wage employment and migration from the view of the law, they have almost certainly concealed it, as well, from the eyes of census officers.

Table 1.2, based on the 1985 census, shows percentages of the female population employed in service and other low-paid occupations. The average for the whole of Lebowa is 5 per cent. Figures for the magisterial districts of Sekhukhune and Nebo, roughly corresponding with the broader region of *Sekhukhune*, both stand at around 5 per cent, similar to the 'homeland' average. Figures for the magisterial districts of Thabamoopo and Seshego, part of *Leboa*, are marginally higher at around 6 and 7 per cent respectively. But those for Bochum, Sekgosese and Bolobedu, also parts of *Leboa*, are lower at around 4, 3 and 2 per cent respectively. The census yielded no consistent contrasts, then, between rates of female employment in northern and southern areas.

The alternative thus seemed to require investigation: that only female migrants from *Leboa*, or certain female migrants from *Leboa*, experienced the desire or need, or were able to develop the autonomy, to join migrant associations in their own right. I found evidence to support this claim from discussions with, and observation of the experience of, individual women *kiba* performers themselves. Combined with information from these life-histories, what the archival record does provide is some sense of the historical background to the circumstances in which many of these women, and their forebears, had lived before migrating: circumstances of considerable social dislocation which had precipitated them into migrancy,

Table 1.2 Lebowa women in employment: 1985 (RSA Population Census 1985, 02-85-05: 531-4)[34]

District	Rural female population	Women in low-paid employment	Percentage of rural population in low-paid employment
Benoni	20 893	135 481	15.4
Bochum	50 573	1 990	3.9
Bolobedu	77 614	1 641	2.1
Mokerong	144 184	7 753	5.4
Namakgale	9 868	586	5.9
Naphuno	49 985	2 380	4.8
Nebo	122 501	6 158	5
Sekgosese	47 622	1 314	2.8
Sekhukhune	177 944	9 618	5.4
Seshego	105 418	7 490	7.1
Thabamoopo	119 652	7 294	6.1
TOTAL	985 888	49 557	5

which had isolated them from other workers when they first began to live in town, and which had subsequently driven them to seek the companionship of migrant women in a similar predicament.

The female migrants who became urban performers of this music came from a very different kind of socio-economic background from their male counterparts. Even looking at a *kiba* group representing *Leboa*, the family backgrounds and orientations of its men are in strong contrast to those of its women. Stated most starkly, this is the contrast between mostly reserve-dwelling traditionalists on the one hand, and mostly farm-dwelling people, relocated into the reserves, with more modern aspirations and/or with a Christian orientation, on the other.

Earlier in this chapter, a contrast was presented between the heartland of *Sekhukhune* and the eponymously named reserve areas of *Leboa*. In the first few decades of the twentieth century, these northern reserves had been thought inadequate to the farming and grazing needs of their intended African populations. Although the chiefs after whom these reserves were named lived within their allocated areas, their subjects were dispersed on surrounding farms. The response of some of these people to the over-population and overgrazing in the region had been that of grouping together and buying or renting their own land, beyond the sphere of chiefly control, for advanced agricultural use. For some of them, the desire for education acted as a spur to remain as, or to become, tenants or freeholders on state, private or mission land.[35] Most of the women who later joined *kiba* clubs in town came from this kind of background.

It was people like these who, living outside of the official reserve areas on African- or white-owned farms, were to bear the brunt of the infamous population removals of the 1950s and 1960s. Thousands of Africans living within 'white' South Africa were relocated, mostly onto the lands which had been purchased by the state's South African Native Trust for the purposes of augmenting the size of the original reserves. The word 'Trust' eventually came to denote, not only this additional land, but also the total package of interventions into rural existence – administrative, agricultural, and demographic – which *apartheid*'s planners were determined to implement. It was the experience of dislocation resulting directly or indirectly from these interventions which had forced some future female *kiba* singers into the labour market, where many belonged to the first generation of migrants, male or female, from their particular families.[36]

The contrast between male migrants who dance *kiba* and their female counterparts is thus a contrast between long-standing reserve-dwellers from both *Sekhukhune* and *Leboa*, on the one hand, and people who had lived as peasant producers and labour tenants on farms outside the reserves, and who had subsequently moved onto the Trust surrounding these reserves, or into the reserves themselves, on the other. Linked to these different socio-economic backgrounds is a series of other contrasts.

Male players, while many have worked their way from employment in mining into better-paid jobs in the industrial and service sectors, still mostly belong to that class of reserve-dwellers thought of as *baditšhaba* (tradition-alists/low-paid migrants). Where they have progressed beyond this social category and moved into the echelons of *majekane* (Christians/middle-class), they have invariably abandoned this style of dancing since it appears as inappropriate to the holders of a higher social status, and as incompatible with adherence to Christianity. Female players, in contrast, are almost all from Christian backgrounds. Those who had lived as peasant producers outside the reserves belonged to the category of earlier converts known as *majekane*, while those from labour tenant backgrounds were *baditšhaba* more recently converted to independent churches. A very few had been raised in Christian communities within the reserves themselves.

The fact that these women come from a totally distinct area of the country, and from rural backgrounds very different from those of their male counterparts, illustrates a point made by Bozzoli about female migration: 'one cannot assume that the later women who leave the land "belong" to the men who left earlier' (1983: 156). For the men in *kiba* groups such as *Maaparankwe* and *SK Alex*, the women who 'belong to' them – mothers, sisters, and particularly wives – are thought of as being situated, together with these men's children, in the villages of *Sekhukhune*. These women are characterised as being rurally resident, even though many visit their husbands regularly and although some have moved to stay in town on a more permanent basis. None of these wives has acquired the degree of independence from conjugal control associated with female membership of an urban-based *kiba* group. When they attend and participate in urban-based *kiba* occasions, they do so in a way associated with earlier female participation in this male genre, as peripheral 'praisers' of the male-dominated central event. Those male migrants' wives who do perform *kiba* are members of rural-based groups such as that described in Chapter 5.

In contrast, the women from northern areas who sing *kiba* in town, sometimes in partnership with male migrants, do so as members of largely independent groupings. Beginning their migrant careers as isolated individuals who were dependent on male 'home boys' for social interaction, they have evolved an autonomous and a specifically female version of 'migrant association', and have used apparently traditional music as a means of expressing their rather less than traditional outlook on life.

'THOSE OF MY HOME': MIGRANT WOMEN ON THE REEF

The images of migrancy yielded by the literature in southern and other parts of Africa portray a world peopled almost exclusively by men. In the literature on migrant associations, particularly, almost no attention has been paid to the role of female migrants as actors in their own right. If they are not altogether absent from the picture, they appear as dependent beings whose activities male migrants are determined – partly through home-based associations – to control. Their escape from such restrictions appears necessarily to entail an escape from these associations, and a loss of interest in maintaining their connections to 'home'.

This image of women in migrant associations as either firmly dominated or as desiring their freedom is linked to a set of central themes which emerge from the broader literature on female migrancy in Africa. Women's options of remaining at a rural home or of leaving this home to work in the cities have been seen as constrained primarily by their relationships with, and especially their dependence on, men.

In some instances, female migration has appeared as an opportunity for total escape from this control, and from the strictures of patriarchal rural society in general. This was so in South Africa prior to the extending of influx control to women (Bozzoli 1983; Walker 1990b: 188, *passim*), and also in towns in West and East Africa and on the Copperbelt (Little 1972; Cheater 1986: 159; Parpart 1991; Parkin 1975b). But in those cases where strict controls on women's movement were introduced – often with the overt collusion or tacit approval of tribal elders and of migrant men – the dependence by women on their husbands or other male kinsfolk was vastly augmented.

Under conditions like these, the entry of women into the migrant labour market is seen as inhibited by the need of their husbands to maintain them as the custodians of production and reproduction in the rural areas (Stichter 1985: 145). In southern Africa it is precisely this kind of conjugal interdependence which has been thought to underpin the existence of the 'migrant labour system' (Murray 1981: 165–70). When women – against the most difficult of odds and in defiance of the law – do enter the migrant labour market, it is the breakdown of conjugal relationships, and thus of their ability to depend on men, which forces them to do so (Gay 1980: 41; Murray 1981: 156).

These structuralist accounts of the centrality of women's dependent role within the logic of labour migrancy are indisputably accurate in broad outline. But, in omitting to examine how female migrants see themselves, they sideline women as agents engaging in their own strategies of survival, or grouping together with other migrants in an attempt to cope with the pressures of urban existence.

There are a number of reasons why an account written from this kind of structural perspective would be predisposed to ignore female home-based association even if it existed. In situations where female migration is relatively uncurbed there is a tendency to exaggerate women migrants' desire to be free from all strictures: they have been portrayed, for example, as promiscuous, or as entering into only fleeting sexual relationships. The readiness to portray women migrants in this light, according to Brydon, may say more about the desire of male vested interests to control these women than about the actualities of their experience (1987: 171–2).[1] This exaggerated emphasis on female unconstraint has led to an assumption – inaccurate, as Brydon indicates (*ibid.*: 176) – that the relationship of such women to male migrant associations is one of distance, or of distinct avoidance: particularly since one of the focal points of male migrant activity appeared to be the desire to control or curb the activities of such women in town (Parkin 1969: 165), or to procure exclusive access to their sexual services (Bonner 1990: 241, 247–50).

On the other hand, in situations where the existence of male migrancy is predicated on the existence of a more-or-less viable rural economic base, and on the stable presence of men's wives to manage the rural economy, male organisation is thought to be dedicated in part to keeping such women in their rural place. The strength of ethnic identity as a focus of association among migrants in southern Africa, according to Vail, is partly based on a powerful primordialist ideology in which the maintenance of control over land and women is central (1989b: 14). Such an ideology may be para-doxically strengthened under the conditions of lengthy male absence from home (Gay 1980: 52). This perspective, like the one previously discussed, excludes women as the possible members of migrant groupings. If they are the objects of control by these associations, they are unlikely also to be active subjects initiating or perpetuating them.

We have heard little, then, about women as beings who actively consti-tute themselves into groupings on the basis of sharing a common rural home. But we have heard even less about the ways in which such women conceptualise, imagine, and reconstruct their relationships to such a home. Describing the experience of the male migrant performers of *kiba*, I claimed in Chapter 1 that the rural homes which serve as a basis for migrant association are not so much pre-ordained as they are creatively invoked. For *kiba* women, even more than for their male counterparts, their communally experienced relationship to a rural area conceived of as home is an imagined one. It is a relationship constructed less out of a shared rural background than out of shared urban experiences. On the basis of certain elements objectively present, such as a common language and a common origin in a very broadly defined rural area, these women have assembled an identity and a consciousness of commonality.

For the Northern Province migrant women who sing *kiba*, their membership of these originally exclusively male groups is neither a sign of dependency nor one of an acceptance of control by migrant men. Although their membership of burial societies was shaped by the influence of husbands or male relatives, they were later to move away from this reliance on male kin, and to team up with other women. They developed considerable autonomy as members of these separately structured female *kiba* groups, with female leaders and office-holders. At the same time, they developed a sense of home as a kind of mythical charter underpinning this membership. It was in the process of identifying themselves with this home that they entered into new partnerships with men's music groups, and – inevitably – involved themselves in some of the ambiguities which such partnerships entailed.

MIGRANT WOMEN: MARRIED AND UNMARRIED

If women's eventual membership of *kiba* reflected their growing autonomy, this was built up only slowly through several years during which they were dependent on husbands or male relatives. The reasons why these women left home to work, then, do reflect the existence – or the rupturing – of dependence on men. It was the women's later joining of *kiba* which occurred once this dependence had lessened or disappeared.

For future female singers of *kiba*, the initial trip to Johannesburg was made for one of two contrasting reasons. A woman migrated either at her husband's suggestion in order to keep him company in town, or because of the lack of support from a wage-earning man – husband or father.

Migration by women to join their husbands has been noted in the literature, where it has been interpreted as 'social' rather than 'economic' in nature.[2] Discussing this kind of migration in north India, Sharma criticises such a categorisation. She points out that a woman whose migrant trajectory is dictated by her husband's presence in a particular urban area, but who then engages in wage labour in that area, is no less guided by economic considerations – and no more guided by social ones – than a man who allows his choice of urban workplace to be influenced by that of a relative (1986: 42). In similar vein, Stichter argues that economic factors cannot be arbitrarily separated from social ones (1985: 6). In the case of future *kiba* singers who did cite their husbands' wish for their companionship in town as their main reason for migrating, the economic dimensions of their move were at least as important as the social ones. Mary Lebogo and Phina

Komape, for example, called by their husbands to join them in Johannesburg, allowed little time to elapse before they had found work in domestic service to help with the family finances.

It is the second of these two reasons, migration because of the lack of a male wage-earner in the family, which is most often cited in the literature on southern Africa as the major cause behind female migrancy (Preston-Whyte 1981: 161; Gay 1980: 41; Murray 1981: 156; James 1985: 178). This claim is supported by the presence, among *kiba* singers to whom I spoke, of a category of women who married young and whose subsequent experience of conjugal separation around five years later brought them back to their parents' village. But the category of women who never married is preponderant numerically. For some of these, their single status was not so much a result of being overlooked by some eligible suitor as because of their feelings of obligation and duty to their family of birth or orientation. For a woman like this it was the absence, not of a husband's support for her children, but of a father's support for herself, her mother and siblings which had initially engendered a sense of responsibility for her family in the rural areas, and which led her to come to town. At least in one case there was a definite aversion to marrying, while in others the idea of acting 'as a son should' was seen, at least in retrospect, as incompatible with the reorientation of duty and responsibility towards a husband and his family. For women in this category, it was only later, when they bore children of their own, and when some of their siblings married or went to work in turn, that the profile of their rural dependents came to match more closely the usual stereotype: children at home in the country, supported by mother working in town.[3]

Many of those who never married, then, were driven by specific rural circumstances to view themselves from adolescence as playing the role of primary breadwinners for their families, whereas most of those who separated from their spouses began to play such a role only after moving back home after a period spent as married women at the home of their in-laws. Both the unmarried and the more recently single, however, migrated for what might appear primarily 'economic' rather than 'social' causes.

But, while the two separate causes of women's migration outlined above might be thought to have given rise to two rather different constituencies, their gender gave the members of both a feature determined very definitely by 'social' considerations. This was their handicap in making independent connections to migrant networks in town. All these women, whether married or not, relied on individual, usually male, family members, related either by blood or by marriage, to bring them to town and to connect them into broader networks after arrival. It was because female migration from the Northern Province was not undertaken by groups of people – youths socialised together, or clusters at particular factories or hostels of people from specific areas – that they were tied, at least at the start of their migrant careers, to husbands or male kin and to the home-based networks to which they belonged.

The women who came to Johannesburg to join their husbands, like Phina Komape, Martina Ledwaba, or Mary Lebogo, were incorporated into their husbands' networks of burial society members and worshippers in the Zionist Christian Church (ZCC). Unmarried women, like the Machaba sisters, or widows like Rosina Seshothi, came to Johannesburg at the suggestion or under the initial protection of a brother or uncle. To the extent that their isolation as domestic servants permitted them any social involvement, they were likewise subsumed within the area-based burial societies or church groups to which these male relatives belonged.

The contrast between the two female migrant constituencies was not, however, a permanent one. The criterion of marital status, initially differentiating between two contrasting reasons for female migration, became less important as wives became widows, divorcees became independent breadwinners, and unattached women developed casual liaisons with male companions in a manner which did not alter substantially their relationship to their rural families. When the women who had come to town for the sake of conjugal togetherness were deprived of this source of companionship and financial support through widowhood, and were simultaneously freed from the necessity of sticking within their husbands' migrant networks, they experienced the necessity but also the independence of selecting a network of their own. Likewise, when the single women driven to look for work had overcome the initial isolation of domestic service, and had begun to make their own female friends as an alternative to the male-dominated social circles to which male relatives had introduced them, they began to construct new networks from assemblages of these individual friendships.

The fact of being a single woman without male support was not, then, a uniform cause of Northern Province migrancy in the way suggested by much of the literature for other areas, but it was a major factor underlying the later coming together of these women in *kiba* groups. For both categories of women – those widowed or separated, and those never married – the link between being single and joining *kiba* had two aspects. It involved opting out of, or relying less heavily on, the forms of group support previously relied on which had been automatically provided to them by their connections to husbands or male kin. These forms were then replaced by, or combined with, new sources of help and succour entered into on terms of their own choosing.

FEMALE MEMBERS, MALE ASSOCIATIONS

The associations to which these women belonged before joining *kiba* were independent churches and burial societies. Over half the women with whom I had detailed discussions had been raised as members of independent churches, or had become members when marrying. Others grew up as members of mainstream churches. Their background in Christian peasant or tenant families, or on and around the farms of Pietersburg and areas further north where they were subject to extensive mission influence, is described in Chapter 6.[4] But most of these women allowed their church membership to lapse when joining a dance group. Some, like Phina Komape and Martina Ledwaba, were able to become dancers only after widowhood, since their husbands, strongly oriented to the ZCC, actively disapproved of what they saw as pagan dancing. For these women, widowhood was both the spur to and the facilitator of their orientation to a new group, which they found to be more supportive and companionable than the church members to whom they had been linked through their husbands. The rejection of church membership by both the widows and the single women to whom I spoke suggests that the independent churches, characterised as an important source of identity for migrants and rapidly proletarianising communities (Comaroff 1985: 241), were more effective for male migrant workers than for women in this respect.[5]

Most future *kiba* singers joined a burial society soon after arriving, either subsumed under their husbands' membership or at the instigation of the same male relative who had brought them to town. When attending the monthly burial society meetings, these women found themselves in a strongly male-dominated world. The leaders and members of the *kudu tamaga* (executive) were then, and are still, men, and although in some cases women were admitted to titled positions in parallel with men's ones, their influence lay in the right to veto rather than to make decisions. Women, as lower earners, felt that men's insistence on raising the monthly contributions in order to pay exorbitant *matshedišo* (condolences) was based on their higher earnings and was thus unfair. Another area of disagreement, in which men's opinions usually predominated, concerned the status of dependents. The dependence upon a man of his wife and children was, and is, officially sanctioned in the burial societies, their membership being thus automatically guaranteed by his own. In the case of a single woman, or one who though married had an independent membership of such a society rather than being incorporated within her husband's group, there was a reluctance officially to acknowledge her dependents as having an equivalent status to those of men. Although money may be given in the event of death, it would be less than that given in respect of the death of a male member's official dependents. In similar vein, women would argue heatedly about the fact that their dependents, consorts or husbands could not qualify for free transport to funerals or for free society badges, whereas men's dependents and wives would automatically be given these things.[6]

Despite the perceived inequalities in these burial societies, Northern Province women who had newly joined the ranks of labour migrants derived significant benefits from belonging to them. But the benefits did not include a sense of continuing companionship, since the societies met only on the first Sunday of every month. Women were left lonely on the other three Sundays, often spending most of their pitifully inadequate leisure time sitting in their rooms. This pattern of isolation was broken only by activities such as the sewing lessons provided at various churches for domestic workers, infrequent visits from people working as servants in nearby houses, and occasional trips to watch soccer.

In the days before the founding of *kiba*, one of the things which made it difficult for women to sustain a connection – above and beyond the monthly burial society meetings – with male migrants from the same home areas was the fact that these and other less formal gatherings were held in or around the hostels where most male migrants lived, in such townships as Alexandra or Tembisa. During the 1960s and early to mid-1970s, when most future *kiba* singers first came to Johannesburg and established themselves in the job market there, transport between the white suburbs and the black townships was provided only by buses which operated on major arterial roads, and which were thus inaccessible to domestic servants in their scattered accommodation. On weekends and Sundays, especially, these buses ran infrequently.

This limited system of transportation was to be transformed with the development of the black-owned taxi trade during the late 1970s. A proliferation of mini-buses began to operate on routes and at times dictated largely by demand and hence by profit. As in cities in other parts of South Africa, the burgeoning of this taxi trade made it possible for domestic servants, from their isolated suburban enclaves, to establish and maintain contacts, during their scarce leisure time, within the broader world of the township.[7]

In the case of Northern Province female migrants working in the northern suburbs of Johannesburg, it was these new opportunities for transport in the late 1970s, and their facilitating of more regular visits to Alexandra, that were an important factor in the genesis of women's *kiba*.

THE MOVE TO RELATIVE AUTONOMY

These female migrants were, then, initially constrained by need and by social expectation to rely on the mediation of husbands or individual male relatives, and to join the home-based associations to which their husbands or brothers belonged. Their move towards greater autonomy, which eventually enabled them to initiate female migrant associations on their own terms, was engendered at both the rural and the urban poles of their lives.

At the rural pole, these women possessed, or developed, a strong commitment to their natal families. Those who had remained single had mostly done so out of a strongly developed sense of filial obligation to their parents. Owing partly to the particular rural circumstances of their upbringing, they

Figure 2.1 Elsie Lekgotwane, leading *SK Alex* in performance (Photo: Santu Mofokeng)

viewed themselves from the outset as behaving 'as sons' should. In looking after and providing financial support for their parents and siblings, they were coping not with the absence or loss of a husband's income, but with the effects on their natal families of the population movements engendered by or indirectly linked to the policies of *apartheid*.[8] For these women, then, a strong sense of commitment to natal family had been intact since childhood.

Those who had married had mostly done so while young, often by parents' arrangement rather than by their own choice. After residing for some time with their in-laws, they had separated from their husbands, between three and five years later, to return to their parents' village. For these women, re-establishing a position at the heart of their natal families required some effort. Some, like Elsie Lekgotwane and Joanna Maleaka, had taken the initiative in leaving their husbands' homes and in relocating, together with children, to their natal villages once more (see Figures 2.1 and 2.4). This could not, however, be a decision made completely independently: for Elsie it necessitated the approval of her parents who paid back the *bohadi* (bridewealth) so that custody of her child could be transferred back to her and to them. But she stressed that she was an active agent in, rather than a passive recipient of, the decision.[9]

When women in this position married again or established relationships with men met in Johannesburg, this second union did not prompt a second severing of natal ties or a subordination of these to marital ties. They retained their houses, continued to remit money for the care of their children to their parents, and sent the children from these second unions home to be cared for alongside those from the first. While the women in some cases received financial support from their new husbands or lovers to contribute to the raising of their children with these men, they retained their independence from them in other ways. After being widowed, Rosina Seshothi, for example, married a second husband whom she met in Johannesburg. He has a first wife and children living in his home village, and so has put no pressure on Rosina to move herself and her children away from the house which she built before meeting him. In 1990 he was contributing R100 a month to help with the upkeep of her four children, although only one of these is his own.[10]

From the urban end, the gradual building up of a female migrant's autonomy was achieved, with a great deal of individual effort, in moving from poorly paid employment into better-paid jobs. While an initial job was procured with the help of a relative, the exertions made by these women to better their position were often made on their own initiative. In some cases this involved walking from door to door and asking for a job in areas where salaries were known to be better, but in others women used social contacts which they made through their employers.

A good example is that of the Machaba sisters, Salome and Andronica.

Figure 2.2 Andronica Machaba, leading *Ditšhweu tša Malebogo* in performance
(Photo: Santu Mofokeng)

Salome was first taken to Johannesburg from her home in the *Malebogo* area by her uncle in 1970. Typically of first-time female migrants, she was unable to speak English and her pass-book was not appropriately endorsed for residence in an urban area, so her aunt found her a job with a family in the Indian 'group area' of Lenasia, earning R20 a month. This was a route favoured by illegal female migrants from other areas of southern Africa as well (Murray 1981: 154). Salome's move into the employment market of the better-paying northern suburbs began soon afterwards with her employment in Parkhurst at R80 a month, but was temporarily interrupted by the birth of her child. Dismissed by her Parkhurst employers because of her pregnancy, she was later forced, after the birth of her baby, to seek work in Lenasia again, with an accompanying drop in pay.

At this stage, she arranged for her younger sister Andronica to join her in Lenasia, where Salome found Andronica a job with another Indian family. Here, Andronica too started with a monthly salary of R20, and had to sleep on the kitchen floor at night since her employers provided her with neither a room nor a bed. The two sisters moved from the poor pay and discomfort of Lenasia into domestic service in the northern suburbs of Johannesburg, where by 1990 both were earning monthly salaries of R350.[11] Once within the Johannesburg suburban ambit, they shifted through a succession of increasingly better-paid jobs, using contacts established through white employers.

Much of what has been written about domestic service in South Africa emphasises the extreme disadvantage experienced by those employed in this sector: their dependence on the whims of employers, and the absence of any defined rights or conditions of service (Gaitskell *et al.* 1983: 103–7). The life-histories of individual servants certainly demonstrates the truth of such a claim.[12] One area of uncertainty has been the lack of formal employment contracts or assurances of long-term employment in the future. A reason for this, in the case of future *kiba* singers, was the considerable geographical mobility of Johannesburg's white population in the 1970s and 1980s. Many women's employers moved between cities or emigrated from the country, leaving them temporarily without work. Once Salome Machaba had made the initial move from Lenasia, for example, she had to change jobs twice because of her employers' departure from Johannesburg. When her Sandton employer left for Switzerland, she went to work for a colleague of this employer, who lived in Parkview. And when the Parkview family then moved to Durban, the estate agent who had sold their house employed Salome as a domestic servant, on the basis of the good reputation she had established with her previous Parkview employer.

If 'white madams' enjoyed the privilege of dismissing their servants without notice, one should not ignore the extent to which their employees, albeit disadvantaged within the overall relationship, could use the unheralded withdrawal of their labours as a last line of defence. Elsie Lekgotwane, without warning, left the communal house where she was working because she was required to do eight adults' ironing every week, which she felt was unreasonable. A strategy used by some, like Flora Mohlomi, was to spend the Christmas vacation period looking for another job, and simply not to arrive for work at her previous employer's place when the holiday came to an end.

A migrant woman did have some opportunities, then, to try to secure herself the best possible conditions of service. But one circumstance which interrupted the most energetically pursued strategies was that of childbirth. The story of Salome's setback in her career as a domestic worker, in which pregnancy and childbirth caused her to have to 'start again' in Lenasia, is echoed in the accounts of many other *kiba* singers. Some women attempted to minimise the interruption to their working lives by arranging for a temporary replacement during the first few months of a baby's life. It was through such a strategy that some women – like Joyce Ledwaba, filling in for her sister who had had a baby – gained an opening into the world of wage work. But it was not always an unqualified success, because the 'replacement' in some cases would refuse to relinquish the job to its original holder.

When Salome Machaba's younger sister Andronica was faced by the setback of childbirth, she found an easier solution to it than Salome had done. Andronica's four-year absence at home to bear and look after children was followed in 1980 by her sister Salome's finding her a job near to her place of employment in the northern suburbs. This help by a sister was a foretaste of the kinds of benefit which the emerging female migrant networks were soon to be able to offer their members more generally. The *kiba* group *Ditšhweu tša Malebogo*, of which both Salome and Andronica were later to be founder members, was able to secure employment for several of its other members on the cleaning staff of Redhill school in Morningside, Johannesburg. This was done informally, through contacts made by a single member who already had a job at the school. The shorter hours, companionable accommodation arrangements, and better pay offered at the school made it an employer preferable to the white 'madams' for whom these women had previously worked.

The first few years of migrant existence for these Northern Province women were characterised, then, by a gradual move away from dependence on men. They shifted into better-paid and more stable forms of employment in the urban milieu, and entrenched their roles as principal breadwinners for their rural dependents. Accompanying these changes, identities based on a narrowly conceived sense of home – as members of burial societies representing specific villages or regions, or as connected to the same churches they had belonged to in the countryside – were to be transcended by a broadening vision of shared origin. Individual friendships,

Figure 2.3 *Ditšhweu tša Malebogo* in performance (Photo: Santu Mofokeng)

tentatively formed with people met in town who spoke the same language, came to be formalised in the founding of women's *kiba*.

FEMALE MEMBERS, FEMALE ASSOCIATIONS

It was around the activity of male *kiba* dancing that the first women's *kiba* groups were formed. But informants' accounts of this process indicate that it involved, first and foremost, a linking of female migrants in similar predicaments. Although male groups provided a focus of and a model for association, as well as access to instruments, an audience, and a perform-ance space, men were not implicated in the initial set of relationships out of which women's *kiba* was moulded.

By the late 1970s, the development of the mini-bus taxi trade had made it possible for Northern Province migrant women working in Johannesburg suburbs to overcome their sense of isolation on weekends by travelling to the African townships of Alexandra, Tembisa or Daveyton. The area and social constituency to which they gravitated was not primarily that of the 'township' people who owned permanent homes in Alexandra, but rather that of the migrants living in shacks or men's hostels.[13] Similarly, Northern Province migrants based in Germiston and Kempton Park gravitated towards the men's hostel in Tembisa, and those in Benoni to the hostel in Daveyton. These venues became foci of social activity for migrant men and women.

During one of these visits to Alexandra, Phina Komape and her friends developed an interest in watching men's dancing:

> One day while working in Brixton in 1979, I visited my sister in Alex, it was on Sunday. While there I heard that there was a group of *dinaka* playing in 19th Ave. I then developed an interest to go and watch them. While I was there alone, I met Salome and Joyce. By then I knew only Joyce because she is from *Mašašane*, and I did not know Salome. Now Joyce told me that they were looking for a group of women to sing traditional music. They wondered where they could find it, and decided to go to Alex men's hostel. As we discussed I became interested and we agreed to meet the following Sunday. Those who met were me, Joyce, Salome and her sister Andronica. We went to speak to some women from *Matlala* and talked to them about forming one group, and they agreed.[14]

At around the same time, some of the women who were to form the core of the initial group had started to dress in 'traditional' *sotho* attire. Fransina Monyela claims to have been the one who initiated this practice in her particular circle, for the purpose of attending special occasions at the church sewing class. Two of the women she met at the class, later to become co-members of *kiba*, followed her example:

> We asked ourselves this question. Why can't we show our proper tradition and start singing? Let us not just dress like this with no meaning attached to it, let us also start singing to reveal our tradition properly in that attire.[15]

Other migrant women had also begun wearing traditional dress on these Sunday visits. Joanna Maleaka, from *Kgothama* area in Venda, was wearing Venda traditional dress on the day in question. She takes up the story:

> We agreed to meet at Zoo Lake[16] the following Sunday to compose and practise our songs better. We went to Zoo Lake as agreed and brought tins to play on. We practised for three weeks and mastered our songs. Later on we went back to Alex men's hostel and asked *Matlala* men if we could use their drums after finishing playing *dinaka*. They agreed and we played their drums.[17]

The same story, in broad outline, is told by other women, who formed groups at around the same time. There followed a complex set of alignments, splits, and realignments between female and male performers. These resulted in some stable alliances, as with *Maaparankwe*, some fleeting partnerships, as with *SK Alex Basadi*, and at least one wholly independent women's dance club – *Ditšhweu tša Malebogo*.

Especially in its initial phases, then, the creation on the Reef of groups of female migrants sharing a sense of a common rural home was undertaken partly in conjunction with male migrant associations, particularly through women's individual membership of burial societies. But when women later became performers of *kiba*, it was as members of separately structured groups with female leaders and office-holders. They formed their own clubs, using the template provided by men's ones.

The initial founding of these clubs, on the model of their male counterparts, is characterised by participants as having required a great deal of initiative. But, by a decade later, joining women's *kiba* had become something more of a standard option available to Northern Province female migrants. Julia Lelahana, for example, after watching women's weekly practices in Alexandra for some years during the 1980s, joined a group in 1988. One might suppose, then, that the founding of the initial women's group was typical of the early stages through which any migrant association must pass before it becomes established.

It is certainly true that these women's *kiba* groups have provided the same kinds of practical and financial assistance to their members as other migrant associations have been documented as doing. Singers have helped other singers by using their informal contacts to get them jobs with better pay and conditions of service, as in the case of Redhill school mentioned earlier. *Kiba* groups have also provided support through their spawning of a range of *mehodišano* (rotating credit savings clubs: lit. 'those which cause each other to save') whose membership overlaps partly but not wholly with their own. In one of these, women buy a specified list of non-perishable groceries – mostly soaps – every month and give them all to that month's recipient, so that she can send them home to her family. In another, each of two members takes it in turn to pay the other R300 monthly out of a total salary of R500. Although some *kiba* singers claim they are 'too poor' to belong to these savings clubs, others claim that the function of the clubs is precisely in helping them to overcome a lack of resources, since the social pressure exerted by the combined membership forces them to save and so to meet their obligation to send money home every month. Many combine the social pressure to save exerted by these clubs with the facility of a savings account in a bank.[18]

This kind of involvement in systems of mutual reciprocity is far more prevalent among migrant women than among migrant men. Asked about the reason for this contrast, one male member of *kiba* remarked that 'these women don't have fathers or husbands. Now they join many associations to secure themselves.'[19] The combined membership enjoyed by a woman like Joanna Maleaka of several burial societies, of several *mehodišano*, and of *kiba*, suggests that she and others like her see their greatest security in a reliance on as many sources of financial, social and moral support as possible.

Less easily measured, companionship is a crucial benefit which *kiba* provides for its members. Singers' accounts make tangible the contrast between the isolation of their early years at the Reef and the bustle of sociable activity which accompanied their later membership of *kiba*. Some enjoyed the opportunity for physical exercise, shared with others, which *kiba* provided. They characterise the dancing as a kind of sport, and claim that missing a practice makes them feel sluggish for the rest of the week. For others, it was bereavement and the attendant emotional suffering which first drove them to seek membership. When Sarah Motswi experienced great sadness at the death of her father, and when Phina Komape and Martina Ledwaba felt lonely after being widowed, they watched the singers for a period and thought that to join them in their music-making would help them to overcome their sense of loss.[20]

But it was not only financial and social advantages which underlay the attraction of women's *kiba*. What made it central in the lives of its members was its provision of a unifying sense of a rural 'home'. And what marks its genesis as different from that of other migrant associations – from that of, say, a Northern Province male association some seventy years earlier – is the degree of effort which its founders and subsequent members had to put into constructing this idea of 'home'. Their origins in a diversity of scattered, and subsequently dislocated, rural communities, from which many had left to find work before a time when female migrancy was considered normal, made this an unusually difficult task. Musical performance was a primary means through which this was achieved.[21]

As I have already suggested, writers on migrant associations in other parts of Africa have drawn attention to the central role played by music and dance in these associations, but few have analysed the message or meaning of these. The reader of such accounts is left with the impression that music, providing entertainment, acts to draw people together so that they may pursue the more tangible benefits of association.[22] But for the women of *kiba*, singing and dancing were more than simply sources of amusement. Performance provided the initial context within which they were to meet, a model on which to base their association, and an opportunity for 'showing off' to others the *diaparo tša setšo* (traditional clothing) which many were beginning to wear. It also provided a means through which they could participate in the expressive modification of a rural-based female genre, and its incorporation within the definition of an urban-oriented male one. But *kiba* performance was to prove itself most potent in defining and elaborating the notions of *gae* (home) and *bagagešu* (people from home), and in associating them closely with notions of *sesotho* (sotho ways) and *setšo* (tradition), even for people whose socialisation might originally have oriented them towards other ways.

KIBA, WOMEN, AND THE CREATION OF HOME

'Home is where this music is sung ... we don't want to forget *setšo sa gagešu* [the tradition of our home people].' This remark, by Fransina Monyela, a founding member of women's *kiba*, echoes the sentiments expressed by numerous other singers. It is common to hear similar feelings expressed by the players and dancers of men's *kiba*. But underlying this statement of straightforward and unproblematic allegiance to an area and a culture of shared origin are important contrasts between male and female performance, and between male and female migrants' senses of what home implies.

Coming from the section of the community known as *baditšhaba* (traditionalists) in reserve areas of both *Sekhukhune* and *Leboa*, men had learned to play *dinaka* pipes as children, and had imitated the accompanying dance which they saw older men performing at home. Their practice of the genre was uninterrupted by their entry into the labour market. In cases like that of Jan Seašane, described earlier, the ability to play this music even gave him some guarantee of a job when he first came to town: he and other players were given preference over those who could not perform it.[23] In contrast, few of the women who came together in urban *kiba* groups had had continuous experience of performing the rural female genres which were later to be transformed into women's *kiba*. While some like the Machaba sisters had learned *sotho* music as children, or during *koma* (initiation), this had been replaced during adolescence, in the strongly school- and mission-oriented areas where they grew up, by a performance culture of *koša ya dikhwaere* or *ya dikhonsata* (choir or concert songs, based on western musical principles). Other future members of *kiba*, like Elsie Lekgotwane, had never sung *sotho* music or donned *diaparo tša sesotho* (*sotho* clothes) at all before coming to the Reef to find work. Only a very few, like Julia Lelahana and Joanna Maleaka, had been active performers of *sotho* musical styles from childhood, through adolescence, into womanhood.[24]

Women's *kiba* did not, then, emerge through simple continuities with past practice. Forged out of a series of disparate though musically compatible rural female styles, for some of its performers it represented a revival of the *sotho* culture of pre-adolescence. But for some it involved an invoking of the musical practices seen as being not of their own but of their mothers' generation, while others had never seen *sotho* music performed by members of their own Christian-oriented families but only by unrelated neighbours characterised as *baditšhaba*. In the ethnically diverse Northern Province, yet others had grown up speaking languages such as Sindebele or Venda, and performing associated styles of music. Women's *kiba*, then, while apparently harking back to a shared *setšo* (tradition), spoke more of a culture women acquired from their friends in town, or at least imbued with new significance there, than of a culture they had personally transported, intact, from the countryside.

For each of these women, the idea of *gae* (home) and its accompanying *bagagešu* was conceived of in narrow terms during the first few years of working in town, and later expanded to accommodate a broader, more flexible and more situationally invoked concept.[25] Some clues as to how this process occurred can be found in group members' retrospective reflections on the individual friendships which were cemented in the founding of *kiba*, or which later brought them into it.

In its initial and limited aspect, home began with the narrow range of acquaintances, mostly from the same village or immediate home area and mostly male, to which each woman was introduced by the male kin who acted as her initial protectors. As the woman established individual contacts with other women met in town, the criterion of a shared language became a crucial one in giving the idea of 'home' a broader catchment area. One *kiba* singer pointed out that any chance acquaintance would qualify as a *mogagešu* (home person) if she spoke northern Sotho.[26] For women whose sojourn on the Reef had been too short and too isolated to allow the learning of other languages, merely overhearing another woman speaking northern Sotho was sufficient to establish a sense of commonality. Flora Mohlomi and Grace Shokane met by chance in a shop, and discovered that they spoke a mutually intelligible language. Through this means, Flora Mohlomi was later introduced to women's *kiba*, of which Grace Shokane had been a member for some years.[27]

Although language provided both the means for making such encounters and an image of commonality in terms of which these could be explained, there were other considerations, as well, which made home people – broadly defined – more important than other casual acquaintances. As Julia Lelahana said, it would be in adversity, especially, that *bagagešu* could help her. If she became ill, for example, *bagagešu* would be more likely than any other person to ensure that she was taken back home.[28]

Sanctioned by these more broadly defined notions of compatibility and shared rural base, women established the friendships which were to become the basis of *kiba*, or which were to introduce later-joining members to the group. But it was once these women had been thus attracted to the activities of *kiba* that their home-based identities, through the idiom of musical style, became most encompassing.

Despite regional variations, the language of northern Sotho had provided a template for the modelling of relationships between people from diverse areas. This was so even for those who had not spoken it at home in childhood and whose knowledge of it had been restricted to occasional contacts with neighbours. But regional variations in dance genres were seen as more pronounced than those of language, and were initially more divisive. These variations were not so much at issue for the women who since early adolescence had eschewed rural *sotho* music in favour of church-oriented genres. But they were important for women like Julia Lelahana and Joanna Maleaka who had been active performers in the rural context. When Julia joined women's *kiba*, she found only a few women who danced in the style of her home area, *Moletši*. It was these women only whom, at that stage, she characterised as *bagagešu*. Affronted by what she saw as the others' inability to dance well, she began to try to teach them her own regional style, but they said, 'Wait, we will build each other.' The ensuing process of reciprocal learning moulded the definitive way of performing which people nowadays have come to associate with the women of *Maaparankwe*.[29]

The creation of new home bases transcending the boundaries of smaller regions transformed these women from strangers into *bagagešu*. This involved some change in the actual lyrics of songs, particularly in their references to the features of particular home areas, as some examples in the next section will demonstrate. But more important than the altering of explicit references to geographical landmarks were adjustments in perform-ance, and the simultaneous broadening and standardising of music and dance style. Through this process, diverse styles, known in their rural contexts by a range of names – as *koša ya dikhuru* (kneeling song), as *makgakgasa*, or collectively as *mmino wa sesotho* (*sotho* music) – came to be incorporated within the broader overall category of *mmino wa setšo* (traditional music).[30]

This process of stylistic homogenisation has resulted, in some contexts, in an implied home even more encompassing than that which incorporates the diverse actual homes of a group's members. A complex interaction between urban and rural versions of the style has been involved. Fierce competition between groups in an urban context, and imitation by one group of features seen as excellent in another, has resulted in a homogeneous urban style. This has in turn been transmitted to the countryside; either when a group plays at a member's rural home for a life-cycle ritual, or when it is hired to play by people from another - often very far-flung - village. The resulting sense of acquaintance with a broader region is based not only on a pattern of frequent and frequently reciprocated visits by performers from one local area to audiences in a variety of others. It is also forged through the blurring of specific area-based sub-styles to form a broader and more widely accessible genre.[31]

HOME: SPLITS AND REALIGNMENTS

It was not only the initial formation of women's *kiba* groups and the broadening of their style of singing which involved the re-elaboration of a common home base. Their fissions from and fusions with other groups also entailed a redefinition of separate and distinguishing, or shared and unifying, geographical origins. Where these splits and realignments occurred between men's and women's groups, they reflected conflicts over the deployment of performance resources – instruments, audience, style of singing, payments for public appearances. At the same time, such conflicts often led women singers to take decisions which gave them greater control over their own performance environment. From this position of increased strength, they elected either to remain independent of male partners, or to re-enter such partnerships on terms of their own choosing.

Ditšhweu tša Malebogo was a group whose members decided to separate from their original male partners, and thereafter to stay unaligned. Their split from the men of *Matlala*, whose drums they had initially asked to use when first founding their group, was provoked by disputes over the use of these instruments. It was a split made possible on a practical level by the women's acquisition of their own drums, of a separate storage space for these,[32] and of people willing to commission and to support performances despite the group's lack of male partners. But the division was characterised as one between people of incompatible home areas and customs:

> '*Matlala* men chased us away. They said we are many and they don't know where some of us come from. They wanted only women from *Matlala*.'

Another member accounted for the split in terms of style of dress:

> 'The people from *Matlala* don't dress like us. We did not agree about the manner we dress.'

A further comment similarly stressed the importance of differences in culture of origin:

> 'we realised that *Matlala* women were discriminating against us because they did not want us to sing our own songs, so we decided to split.'[33]

The extensive reference to different homes and cultures of origin in this description of group fission displays a notion of home more imaginatively invoked than based on real rural affiliations. The group which separated from men's *Matlala* to become *Ditšhweu tša Malebogo* in fact retained two women from *Matlala* area, left behind in the *Matlala* group one from *Malebogo* who was 'troublesome', and eventually incorporated a range of others from homes far beyond the borders of the *Malebogo* area which gave the new group its name. Two or three of the group's founder members, including the Machaba sisters, were from villages in *Malebogo*. But the definition of *Malebogo* as home base proved wide enough to include people of Tswana, Venda, Ndebele and other origins.

One of these is Phina Komape. Her rural home is in the *Mašašane* area, in the Sindebele-speaking section of Komape village. But her version of the song *Sekhekhe sa go nwa bjalwa* (a drunkard who drinks beer) refers in its concluding verses to a more broadly defined northern area:

Sekhekhe sa go nwa bjalwa	A drunkard who drinks beer
Ke a le bona le sobetše	I see it is sunset
Ba ipshina ka go re sega	They enjoy laughing at us
Le a re bona re tagilwe	You see us, we are drunk
Legodimong re tla no ya	Heaven is where we will go
Legodimong go bo kgaule.	Heaven, the place of forgiveness of sins.
Mathiri ge la kgobokgane le sang go nwa bjalwa	Young women, when you are together, stop drinking beer
Nkwenya ya lena ke mang?	Who is your leader?
Nkwenya ke Maleaka.	Your leader is Maleaka.
Le a re bona re tagilwe	You see us, we are drunk
Felegetšang Mmanotwane sa go nwa bjalwa	Go with Mmanotwane, the one who drinks beer
Ke bana ba Mamotswiri	They are Mamotswiri's children
Kgane ga go na Masogana a go nwa bjalwa?	Are there no young men who drink beer?
Dirang ka pela le tloge	Hurry up so that we may leave
Se apa bošula o etla	Bad people are coming
Le a le bona le sobetše	You see the sun has set
Banna ba bangwe ba a betha ge se nwele bjalwa	Some men beat their drunkard wives
Dirang ka pela le tloge	Hurry up so that we may leave
Blouberg Makgameng	Blouberg Makgameng
Ditšhweu tša Malebogo	The bright ones of *Malebogo*
Lebelela Rita o bone.	Look and see Rita Mountain.

She has personalised the lyrics of an existing song by adding references to her group and its leader, and to the area to which it claims allegiance. She weaves together allusions to a variety of geographically disparate landmarks: the Blouberg, the range of mountains within the *Malebogo* area from which the group takes its name, and Rita, the large mountain north-east of Pietersburg which serves as a symbol of the whole of *Leboa*.[34]

Another such member is Joanna Maleaka, the group leader referred to in the song above, who comes from the *Kgothama* area in the homeland of Venda. While she subscribes to the idea that she and the other members of her group are all bound together by their sharing of a common rural base, the praises she recites express both her admiration of *Malebogo* and its clear contrasts with her own 'real' home in Venda.

Re bina koša kua Alex	We dance in Alex
Koša re a bitša Ditšhweu tša Malebogo	Our group is called the bright ones of *Malebogo*
Malebogo ga se bodulo	*Malebogo* is not a place for settling

Go dula dikokoto	It is a place for heroes
Go dula banna ba mosadi	It is a place for the children of a woman
Iiuu! Ke motswetla, ga ke iphihle	Iiuu! I am a Venda, I don't despise myself
Ke tswa GaRamapulana	I am from Ga-Ramapulana
Go na kua ga bo Mphephu.	At Mphephu's place.

The 'place for settling' refers to her own home, in a Trust area where the implementation of the government's plans for agricultural 'betterment' led to massive relocations of people into *dilaineng* (lit. 'the place of lines'; the grid plan imposed by Trust officials). She contrasts it with *Malebogo*, a reserve area in which people's antipathy to this planning led to its abandonment by the authorities. The lyrics serve both to highlight the heroism of *Malebogo*, the chosen rural reference point of the group to which she belongs, and to announce her dogged defence of her own home area in the 'Trust'.[35]

After experiencing such separations from male partners, there were other women's groups which did elect to re-enter partnerships with men on terms of their own choosing. The women who now sing as part of *Maaparankwe* are an example. They, too, began their careers as urban singers in alliance with the men of *Matlala*. After their separation from these men, provoked partly by demands from them for sexual favours, they spent some time unattached to male performers. But their sense of physical vulnerability, especially when travelling to the countryside or to unknown urban locations to perform, drove them to seek out a partnership with the men's group *SK Alex*. The subsequent termination of this alliance was caused largely by the women's dissatisfaction at their partners' lack of commitment to the performance enterprise. They accused them of attending practices only '*tšatši le rata*' (when they feel like it).[36]

For these women, all *Leboa* migrants, the seeking out of an identity as the female representatives of *Sekhukhune* in Tembisa reflected, in part, a desire for higher standards of performance. It was the wish for a semi-professional alliance with male dancers which underlay their separation from *SK Alex* and their approach to *Maaparankwe*. Their identity as representing *Sekhukhune* also gave them certain benefits as performers – a performance space, an audience, protection in the townships, jointly organised transport. In short, many of the advantages which first drove women into these partnerships remain as powerful incentives for continuing with such relationships. But their involvement in the moral economy of *kiba* has more to it than merely a partnership instrumentally entered into. Despite their independence and autonomy as a group of female performers with their own leadership and hierarchy of positions, they are deeply involved, together with *Maaparankwe* men, in the continuing recreation of 'home' through a

Figure 2.4 Joanna Maleaka (Photo: Santu Mofokeng)

creative use of performance scenarios and contexts.[37] As part of this, the evocative and frequently invoked symbols of the Pedi chiefship provide a powerful rallying cry, both for the men born in the area where this chiefship once held sway, and for the women born far beyond it.

On the level of style, there are significant differences between men and women in their use of the heroic discourse and symbolism associated with the chiefship. Women's *kiba* both subscribes to and distances itself from the epic quality of this discourse. Similar ambiguities affect the very definition of female migrant performance as part of the genre of *kiba*. Women's music, very different from the men's version in most respects, appears to depend on its definition beneath the sheltering rubric of an originally male style for its broader acceptability in the migrant constituency. These and other ambiguities which surround the relationship between women's and men's *kiba* as sub-styles within an overarching genre will be dealt with in the next chapter.

The co-operative venture undertaken by men and women such as those of *Maaparankwe* was pursued, then, in the interests of polished performance and of harmonious social relationships, but given shape through the search for specific home-based identities. In this way, women from northern areas of *Leboa* have come to be thought of, by themselves and by others, in association with the Pedi heartland of *Sekhukhune*.

Through all these shifting partnerships and changes in membership, notions of an appropriate 'home' have been invoked and activated. In the case of *Ditšhweu tša Malebogo*, this was to justify the hiving-off of a group from its former partners, while in the case of *Maaparankwe* it legitimated a group's cementing of a new partnership. It can be seen that these shifts of membership and identity have been very different for migrant women and for migrant men. For men, a knowledge of a constant rural home underlay all these changes. Women, on the other hand, have created a sense of cohesiveness out of a situation of scatter and diversity. Some, like *Maaparankwe*, have relied in the process on the prior and 'ready-made' identities provided by men's groups as an important template upon which to build. Others, like *Ditšhweu*, have constructed identities quite independently of men. But both have used *kiba* as a loose and flexible system for associating with other migrant women in town.

CONCLUSION

If we are to move beyond the view with which we are provided by much of the literature on women and migration, we must begin to see women as agents with some control over their own destinies, rather than as submitting passively to, or alternatively driven solely by the desire to escape from, the control of their 'home boys'. The rural backgrounds of many of the singers of women's *kiba* predisposed them, as major breadwinners for their natal families, to view the world more as if they were sons responsible for family upkeep than as if they were daughters or wives escaping from patriarchal structures. Even those who had been married prior to migrating subsequently established strong ties to their natal families. Women of both these types invested financially and emotionally in the establishment of a rural domicile. As principal wage-earners, they sent money home to a mother who in turn managed the land and undertook to care for children.[38]

The strong links to a home region which have been documented as a feature of male migrancy are predicated on two linked conditions. One is men's absence from home for lengthy periods in order to earn the wherewithal for its upkeep. The other is their secure knowledge that this home is being maintained in their absence. It is normally a wife who is expected to undertake these processes of maintenance sometimes summarised as 'reproduction'. Home-linked association, appearing as the prerogative of male migrants, thus entails men's concern for home from a distance, combined with their reliance on a wife to take care of this home at close quarters. Women who became singers of *kiba* came to approximate these circumstances, usually relying on a mother to maintain their homes and families in their absence.

Kiba women thus became 'as men' in their combining of specific concerns with the welfare of particular homes and families with a generalised attachment to a distant home conceived of and represented in heroic and even epic terms. But in order to have the freedom to associate with other female migrants on terms of their own choosing, women had to develop some autonomy from their 'real' home-boys: brothers, husbands, and the members of home-based churches and burial societies. When they joined *kiba* groups, and engaged in the pursuit through musical style of a new concept of home, necessity dictated the continuation of some links to migrant men. But if these links became irksome or stood too squarely in the way of women's freedom of performance, they severed these in the name, once again, of a more accurate and faithful reflection of home.

The home which *kiba* performance creates, then, enables a distance from 'home boys' while maintaining a professional connection to some of these. Home in this context is an idiom of solidarity between women who value their acquaintance with fellow-migrants encountered in an urban context, and who are committed to the same enterprise of caring for a rural-based family. Between them, they have created a home, symbolically predicated on a northern country area, in town itself.

3

'WE ARE VISITORS': MEN'S AND WOMEN'S *KIBA*

Designated as part of *mmino wa sesotho* and more recently *mmino wa setšo*, *kiba* is recognised as being a genre rooted in the past. Its continuities with past performance, insisted on by practitioners and audiences, can be demonstrated by comparing its melodic and rhythmic structures with those documented by earlier researchers (Kirby 1934; Huskisson 1958). Its complex rhythmic patterns, and the descending melodic sequence with the distinctive northern Sotho five-note scale, are much the same today as in the Gallotone recordings of the 1940s, and probably much the same as when, decades earlier, migrants from the Northern Province first began to migrate to the Reef. Its use of polyrhythm and call-and-response, and its integration of individual players in a broader melodic pattern through the technique of 'hocketing' (whereby the notes of what appears as a single melody are sung or played by several different players), are features typical of traditional music from other parts of sub-Saharan Africa (Chernoff 1979; Nketia 1975). Unlike the more eclectic forms with which it is usually contrasted – *mmino wa kereke, wa sekolo*, and *wa sebjalobjalo* (church, school, and modern music) – *kiba* has not taken on the ubiquitous three chords of the Wesleyan hymn, and its structure of endlessly repeated rhythmic and melodic cycles shows no signs of giving way to the finite song-form of tin-pan alley or to the four-square rhythmic patterns of radio jive music (Manuel 1988: 22–3, 85–6, 108).[1]

But despite these remarkable continuities of musical form, the genre is not a static or unchanging one. The past, while important to *kiba*'s constituents, is not unmediated, but becomes evident in its refraction through the lens of contemporary performance, and in its reinterpretation by composers, performers and audience. *Kiba* lyrics thus share with other southern African oral poems a propensity to situate their commentaries on the immediacies of contemporary experience within a structure whose links with previous performance renders them durable and permanent (Vail and White 1991: 42, 76–8). Like the words of West African *oriki*, these lyrics indicate the relevance of the past in the present, and show that the present is interpreted in the light of the past (Barber 1991: 15).

The giving of new significance to older songs, and the interpreting of new features against the backdrop of long-established conventions, occurs in the aesthetic of men's and women's *kiba* dance. Through performance, heroic themes seen as belonging to the pre-colonial era are transformed into expressions of the friendly rivalry which underlies much home-based migrant association. But it is in women's *kiba* – also called *koša* or, mostly in its rural version, *lebowa* – that the most flexibility exists for the creative transformation of older themes. Women's *kiba*, as a sung rather than an instrumental music, has lyrics which can be heard, recomposed and reinterpreted. Being sung rather than instrumental, it is stylistically as close to its rural female precedents as it is to the men's genre alongside which it has recently sought reclassification. This is so despite the fact that many of its migrant performers have adopted it only recently, in the spirit of a kind of cultural revival. And as a sung genre, it facilitates some subversion of the grandiose and heroic emphases of its male equivalent. This chapter seeks to explore both the commonalities between men's and women's performance, and the new flexibilities and unorthodoxies which women have introduced into an originally male genre.

BORROWED INSTRUMENTS, OLD SONGS

Two assumptions have underlain much of the ethnomusicological study of southern African societies. The first is that music was thoroughly integrated into the structures and activities of rural life. The second is that this music obeyed relatively fixed stylistic canons. These combined assumptions focused attention away from the phenomenon of stylistic change and from the existence of styles which might be less central to a community's life.[2]

Assumptions of this kind have been shown to be flawed. Our attention has recently been drawn to the existence of marginal or peripheral arts which exist alongside mainstream ones in rural society (Barber 1987: 16, 105): to the existence, for example, of personalised commoner praises alongside those with which chiefs and rulers celebrate their power (Gunner and Gwala 1991). It is often these unofficial genres which become the basis for transformed cultural forms in an urban or migrant context. Miners from Lesotho announce and elaborate their identity as workers through *lifela*, which originated in boys' initiation songs rather than in chiefly praises (Coplan 1987: 414–15). Zulu men's migrant guitar styles transform an individualised tradition of women's songs of love and courtship, rather than drawing from songs of communal or political import (Clegg 1981: 2–3). In similar vein, the Northern Province-based genre of *kiba*, in both its male and female versions, grew out of rural performance styles which were neither under chiefly control nor tied to events of general ritual significance. Both were thought of as *dipapadi* (games), and were performed by groups or teams of youths at occasions such as weddings, or at competitions held at neighbouring villages at which a rich patron might supply beer or present a goat as a prize for the winning group.[3]

Figure 3.1 *Dinaka* (pipes) resting on the top of a *moropa* (drum) (Photos: Santu Mofokeng)

In its male form as a pipe dance, *kiba* is said to have been imported. Its place of origin varies with different accounts: some say it comes from Venda (where a similar dance has long been linked to national political occasions), some from Zimbabwe, and some simply from 'the north'. Although the details of its origin need not concern us here,[4] the fact that players are so insistent on its provenance outside their own area seems to endorse its status as a peripheral form of cultural expression, free to be defined as 'play' and later to become the major vehicle of a new migrant identity since, unlike its Venda counterpart, it has remained beyond the ambit of rulers' jurisdiction.[5]

This stress on importation is even more pronounced in the case of women's music, whose modern form, *kiba*, developed out of a succession of female rural styles. Accounts given by singers and audience emphasise each new style as having been acquired by local populations from some other area – 'We got it from GaMphahlele', 'One of us saw this being danced at GaMasha, and the others learned it from her.' Newer women's songs, imported into villages and replacing older ones in this way, were thought of as 'fashions'. They swept through the countryside, and often contained lyrics of great national topicality alongside those referring to more domestic and area-specific concerns. In the Pedi heartland *Sekhukhune* during the 1940s, girls spent most of their leisure time between initiation and marriage singing *mararankodi*, with lyrics commenting not only on the trials of coping with in-laws, and lamenting the absence of migrant brothers, but also singing of the dangers of the Germans whom many of their men had gone to

Figure 3.2 Drum belonging to *SK Alex* being carried from the men's hostel to the piece of open ground where *kiba* performance takes place (Photo: Santu Mofokeng)

Figure 3.3 *Harepa* player at the Tembisa hostel (Photo: Santu Mofokeng)

fight.[6] Women of a slightly younger generation sang *tšhutšhumakgala* (train), which referred to the struggle of Pedi cultivators and migrants against attempts by the South African state to govern them through the Bantu Authorities system. Subsequent fashions, sung by a succession of younger women, were *makonkwane, eya, mankgodi, marashiya* and *makgakgasa*.[7]

Local accounts, in describing the origins and development of both men's *kiba* and women's rural styles, thus emphasise their exotic origins. Such an emphasis might seem to contradict the insistence on the music's long-standing association with *sotho* tradition. But the borrowed or imported elements have not intrinsically altered musical content. Rather, they have provided novel ways of rendering old songs.

When *dinaka* (pipes) were adapted from Venda or from 'up north', they were used to play songs phrased in the five-note scale of northern Sotho/Pedi music, rather than the eight-note scale of the Venda pipe dance. The borrowing of the instruments did not change the songs, except by 'submerging' their original lyrics, as will be shown further on.[8]

A similar adoption of a new instrument to play old melodies occurred with the later introduction of the *harepa* (German autoharp or zither). When Kirby did his survey in the 1920s, he found that 'whenever possible the native owner of an autoharp has his instrument tuned by a European' (1934: 257). But by the time of the first Gallotone recordings in the 1940s, northern Sotho musicians were tuning the instrument with their five-note scale. The *harepa*, although western in origin, became assimilated as part of pagan or traditionalist culture, and was shunned by members of the mission elites: a process which was repeated with trade-store instruments in other areas of the country as well (Clegg 1981: 3, 7; Coplan 1985: 362–3). Rather than imposing or suggesting a switch-over to European melodic or harmonic forms, this instrument in Sotho hands allowed for a more effective realisation of indigenous musical principles than did the original instrument – in this case the plucked reed *dipela* – which it replaced (Rycroft 1977, cited in Coplan 1985: 363).

The adoption of new forms, or the reliance on new fashions, does not then represent a rejection of older songs but rather a revitalisation of these. The development of women's rural genres which resulted eventually in the emergence of women's *kiba* illustrates this point. Through a complex series of reciprocal interactions between town and country, women in both rural and urban arenas began to perform in a style previously recognised as the preserve of men. This has been the most recent and certainly the most radically different of the 'fashions' which women's music has taken unto itself. Once again involving borrowed instrumentation, this change has led to women's use of the full set of four drums (*meropa*) where a women's song/dance was previously accompanied by a single long drum. But despite its naming as *kiba*, the genre has not borrowed the *dinaka* (pipes) of men's music. Its notes are sung ones.[9]

The naming of the new fashion or style shows something of its gender ambiguity. Sometimes termed *koša* but mostly *kiba* when performed by migrant women, it claims an equivalence with its male counterpart. Played by village women, it is often referred to as *lebowa*, indicating the frequent use made of it by new political elites in the homeland of the same name. A village women's group is called upon to represent its village at the Lebowa agricultural show, to make memorable the opening of a new school or tribal office, or to accompany its chief to the opening of parliament. It is in its rural women's version that the genre has come closest to becoming subordinate to the demands of local chiefs, largely because of the quasi-clientelist dependence of rural women on these chiefs (James 1990b).

The eventual merging of women's with men's music under the rubric of *kiba* was thus the most recent stage in the sequential development of women's rural styles. For decades before this, men's *kiba* had undergone its own development, in the context of the industrial compounds and hostels where most male migrants from the Northern Province were living.[10]

KIBA IN AN URBAN CONTEXT

It was on the Reef, and particularly on the mines, where men were sometimes 'hired because of their art' in performing *kiba*, that the genre acquired many of its present features. Here, performers began to be provided with parts of their gradually evolving uniform by employers: durable plastic shakers to replace the indigenous ones made out of cocoons, headdresses with ostrich feathers and horns, white tennis shoes, and the like. It was on the Reef in the late 1940s and early 1950s that *dinaka* players, originally wearing the black trousers of the *Malaita* gangs,[11] or *thethwana* – a rather restrictive skirt-like garment made of appliquéd and beaded cloth – first saw Scottish kilts, and adopted them as part of the uniform for their performances:

> We saw white soldiers wearing Scotch. *Kiba* is like soldiers organised against something, so we too wanted to wear one thing which was similar.[12]

The adoption of kilts was to have a marked effect on the aesthetic of the dance due to the freedom of movement it allowed and encouraged. One of the most applauded effects in current usage is a tossing of the kilt from side to side over the buttocks 'like a peacock', ending with a flourish in which the kilt remains up to reveal (in contrast to the famed Scottish practice) a pair of white boxer shorts underneath. Such a gesture would have been impossible in the restrictive *thethwana*, and would probably never have been thought of without the impetus provided by the kilt's swinging movement.

Not only the uniformity of soldiers' dress but also something of the ethos of regimented soldierly behaviour found its way into *kiba*. Rank-and-file members were called *masole* (soldiers), and the idiom used to describe membership of a *kiba* group – *go joina* (from the English, to join) – is the same as that used to describe enlisting in a military regiment, or 'joining up'. Although none of my informants fought with the Allied forces in World War II, many older *kiba* players did so. It is probable that much of the imagery of soldiery to be found in present-day *kiba* performance derives from this experience.

In men's *kiba*, these trappings and ideas drawn from the experience of modern soldiery have been combined with the military idiom of an epic pre-colonial past. Although men's songs have had no words since singing was replaced by the introduction of *dinaka* (pipes) from 'the north', the original words are still known to some participants. These submerged lyrics form the basis of elaborate reflections on the significance of individual tunes, as in this interpretation of the song *madikoti*:

> On arrival home at the *mošate* [chief's kraal] the warrior will have to dance *kati* [a rejoicing dance] and say a *sereto* [praise] about himself. The chief ... will say 'a brave man amongst brave men, when I say I am a chief, I am a chief because of you'. He will go to one of his houses, and take one of his daughters who will then be given to the man who made them win the battle ... The chief will praise his daughter, saying 'there you are, my child, there you are with the buttocks of a light-skinned girl who has never walked in bad ways'.[13]

It is not only the lyrics which celebrate the heroic era of the chiefs, but the actions of the dance as well. In *segoata-goatana* (the one who sneaks away) and *magana go bušwa* (they refuse to be ruled) the secession by a splinter group from a chief's dominion is both described in the lyrics and enacted by the performers, who dance backwards in a stealthy way out of the main performance area.

One of the most important songs in the *kiba* repertoire is *monti*:[14]

> *Monti* was a *mogobo*, a situation where warriors from the war will enter the *mošate* [chief's kraal] singing and dancing. When people enter from the war singing it, it will have a double meaning. You will feel unhappy because some have died in the war, but you will also feel happy and satisfied because you have won the war. With us, as we use *dinaka*, we no longer do this *mogobo*, but instead sing *monti*. It is a regimental song, it is for attacking.[15]

It can be seen from this account that *monti* is conceived of, on one level, as a re-enactment of, and perhaps a replacement for, the scenario of warriors returning from a battle. In contemporary use, however, this song serves as a song of greeting by visitors to a host and/or an audience, in which the ideas of respectful praise and pleasing one's hosts are foremost. Its expression of this visiting ethic is tied up with its role as introduction and as finale to the whole sequence of dances of which the performance consists. In greeting/introduction, the dancers group together at some distance from the central performance area (defined by the presence of the drums), and dance slowly onto centre stage (see Figure I.1), where they then assume a circle formation and move around the drums; or, in situations with a more clearly defined inside space, such as the rural homestead of someone who has invited an urban-based group to play at a party, the performers will assemble in the road or public space outside, and dance through the gateway into the yard. At the end of the performance the dancers, having formally greeted and taken leave of their host or audience, will use *monti* again to take them back through the gateway to the public space beyond.[16]

Migrant women *kiba* singers, performing their own version of *monti*, contribute to its transformation from a song of triumphal regimental return to one of migrant visitation. Women dance with a flashlight brandished in the right hand and a glove worn on the left; a practice explicitly thought of as substituting for the weapon and shield which members of a regiment once carried in the right and the left hand respectively (see Figure 3.7).[17] But the right hand may also be used to brandish other objects, such as the bottles of soft drink which the host of the occasion has provided (see Figure 5.7). In this context, the action connotes praising and respectful visiting rather than aggression.

Much creative effort goes into harnessing the potentially disruptive effects of unbridled competitiveness. The men's song *ke rena baeng* (we are visitors) with its women's version *basadi ba baeng* (visiting women) stresses that the host dancers – equivalent to a football 'home team' – should not feel threatened by the arrival of the visiting dance group since it has come in a spirit not of rivalry but of co-operation, not to set themselves apart but to be included in a broader unity.

A situation in which the ritualisation of visitors' competitiveness could be seen alongside a more naked expression of this competition was at a *kiba* annual party.

The annual party of SK Alex

At the piece of open ground next to the No. 1 Men's Hostel in Alexandra, the dance group *SK Alex* held its annual party one Sunday late in 1990. They spent their accumulated savings from the year's performances on a variety of drink and food, of which the most important item was a sheep which was slaughtered at midnight on Saturday and by Sunday morning was cooking in a series of black pots on an open fire. The honoured guests, who arrived at midday, were *Bapedi Champions*, a group also representing *Sekhukhune* but based in the Benoni township of Daveyton. Immediately after their arrival in a hired bus, the visitors alighted and prepared to dance. While the women, already dressed in *diaparo tša setšo* (traditional dress), stood to one side, the men, still wearing their best Sunday suits, did a performance of the regimental song *monti* to greet their hosts. It was accompanied by such invocations as: 'We want to please those who have invited us: whatever food has been prepared here is for us, so we must please these people.' The hosts, *SK Alex*, also dressed in suits, responded with a similar greeting.

It was only later, after both men's groups had retreated into the hostel to change into full dance regalia, that the fierceness of the competition between them started to be expressed in performance. The groups vied with each other in producing a range of special aesthetic effects never seen at regular practices. During a kicking dance step one man created great hilarity by 'losing' a shoe which soared high above the heads of the spectators; another man 'borrowed' a hat from a member of the audience as a dance prop, only to be outdone by a member of the competing group who 'borrowed' a small child from its mother for the same purpose. The man eventually judged best dancer by the crowd, as measured by the amount of money thrown to him, engaged in an acrobatic display which involved equal measures of simulated aggression and comical self-mockery, and which ended with him turning somersaults and falling with mock surprise in the dust.

The women's groups had also kept some of their most striking *dipapadi* (dramatic tableaux; lit. 'games') for this stage of the competition. The host group put on an act in which a sick person, after first consulting a *ngaka* (traditional healer) for a cure, was then taken to a medical doctor in a white coat who examined her with a stethoscope and prescribed some bright pink medicine. The visitors, to the crowd's delight, produced a 'monkey' – a woman clothed in overalls and a gorilla mask – who swaggered among the dancers and made as if to frighten the children in the audience.

The dancing and acting in this second phase of the event was no longer designed to please the hosts, but to outdo them. 'We are two groups, and we must compete, just like Pirates and Chiefs.'[18]

In a *kiba* performance like this one, migrant men combine a number of discourses. By assuming some of the costume and ethos of the Scottish military, they state their membership of a disciplined and purposeful group of urban-based musicians. By referring to the past in which their forebears were ruled over by the chiefs of the Pedi polity, they state their identity as inhabitants of their home in *Sekhukhune*. And by retaining some of the challenge of battle as a residue of meaning behind the actions of greeting and visitation, they use *kiba* as an idiom of competition with other urban-based groups.

Women's performance emphasises many of the same themes: the idioms of soldiery and 'joining', of fierce competition ambiguously co-existing with deference, and of pride in rural-based identity. In some respects, then, women co-operate with men in the construction through performance of a unitary migrant identity: a world of visits, reciprocation, and competition. But in other ways, women's *kiba* performance distinguishes itself sharply from that of men. There are differences of style and subject matter which facilitate the creation through performance of a separate, specifically female, migrants' world.

WOMEN'S LYRICS: COMPOSITION AND INTERPRETATION

Dinaka is not supposed to be sung by women ... Now men have left it and women are trying to bring it back; that is why we say '*lebowa*'.[19]

In the old days of *marashiya* [a rural, pre-*kiba* style], there was no *monti* [for women]. We sing it today with our mouths while men blow pipes.[20]

These two statements capture some of the transformations which have brought female performance into the *kiba* fold. The first was made by Lucas Kgole, a musical entrepreneur who, with a female backing group, has recorded several albums with the company Gallo Africa, and who currently makes a living from herbalism in the village of Sephaku, in a district

Figure 3.4 The men and women of *Bapedi Champions* at the annual party of *SK Alex*, 1990. Alexandra Township (Photo: Santu Mofokeng)

adjoining *Sekhukhune*. It asserts that *dinaka*, or men's *kiba*, is more or less defunct in village life. Previously excluded from the genre, women are now seen as having revived it by starting to engage in its performance (albeit, in his case, under the patronage of a male group-leader). The second observation was made by a rural female singer in the *Sekhukhune* village group *Dithabaneng*. It indicates that, while women's songs like *marashiya* were previously named separately, they now have the status of female parallels to standard items in the male repertoire, distinguished from these by being sung rather than rendered instrumentally and by the much more sedate style of dancing. What women's *monti* shares with men's, stylistically, is a distinctive pattern played on a set of four drums (*meropa*). Similarly parallelled by women's equivalents, and similarly sharing with them easily recognised drumming patterns, are the other core songs in the men's repertoire: *lerago*, *kiba* (from which the style takes its name), *fesi*, and others (see Tables 3.1–3.4).

The standard rhythm for each song in the male repertoire provides a kind of peg to which a range of women's songs adapted from previously existing rural genres have been attached. In some cases, a man's song may have only one female equivalent, but in others it has several, each with its own lyrics, melody and dance-pattern (see Table 3.4). The multiplicity of women's songs reflects two things: the greater diversity and scatter of home areas, and thus of female rural styles represented in a single woman's group, and the

Figure 3.5(a) and (b) *Kiba*: male dancer performing solo, with pipe players in the background (Photo: Santu Mofokeng)

Table 3.1 Core songs documented by Huskisson in the 1950s, and still played today

Monti	A regimental song
Lerago	Buttock
Kiba	(From 'to stamp or beat time')
Fesi	

Table 3.2 Additional songs, played by some of the groups met by Huskisson, and still played today

Madikoti	The girl with dimples
Lekwapa	Shangaan
O le metše	You used to steal
Segoata-goatana	The one who sneaks away
Magana go bušwa	They refuse to be ruled

Table 3.3 Additional songs played today, not listed by Huskisson

Mahlwa le mpona	You have always seen me
Mojeremane/ke epa thaba	German/I dig the mountain

greater improvisational challenge posed – and freedom allowed – by songs with lyrics than by those without. If lyrics can be heard and appreciated, they can also be adjusted to enable the precise expression of particular sentiments. It is in the creation of new lyrics, the re-creation of old lyrics, and the constant process of reinterpreting both that one can see women's music, having sought legitimation within the recognised migrant genre of *kiba*, moving beyond the constraints imposed by this definition to express concerns of its own.

If the features of women's *kiba* suggest its recognition as a separate stylistic entity, this distinctiveness is most apparent in its links to older, rural-based female styles. Although the new style of *kiba* has become popular and has replaced older ones in both urban and rural areas, there is a continuity of musical features and of subject matter. Fragments of older songs are integrated into the context of newer ones, which are then reinterpreted by their performers: new lyrics are added which give older ones a different slant and which then provide the basis for a changed significance to an older song.

This observation provides a key to understanding the contrast between the unheard lyrics of *dinaka* (pipes: men's *kiba*) and the audible ones of *dikoša* (songs: women's *kiba*). At first glance, this appears as a contrast between a nostalgia expressed in heroic and metaphoric terms for grand public occasions in bygone days, and a concern for domestic situations in the more recent past expressed with critical and often comical directness.

Table 3.4 Some men's tunes with women's equivalents

Men	Women 1	Women 2	Women 3
Lekwapa	*Lekwapa*		
Lerago	*Setimela*		
Monti	*Legalane*	*Ke na le ngwana wa mošemane*	
Kiba	*Lebowa*	*Sekopa sa maiesane*	*Mpepetloane*

Dinaka tell of beautiful virgins given to brave warriors in far-off times, while *dikoša*, like other women's genres with similarly domestic preoccupations (Gunner 1989: 13, 33), comment wryly on such matters as the need to conceal an illicit love-affair from one's husband.

But this apparent preoccupation with the domestic and mostly rural setting of women's experience conceals the capacity of these songs to undergo a continual process of recomposition and reinterpretation. They are thus not fixed in structure or in meaning, but are characterised by what Barber and others have called an 'emergent' quality. Lyrics which derive from older songs, and which on one level might be seen as reflecting on rural women's domestic involvements in the past, on another level express a set of very contemporary and often urban-based concerns, and provide comment- ary on extra-domestic as well as domestic issues.

The lyrics of these songs, like the West African *oriki* documented by Barber, consist of different parts which were composed by different people at different times, with the most recent contributions being those of the contemporary performer/composer herself (Barber 1984: 504). In women's *kiba*, the solo singer adds her own new words on to those of an existing song, and sings the resulting combination interspersed with a chorus, usually also the song's title, in which the other singers *dumela* (sing a repeated refrain, lit. 'agree').

The juxtaposition of old and new elements may at first glance appear confusing: some chorus singers, questioned about the significance of lyrical remnants composed by unknown singers in the past, claim ignorance because they are from 'an old song'. This suggests a throwing together of newer with older elements in a spontaneous and perhaps unconsidered way. But the use of these elements in the hands of accomplished composers, and their interpretation by seasoned performers and audiences, reveals a logical structuring which underlies this apparent lack of design. Themes of the lyrical fragments retained from past performance are often echoed, inverted, or transformed in those of the newly composed sections.[21] It is through this structuring that the relevance of 'the past in the present' is made explicit (Barber 1991: 15), and that statements of singers' contemporary pre- occupations, problems and aspirations are given a transcendent quality

Figure 3.6 *SK Alex* women: drummer and solo singer in performance (Photo: Santu Mofokeng)

which links them to the concerns of previous generations, and to 'tradition' (Vail and White 1991: 42; Coplan 1987: 415).

The linking of fragments within a broader structure which gives these meaning can be seen in songs which use 'poetic licence' to utter veiled criticism.[22] Negative comments about the present misconduct of an individual chief within the homeland government are placed against a backdrop in which the abstract and transcendent qualities of chiefship are celebrated. Critical comment of this kind relies on interpretation not only by performers but also by informed and receptive audience response. *Dipalela Tlala*, a women's group from the village of Sephaku in a district adjoining *Sekhukhune*, sings a song of praise to the area and to its chief Jack Mahlangu which at once announces the women's clientelist dependence on him and simultaneously criticises him in a veiled manner:

Dipalela tlala, ko re yeng gae	Defeaters of hunger, let us return home
Bana ba Mahlangu	Children of Mahlangu
Bana ba Jack, ko re yeng gae	Children of Jack, let us return home
Dipalela tlala	Defeaters of hunger
Gopolang Sephaku naga matebele	Remember Sephaku the place of Ndebele
Sephaku, ntsiru ge le ke bone musi	Sephaku, give way, let me see the mist

Ke bone magoši diapara nkwe	Let me see the chiefs who wear the royal leopard skin
A ke bona magoši, ke bona mong a rena	When I see the chiefs, I see our own lord
Mong a rena, le ga le ka molatola	Our own lord, even if you say bad things about him
Mong a rena, le koloni ba mo dumela	Our own lord, even in the Cape they greet him
Mong a rena, le Pretoria ba mo dumela.	Our own lord, even in Pretoria they greet him.

Although this song appears primarily concerned with praise of the area and of the chief, its composer insisted in private discussion that it was critical of the chief, and that village and area audiences would be aware of this on hearing the song. The phrase *dipalela tlala* (defeaters of hunger) is a veiled reference to the chief's support of the introduction into the area of a much-disliked agricultural co-op, which landed most cultivators deep into debt and which forced them to have to face, and defeat, hunger and deprivation. The phrase 'even if you say bad things about him', while appearing to invalidate criticism, in fact substantiates it, and the reference to his acceptance in Pretoria disparages him for his role in the state-controlled structures of government.[23]

It may, then, be not only factors intrinsic to the form of women's *kiba* itself, but also the dependent social relationships in which its performers find themselves inextricably involved, which make this genre so dependent on sensitive audience reception for its fullest appreciation.

Composers thus situate their criticisms within the context of history. The fragments of older songs may, as in the previous example, provide evocative descriptions of a past way of life in which leadership and area loyalty were sacrosanct. But the existing songs from which fragments are drawn may, themselves, describe more recent situations in which the deprivation, harassment and anxiety of the migrant existence are a feature.

Setimela (steam train) is an example which demonstrates this point. The song, today performed by a range of women's *kiba* groups, urban and rural, is presented here in the version sung by the rural-based group *Dithabaneng*:

Setimela sa Mmamarwale	Train of Mmamarwale
Nthshwanyana	Black carrier
Setimela nkabe se rwale buti bokgolwa	Train should carry my brother from *bokgolwa* [i.e.the state of being a migrant who never returns]
Buti e sa le a eya bokgolwa	My brother home from *bokgolwa*
Ngwana-mme o tla hwa ese ka mmona.	My mother's child would die without me seeing him.
Setimela nkabe se rwale	Train should carry women

Figure 3.7 Nkapile Hlakola, composer/solo singer of *Dipalela Tlala*, in performance with her group (Photo: Deborah James)

Figure 3.8 A 'diviner' throws the bones: dramatic tableau of *Dipalela Tlala* (Photo: Deborah James)

Figure 3.9 'Police' making an arrest: dramatic tableau of *Dipalela Tlala* (Photo: Deborah James)

| Se re iseng ka lebowa khutlong sa thaba | It would carry us to Lebowa mountain |
| Ka ntshe gago tsotsi gago mathatha. | Where there are no *tsotsis* [gangsters] and no problems. |

The first part of the song is a fragment which was composed about fifty years ago. The last three lines, recently composed by the leader of a neighbouring group and copied from it by *Dithabaneng*, evoked an elaborate and lively interpretation:

> They mean something that can carry them away from the past into the new style of living where there are no problems. I think they also have education in mind, where an educated person can rid his family members of financial problems. We are no longer, as in the past, milling our own crops, today we take them to the mill or get mealie-meal from the shops.[24]

The original character of this song, with its plaintive cry by an individual girl about the absence of her migrant brother, has been transformed through new composition into a self-aware statement of female group identity, linked with notions of modernity and nationhood. At the same time, this optimistic view of the benefits brought by the 'new style of living' is mediated by linking it to the deprivation which women have previously suffered on account of migrancy and the modern way. Heartland rural singers, while orienting themselves to progress and the future, regard themselves and their performance as firmly situated within the world of *sesotho*.[25]

Another song which juxtaposes its composer's experience with the relatively recent predicament of other women has harassment by police as its central theme. Paulina Mphoka, encouraged by her friends to compose a new song, added new lyrics to the existing ones of *Mosadi wa sepankana*:[26]

Mosadi wa sepankana, mosadi wa diphafaneng	Woman who wears a skin, woman of beer
O rekiša bjalwa	She sells beer
Mapodisa a ka Lebowa aa monyaka.	The police of Lebowa are looking for her.
Tsodio o otile, mokgwa ntshe ga a robala	Tsodio is thin, he does not sleep
O tshwenya ke malome-agwe	He is troubled by [the ghost of] his uncle
E le go Matšhabataga	Who is called Matšhabataga
Tsodio o bolaile Matšhabathaga	Tsodio has killed Matšhabataga
Le yena Tsodio o nyakwa ke mapodisa.	He is also troubled by police.
Basadi ba joinile ke masole	Women have now joined the soldiers
Batšea pasa le banna.	They are getting passes just like men.

The middle section is based on a song which, although part of the corpus of *mmino wa setšo*, was itself recently created by *harepa* player and composer Johannes Mokgwadi, one of the best-known exponents of *mmino wa setšo* in the Northern Province. It concerns the molesting by police of Tsodio, who, having killed his uncle Matšhabataga, is being both haunted by the ghost of his victim and plagued by the less ethereal representatives of law and order.

This fairly neutral reference to the police is made more pointed by its juxtaposition with the last section, of two lines. Deriving from earlier female performance, this refers to the inclusion of women in the late 1950s within the legislation requiring Africans to carry passes. It records a time when, moving to South Africa's urban areas, women became subject to the same indiscriminate raids and arrests by police which men had been experiencing for decades. Paulina's own more recent experience of harassment, this time at the hands of the Lebowa rather than the South African police, is recorded in the first section, of three lines. Like a number of other *kiba* singers before they became migrants, she had supplemented her family's income by brewing illegal liquor, and had been arrested by police for doing so.

This combining of three separate incidents lends a weight to each of them which it could not have possessed on its own. None has the links with pre-colonial rural experience which might be thought necessary to a genre claiming links with the past, but each enshrines a broader view, critical and detached from immediate experience, of such scenarios of harsh persecution. Paulina's addition, here featuring as a new fragment set against an older backdrop, might some years hence appear as part of the collected stock of wisdom passed down from the experienced singers of the past to the novice composers of the future.

But Paulina's song is not only about police harassment. It has also been explained to me in other terms. It is about women's new-found identity as migrants who, like soldiers, form strong collegial bonds, in a disciplined group, with others who share their situation away from home. Another interpretation foregrounds the quality of *botho* (humanity or human goodness), illustrated by default in the story of the murderous Tsodio. Described here in the context of other lyrics which refer to the strength and fortitude of women, *botho* becomes, against this backdrop, a quality especially of women. As with other 'emergent' genres, the audience interprets the lyrics' significance, and may construct the song anew at different performances through their differing interpretations (Barber 1991: 15; Gunner 1989: 21).

The source from which the story about Tsodio comes is not only the well-known song by Johannes Mokgwadi, often played on the radio, but also a hugely popular radio serial of the same name which has been broadcast by Radio Lebowa. It is the topicality and popularity of the radio serial and song on which it is based which enable listeners to attach to this brief reference a range of meanings not set down in the text itself. The flexibility enjoyed by an audience in interpreting a song like this one is inseparable from an imprecision about where one genre ends and another begins.

THE BLURRING OF GENRE BOUNDARIES

A blurring of genre boundaries is common within oral performance culture. Another feature of *oriki*, this is closely linked to its character as an emergent form with no apparent closure or fixity. *Oriki* could be seen as constituting a genre in their own right, but are also performed in the context of various other modes or genres, and rely on still further accompanying genres for their fullest understanding (Barber 1991: 1–7; Coplan 1988: 343–50).

In the case of women's *kiba*, its very emergence, as a set of previously existing rural genres newly incorporated within a male migrant one, is testimony to this lack of rigid genre boundaries. In addition, the process of composing lyrics and devising actions for particular songs entails a perpetual borrowing or importing of elements from sources apparently external to *kiba* itself.

One source is a series of scenarios from real life, represented in stylised form. Central among these are healing rituals, both divination by *dingaka* (traditional doctors) complete with divination mat and *ditaola* (diviner's bones), and the diagnosis and cure offered by western doctors, featuring a white coat, a stethoscope, a telephone and 'medicines' made of commercial soft drinks. Other dramatic tableaux involve uniformed policemen who perform mock arrests and extract fines.[27]

Kiba also draws from parallel forms of expression or companion genres within the realm of *sesotho* (*sotho* ways). Among these are *direto* (praises), a form of expression in which many urban female performers are expert, proverbs, and certain songs from *koma* (women's initiation). These, although strictly secret in their original form, have been incorporated into *kiba* in a disguised form, as in the song *Tšhukutšwane*:

Tšhukutšwane	Female rhinoceros
Mmamogala wa basadi.	The brave one of women.

This comment on the bravery of women, likening it to that of the small but tenacious female rhino, is here taken from its restricted setting within initiation and given a broader relevance. As well as evoking memories of the experience of initiation, the song is thought of in association with the proverb *Mmangwana o swara thipa ka bogaleng* (a mother handles the knife on the sharp side).

As an emergent genre developing within a rapidly changing social context on which its lyrics reflect, women's *kiba* thus draws on parallel forms of *sotho* cultural expression, as well as on popular media such as records and the radio, as its sources. These elements are integrated within the framework of *kiba* songs, and reinterpreted in the light of singers' contemporary experience. One of the key events around which lyrics are explicated, and which inspires the creation of new lyrics and dance-steps to add to existing ones, is the act of performing *kiba* itself. The apparently domestic concerns expressed by some songs, inherited or claimed by contemporary female performers from their forebears, are overshadowed in certain contexts by the immediacy of *kiba* sung and danced in the here and now.

An example is one of the female equivalents of *monti*:

Ke na le ngwana wa mošemane	I have a boy child
Wena o lefšega.	You are a coward.

These lyrics reflect in their original version on a fairly common family situation, and one not unknown to *kiba* singers themselves: a woman is boasting about her son, and mocking the inadequacies of another woman whose inability to produce children is proof of her 'cowardice'. But, in becoming a song of *kiba*, these words have been reinterpreted as a statement of boastful pride in the singers' ability to perform, and of scornful disparagement of their rivals' inability to do so.[28]

Another example is the song *Sekopa sa maiesane*, sung and danced to the rhythm of the men's song *kiba* from which the entire genre takes its name. This song was taught to the group by Julia Lelahana, who learned it at her rural home:

Sekopa sa maiesane	[Meaning unknown]
Bošego bo ja kolobe	At night pigs are eaten
Mošate gae.	At the home village.
Nna nka senwe bjalwa	I will not drink beer
Go nwa bo ntage	As it will make me drunk
Ge ke tagile bo ntira setlaela	If I am drunk I will look like a fool.
Ke melato ya lona lapa le	These are problems of this family
Le tla no šala le e bona	You will see how you solve them when I'm gone.
Le tla no šala lentse le ekiša	You will remain imitating me
Ka gore ge go esa re boya le tsela.	Because when the sun rises we will have to go back.

All but the last section of the song consists of remnants from previous songs. While the meaning of the song's title and of the first three-line section was so obscure that none of the singers could explain it, the next section, like a number of other women's *kiba* songs, reflects on the disgrace of uncontrolled drunkenness. The third section, of two lines, speaks of domestic strife in a rural homestead. Julia's composition, the last two lines, follows on in style from the lines immediately preceding it. But it refers to a visit by herself and her fellow *kiba* singers where they make such an impact with the quality of their performance that local singers copy their songs and dances long after their departure. The idea that the song is about *kiba* itself, imparted by this most recent input, also affects the interpretation of other lines: hence the specific disadvantage of drunkenness in this context is the fact that it impairs the dancers' ability to perform at their best.[29]

Julia interpreted the song *lekwapa* in similar vein. A core song in both men's and women's *kiba*, this refers in its original version to a situation of ethnically based antagonism:

Lekwapa a le bolawe	The Shangaan should be killed
Mamanoko a bo thoka	People of the stick
Tšhagate ga ana taba.	Tšhagate is not a problem.

The ostensible meaning of the song, still present as an underlying signifi-cance in the men's version, is a statement of enmity, set in a warlike context, against a Shangaan who should be killed,[30] and of affinity with '*Tšhagate*' (a proper name, here signifying other Sotho-speakers) who can be left to live. But again, in its women's version, the song is reinterpreted as commenting on the rivalry between a competing dance group (equated with *lekwapa*) and the home team (*Tšhagate*).[31]

In these and many other examples, a commentary which contains reference to the domestically-oriented and rurally based past of *sotho* women is overlaid with new significance. Through a process referred to by perform-ance theorists as 'recontextualising' (Bauman and Briggs 1990), an older text, incorporated as *kiba* and placed within the new context of migrant women's urban association, starts to offer a commentary on the feeling of fulfilment entailed in being a 'soldier' who has 'joined' other working women and who gains a sense of common identity through performance with these fellow members.

Alongside the other concerns documented in this chapter and elsewhere in the book, the capacity of women's *kiba* lyrics to be interpreted as signi-fying pride in a group's own performance is what makes this genre particularly adept at carrying the message of a new group identity for migrant women. This capacity enables *kiba* to refer not only to a range of domestic and extra-domestic issues in the lives or past experiences of its singers, but also to itself as a reflexive performative genre (Baumann 1989: 266). It is through this capacity, too, that women's *kiba* remains firmly linked with the male version of the genre. The themes of self-praise, celebration of performance technique, and friendly disparagement of the inadequacies of rival dancers are common to male and female performance as they transform heroic and domestic concerns, respectively, into idioms for friendly but fierce competition.

MEN'S GENRE, WOMEN'S GENRE

Like men, women remake the past through *kiba*. Where men, through dance and music, transform submerged epic themes into statements of friendly competitiveness, women turn domestic themes into commentaries on their success as polished performers. But there is continual ambiguity about whether women identify wholeheartedly with the common projects of *kiba*. On the one hand, as the earlier description of women's *monti* makes clear, there is a unity of purpose with men's *kiba* in enunciating the ethic of competitiveness combined with respectful visiting. But on the other, as can be seen from the lyrics presented above, there is also an independent initiative in which women's *kiba* marks off its participants as the holders of a specifically female migrant identity, pitting their communal sense of skill against that of other women migrants from the north.

Why has a female version of a male genre developed in the circumstances of labour migration on the Reef? Or, phrased in slightly different terms, why has women's music, by adopting the drum ensemble and rhythms of men's, been transformed into a subdivision of men's music? Why have women's migrant songs, so clearly different from men's in many respects, claimed recognition as a part of *kiba*?

In looking for an answer to these questions, it is fruitful to read some of the still limited anthropological literature that explores the impact of gender on forms of cultural representation. Recent attempts to understand gender divisions in cultural and musical practice have located these within the context of other, broader uses of the male/female dichotomy to divide the social world (Gal 1991; Koskoff 1989b). Based on – and simultaneously confirming – a division of labour, such divisions also confirm and entrench the differential rights of women and men to exercise public power. They even enshrine the very conceptual dichotomies which are thought to underlie social life: public/private, nature/culture and the like (Ortner 1974; Ortner and Whitehead 1981; Rogers 1978).

The oppositional division of musical roles between men and women is thus linked, in specific cultural contexts, to other conceptual divisions in the social world. From one perspective, gender-defined musical practices may be seen as complementary and as relying on reciprocal interdependence for their proper definition. But this division may also be seen as serving to separate women's music off from the mainstream, and as providing women with a socially acceptable but restricted space for musical expression. In this way, a specifically 'women's' music may be one with less of a voice, less of an audience, than that of men (Koskoff 1989b: 8–9).

Despite major disruptions in the form and content of social relationships, dichotomies of this kind are still used to represent gender-role divisions in the world of southern African labour migration. In the Northern Province region of *Sekhukhune* in particular, rurally resident and dependent wives/

Figure 3.10(a) and (b) *SK Alex* on 'home' visits: preparing to depart for, and dancing *monti* on arriving at, Mamone in Sekhukhune (photo: Santu Mofokeng)

sisters play roles conceptualised as specifically female, and thought of as strongly linked to the domain of *sesotho*.[32] In this rural setting, women's music remains in a separately defined sphere of female, *sotho* performance. Despite its use by chiefs and homeland elites on occasions of political importance, and despite women singers' use of it, reciprocally, to utter criticism of the holders of power, in everyday settings it is largely ignored by men since it belongs to a domain of things qualified by the adjectival clause *tša basadi* (of women).

Women's music, even that stylistically identified as *kiba*, is thus in rural circumstances generally assigned to a separate sphere and denied a broader audience. It may be in order to escape the lower status of a female genre that its migrant performers, particularly in an urban setting, have sought to make themselves part of men's *kiba*. Like certain female performers elsewhere they 'have begun to "cross over" into the mainstream', and have enjoyed a corresponding rise in 'musical status' (Koskoff 1989b: 12).

The consequences of a failure to gain such recognition may be seen in the case of the songs/poems of migrant women from Lesotho, whose art has remained generically distinct from men's. Lacking a classificatory label of their own, these songs are excluded from the precincts of *sesotho* within which the equivalent male migrant poems are accommodated: 'within the politics of performance in Lesotho, a woman's genre whose texts are often fiercely critical of the behaviour of men and governments is being denied a public identity' (Coplan 1991: 174). In contrast, the women's songs redefined as *kiba* have undoubtedly gained broader recognition from their inclusion within a previously exclusively male genre. The adoption of the drum ensemble and rhythms of this men's style has allowed women to continue singing and improvising on specifically female songs, but under the rubric of an established male migrant cultural form.

If women's migrant song is part of the male migrant genre of *kiba*, and if it evokes an enthusiastic audience response commensurate with that enjoyed by the male version, it is primarily the highly polished, vibrant and exciting quality of the dancing and drumming which gives it this shared identity. And if, despite its inclusion within *kiba*, it remains distinct from its male equivalent, it is in the importance of lyrics and the freedom to improvise on these that this separateness can be seen. In the sung and danced aspects of men's and women's performance, there are contrasting variations of restriction and freedom. While men's *kiba*, lacking lyrics, provides fewer opportunities to express comment than women's, the effectiveness of women's ability to do so is curbed by the fact that the audience's attention is in any case focused away from their lyrics and on to the dancing, which can be more immediately appreciated. On the other hand, men while dancing have more freedom than women to improvise as individuals, each showing off his own distinctive style. The same rhythmic free flights played

Figure 3.11(a) and (b) Rural women singers performing to greet their urban
visitors, *SK Alex*. Mamone, Sekhuhkune (Photo: Santu Mofokeng)

on the solo drum which prompt such improvisations from men, from women elicit a set of movements apparently improvisatory in nature, but carefully co-ordinated together as a group.

The creation of a female version for a male genre, or the recasting of a female genre with male instruments and in a male guise, thus represents a seeking of higher status for a style otherwise thought of – especially in a rural context – as being of little account. As a musical reclassification it does not, however, represent a mere sleight of hand. The migrant singers of *kiba*, unlike their rural stay-at-home equivalents, are constructing a new gender identity in terms other than merely musical ones. The roles they play 'as sons', and as primary breadwinners within their natal families, call into question the criteria conventionally thought to differentiate men's behaviour from that of women. The adoption of these new roles, within the context of existing family relationships, will be seen in the chapter which follows to be one of the concerns which *kiba* lyrics express.

4

WOMEN AS BROTHERS, WOMEN AS SONS: DOMESTIC PREDICAMENTS UNRAVELLED

Changes in domestic relationships resulting from labour migration in southern Africa have been documented in some detail. Emphasis has been placed, in particular, on the effects on women of marital breakdown. In the worst scenario, the conjugal dissolution or reluctance to marry which conditions of migrancy engender has led to the emergence of small female-headed households: the most deprived of all family types in the southern African labour reserve (Brown 1983: 375–80; Murray 1981: 154). But alternative developments have seen unmarried women provided with some security within agnatic structures (Schapera and Roberts 1975: 267; Murray 1981: 110; Izzard 1985: 268–9). Another possibility, particularly for migrant or working women, has been the creation of households based on structured co-operation between sisters, between siblings of both sexes, or between mother and daughter (Izzard 1985: 272–4; Niehaus 1994; Preston-Whyte 1978). The documenting of the 'reconstruction' (Schapera 1940: 356) of families, while thorough, has shown us little of the way in which gender roles, thus radically restructured, are conceptualised. We do not know whether women, newly centred within families in which the various ties of blood provide continuity where those of marriage have failed to do so, continue to think of their relationships to men in the conventional terms laid down by previously established gender stereotypes. In the case of migrant *kiba* singers, certainly, convention combines with reconceptual-isation to provide a complex and equivocal view of gender relationships.

As I claimed in the previous chapter, women's *kiba* clothes new themes in the trappings of tradition. In addition to expressions of pleasure and pride in its performers' ability to outdo rivals through virtuoso performance, it offers comments on aspects of the broader social environment. Aspirations to live in 'the new style', criticisms of chiefly misbehaviour and complaints about police harassment are grist to the mill of both rural and migrant *kiba* com-posers. Lending these utterances greater weight, at least when used by migrant women in the urban context, *kiba* eludes the stigmatisation of a women's-only style by claiming broader recognition alongside the perform-ance of men.

This suggests a challenging of the received wisdom about male and female behaviour. But the intricacies of domestic relationships, in the context of which such conventions are forged and reinforced, have not been a concern of any of the lyrics presented thus far. On the contrary, I have claimed that these lyrics succeed in transcending the limitations of the strictly domestic preoccupations which were a concern of earlier female styles.

It will be seen in what follows that where *kiba* or proto-*kiba* lyrics do present and comment on relationships within the household they appear to depict women in the role of the dependent, stay-at-home wife, sister or daughter-in-law. Apparently enshrining conventional womanly roles, they often direct themselves to correcting wayward or unfeminine behaviour. The migrant singers of these lyrics, however, while seeming to comment about the conduct befitting a dependent wife, are actually conceiving of their own roles in terms of the dependability associated with a brother or a son. But their assumption of such responsibilities is not phrased directly through *kiba*. It is expressed, rather, by means of a reconsideration of 'proper *sotho*' kinship roles. Here, the pertinent domestic relationship is not that between a dependent woman and a male provider, but that between a brother and sister within a natal family. The co-operation that should exist between such siblings, and the antagonism and competition which may result from their attempts to occupy similarly central roles within a family, are the main areas of contestation. If we examine *kiba* lyrics in the light of this redefinition of gender roles, we find that they do, indeed, contain strident criticisms of male behaviour, albeit phrased in terms of the marital-style relationships which are of little pertinence to most migrant women performers.

KIBA: MEN AS HUSBANDS, MEN AS BROTHERS

In the rural women's songs on which *kiba* is based, and in later *kiba* songs themselves, the lyrics express apparently conservative views of womanly roles. The necessity of being courted and chosen in marriage is sung about in the song *mankgodi*:

Mankgodi o a pholo ke saletšwe	I, the vulture, am delayed
Ke saleditšwe ke go hloka diphego	Delayed by not having wings
Ke nna kgarebe ke a bina	I am an initiated girl, I am dancing/ singing
Ke bina koša ye.	I sing this song.
Bjale thaka tše tsaka mo lekgotleng	Now my peers in this group
Ba tlo no ferewa nna ke saletše	They will be courted, and I, delayed
Wa nkwa gore ga ke na diphego	Hear me, I have no wings
Ka gore nka sere ke a go rata.	It's because I cannot say that I love.
Esita motho ge a robetše o wa tsoga	Even if you are lying down you can rise up
Sella tša gago, tša gago di tla tla.	Do not cry for yourself, your turn will come.

The vulture left behind without wings to fly with is the *kgarebe* (initiated girl) who, unlike her fellows, is not approached by a suitor: as she is a woman she cannot propose love or marriage to a man. 'As I don't have wings, I will just stay behind until maybe someone comes to me.' Others advise her, 'Don't cry, wait, your turn will come.'[1]

Linked to this theme of dependency on men to initiate courtship is the preoccupation with the necessities – clothes, cash, and other material goods – such men are relied upon to provide.[2] And a further theme, intrinsically connected to this dependency on a husband or suitor, is the importance of child-bearing to give a woman her proper status in society:

Makonkwane sebata makonkwane	Makonkwane the beast
Moswari wa theka laka	The holder of my waist
O sa ile Mabulane	Has gone to Penge mine
Theka laka le ge le se ne sebako	My waist, even if it has nothing around it
Theka laka le tseba ke wene	My waist, the one who knows it, is you
Makuku we, maraga theto	Makuku, you, the ones who kick away string aprons
Ke bommago Joubere	The people of Joubert's mother
Mošimanyane wa sekolo	The school boy
Re re o a lla legokgolana	We say he is crying
O a lla Joubere wa Hlabirwa Mmamorei	He is crying, Joubert, son of Hlabirwa Mmamorei
Hlabirwa ke monna yo elego rragwe	Even if he is a short man and holds me
Leba shoti ge ba ntshwana ke aya	I will go with him to hear what news he has for me
Ke yo ekelwa mehlamo ka mo nthago ga Meswana	I went with him behind the thorn trees
Ntemogeng ke imile	Notice me, I am pregnant
O tla mpona ka foiye ge dumisiwa.	You will see me with prickly pears [i.e. pregnant].

This song celebrates courtship and child-bearing. The ones who 'kick away string aprons' are the recently initiated youths who cause young women to become naked: that is, their lovers. The song was accompanied by a dramatic tableau in which one female singer played 'mother', another played 'father', and a doll was assigned the role of 'baby'. The baby was named Joubert, and his father was given the *sereto* (praise name) Hlabirwa Mmamorei. The use of the praise name was an acknowledgement in general terms of a young man's achievement of fatherhood: but it also had the effect, according to informants, of concealing the specific identity of the lover of the song's original protagonist. The song as a whole stresses not only the importance of child-bearing to giving a young woman (and her suitor) their aspired-to status in society, but also the importance for both of fidelity: he, as her lover and intended husband, should be the only one who knows whether there is anything tied around her waist.[3]

When the excitement and risks of early courtship give way to the burdensome and even lonely experience of being a daughter-in-law, the songs assume a critical dimension. They explore the ambiguous links between a woman, her place of birth where she feels at home with her siblings, and her place of marriage (*bogadi*). In *ngwana o tšhabile bogadi*, a 'child' (young woman) has run away from her in-laws. Her siblings chase her back again, saying that although marriage entails many pains, she should not run away from these. In their turn, they have had to put up with these sufferings, so they advise their sister to return to her in-laws' place and endure her hardships in silence. A similar theme is contained in a version of the song *mararankodi*:[4]

Mararankodi, taba tša lesego	Mararankodi, news of laughter
Taba tša bogadi le bagaditsong	News of marriage and of being a co-wife
Ebego ke dibotša mang?	To whom will I tell this news?
Ebego ke dibotša mang, taba tša bogadi ye?	To whom will I tell this news of marriage
Bana ba bogadi ba nkgowa-bjang	The children at my husband's place are shouting about me
A ba nkgowa bjang ba sa bone mpa mantsha	They are shouting about me because they don't see stomach [i.e. I am not pregnant]
Ke bolabolong ngwana sešuana?	What will I say as an orphan?

The idea of a daughter-in-law as an orphan, deprived of the support and friendship of parents and siblings while living at her place of marriage, is found as well in the laments of Tumbuka women in Zambia and Malawi (Vail and White 1991: 251–2).

Images of appropriate womanly behaviour are celebrated in some proto-*kiba* and *kiba* songs, while unbecoming or disorderly behaviour is sharply criticised in others. Of a series of songs about beer and its consumption, for example, some, like *sekhekhe sa go nwa bjalwa* (a drinker who drinks beer), celebrate the act of drinking if it is done in appropriate circumstances by older women, while others, like *o tla loiwa ke batho* (people will bewitch you), warn against the loss of self-control, particularly inappropriate to a woman, during excessive drunkenness, and about the possibility of being bewitched by an enemy while in this state.

But many of the most strident criticisms of unfeminine behaviour in these songs are interpreted as being directed, not towards women in general, but

towards the woman a brother is planning to marry. One of these is *sebodu*
(lazy person), a contemporary *kiba* song:

Sebodu sa go rata go ja	Lazy person who likes to eat
A sa sile a sa reng	Who doesn't grind meal
Sehlwela boroko	Sufferer of drowsiness
Sebodu o mmotše tee, o mmotše seturu-turu	Lazy person who likes to be told about tea, about a big tea-pot
O mmotše 'condense',	Who likes to be told about condensed milk,
basadi baraga-theto	women who kick away string aprons [i.e. young women who immodestly expose themselves]
Ke sebodu mahlwela boroko	It's the lazy person who suffers drowsiness
Masogana kgaetsedi tša ka	Young men, my brothers
Le mo tsee lang le mmona a le sebodu?	Why do you take her knowing she is lazy?

Similar slovenliness in a sister-in-law is criticised in the song *dinala di a rotha*
(long nails), which tells of a woman who grows her nails to an unreasonable
length and refuses to go with her fellows to fetch water, but who will want to
drink once the water has been provided. A rural version of this song
expresses similar sentiments:[5]

He wene mosadi wa sebodu mammabjang	Hey you lazy woman who is always sick
O reng o babjwa ge o bona go engwa?	Why do you get sick when you see people plough?
Ge re sola o wa tsoga.	When we dish out food you get well again.

The sharp criticism of these songs has a poignancy since it anticipates a
sister's immanent loss, not only of the companionship of her brother, but
also of his earning power as a migrant.[6]

The themes in *kiba* and proto-*kiba* songs of sisterly reliance on a brother,
and of jealousy and antagonism between sisters-in-law, point to the
centrality of the brother–sister relationship in Northern Province communities. But this is a bond of closeness from which strains arise when sisters
begin to play an active role as breadwinners. *Kiba*'s portrayal of men in the
role of lover/husband in these songs is certainly not without relevance to the
lives of *kiba* singers. Salome Machaba, for example, has a male companion
in town, while Rosina Seshothi and Flora Mohlomi are married to men
whom they met while working in Johannesburg. But in terms of their
structural relationships with the rural families which they support, the link

to a man of most significance is that with a brother. The role of major breadwinner, responsible formerly for siblings and presently for their own children and mothers, makes many *kiba* singers central in the continuity over time of their own families of origin or orientation. Their brothers, occupying a similarly central role, are co-operators but also potential competitors with them.

THE KINSHIP ROLES OF *SESOTHO*

Even at a time before female migrancy was common, an adult sister had considerable importance in her natal home, and especially in relation to her brother. Anthropologists documenting rural life among the Lovedu and Pedi have pointed to the central role played by a *kgadi* (eldest sister) in ritual and in intercession with the ancestors (Mönnig 1967: 56–7; Krige and Krige 1943: 235): she became 'the ritual head of a family, just as the eldest brother [became] the jural head' (Kuper 1982: 60).[7] The pivotal import- ance of a sister to her brother was evident in the practice of the 'cattle- linking' of these siblings through cross-cousin marriage. The bridewealth paid to a family for a girl's marriage would be used by one specific brother when he required cattle with which to pay bridewealth in turn, and this linking would give the sister particular ritual rights and duties over the house established by the brother through his marriage (*ibid.*).

With these precedents in the Northern Province, bonds between siblings have become increasingly important throughout southern Africa's labour- sending areas under present conditions of conjugal collapse. Being more flexible and informal and having 'a greater component of willing reciprocity' than marital bonds, sibling bonds have even served as a model for the formation of households in situations where maritally based domestic units have proved unviable (Niehaus 1994: 118).

This broader reciprocity within the natal or agnatic family has been of considerable significance in ensuring continued support for women whose desertion by their husbands would otherwise leave them without support (Schapera and Roberts 1975: 267; Murray 1981: 110; Izzard 1985: 268–9, 272–3). Among village-dwellers of the Northern Province, for example, stay-at-home women unsupported by husbands or lovers often receive some support from men in the broader agnatic group into which they were born (James 1994: 158–98). A sense of obligation originating between siblings even extends to members of the descending generation. It is considered appropriate for a brother to provide support not only for his sister when her husband dies, but also for this sister's children and even for their children in turn.

But for a wage-earning woman such as those who sing *kiba* in town, the situation is more complex. Although she may be bonded in co-operation and amity with her brother as custom dictates, she occupies a position of great structural similarity to him which often results in rivalry and even displacement. Through becoming a wage-earner she has taken steps to count-eract her dependency on her brother, and to be like a brother/son herself, but this assumption of a leadership role within the family may put her in a position in which she has to compete with him for a variety of resources.[8]

The means by which these migrant women singers think of themselves as family wage-earners, and thus as almost-brothers, are complex. *Sotho* custom enshrines the obligation of an oldest son to support his younger siblings, and, later, of a youngest son to look after his parents. But a son, whether older or younger, acquires alternative obligations towards his own wife and children, which render him unable or unwilling to offer full support to parents and siblings. Where a daughter succeeds in fulfilling these obligations in her brother's place, and thus in redefining a role sanctioned by custom as that of a son, this gender interchangeability shows a distinctly modern character. But her capacity to perform this role of support where her brother has failed to do so indicates her success in behaving in accordance with 'real *sesotho*'.

'In *sotho*, the oldest child should support the younger ones.' Thus *kiba*-singer Helen Matjila invoked the expectation that a family's oldest *son* will hold family assets such as cattle in trust for his younger siblings (Mönnig 1967: 336–7; James 1988: 39–40),[9] by way of a justification for her entry, as an oldest *daughter*, into migratory wage labour as a domestic servant. But women like Helen appeared in their parents' eyes as not simply 'like' but 'better than' a son. Becoming wage-earners and later having children of their own placed them ideally, like migrant daughters elsewhere, to offer financial support to their mothers while relying on them for child-care (Izzard 1985: 273–5; Preston-Whyte 1978: 62–9). This reciprocal inter-dependence meant that the wage-earning capacities of a family's daughter were less likely to be lost to her relatives than those of a son who acquired his own wife and children to feed.

Certain married brothers, like Helen's, did help with the upkeep of their natal family. But this was possible because they had not yet built their own house, established a separate household, and so undergone the transform-ation from *lesogana ga na le lapa* (young man without a yard) to *monna o a lapa* (adult man with a yard). A man's metamorphosis from one to the other was often, indeed prematurely, precipitated by conflict between his wife and his natal family over who was entitled to claim support from him (Molepo 1983: 81).

From the point of view of a brother, the contestation over whom he should support is expressed through a redefinition and a narrowing of his proper – *sotho* – duties:

> Let's say [your sister] is old enough but not married, and on top of this she has got some children. You on the other hand have got some

children and a wife, and in this situation you won't be able to manage both – your sister and her children together with your wife and your own children. Another thing is that my sister's child is not that much connected to me.[10]

The sloughing off of responsibilities by brothers/sons for their sisters, sisters' children, and parents, like the assuming of these responsibilities by these sisters/daughters in their place, is much discussed and contested. Both processes involve a change in roles formerly played by men and women but are none the less justified in terms of custom and *sotho* tradition.

There are other matters for continual renegotiation between *kiba* singers and their brothers. Some men, like Anna Dikotlo's brother, do assume responsibility for broader natal family upkeep and so enter into potential competition with their sisters over access to family land and the right to negotiate over and receive bridewealth payments. Others, like Sarah Motswi's three brothers, monopolise the available child-care resources and leave the unmarried daughter without help from her parents.[11] And it is perhaps not surprising that the least ambiguous position is enjoyed by those migrant *kiba* singers, like Julia Lelahana and Joanna Maleaka, who have no brothers or male relatives in the immediate family. These women feel that the role they have played as breadwinner during difficult times entitles them to an uncontested authority within the family, and to have sole access to bridewealth payments when their daughters eventually marry.[12]

When defining domestic relationships within rurally based families, migrants thus make extensive reference to *sesotho*. Bonds between siblings have precedents in rural society, drawn on to sanction co-operation between brother and sister in the present. A brother's responsibilities to his sisters and their children are either validated or avoided by reference to the *sotho* kinship roles of *kgaetsedi* (brother) and *malume* (mother's brother). And a sister's assuming of new responsibilities, substituting for or adding to her brother's position in the family, is conceived of in terms of the duties expected, in *sesotho*, of an oldest or youngest child. New roles are thus defined by reference to the domestic relationships of old. But how do these claims to position, phrased in kinship and domestic terms, relate to the domesticity and dependency of the *kiba* lyrics with which this chapter began?

KIBA: DEPENDENCY AND CRITICISM

Although many *kiba* lyrics transcend the concerns of domesticity as documented in the last chapter, others, especially those of the older songs from which women's *kiba* has evolved, do contain comment on relationships within the immediate household. Those cited earlier in this chapter reflect on situations both of courtship and marriage, and of sibling affection and the concomitant jealousy of a sister-in-law.

Despite the apparent preoccupation in these songs with the praise or censure of other women, they also concern themselves with the behaviour of men. Unacceptable male conduct appears in *kiba* lyrics as that of a husband or lover – unfaithful, unreliable, or incapable of behaving as a proper husband should – towards his dependent wife or consort. In some songs the criticism is direct. A man is castigated for failing to work and support his family[13] –

Mme a bolawe ga ana mošomo	Mother, he must be killed, the unemployed man
A swanetše a bolawe.	He should be killed.

– or for trying to restrict his wife in her pursuit of independence and entertainment, as in the song *sekgalabjana* which recommends a treatment of similar severity for an old man who will not let his wife stay out late singing with her group. Complaints about men's restrictions on their wives' activities are contained as well, though less stridently, in *sekhekhe sa go nwa bjalwa* (a drunkard who drinks beer).[14]

But comments on men's behaviour, like those on the misconduct of a chief, are often veiled. Appearing more in audience interpretations than evident at face value, the meanings of these songs are open to contestation. Lyrics apparently enshrining conservative views of women's roles can prompt explanations more contemporary in import which challenge established norms about passive female behaviour. *Mokankanyane*, a favourite song about beer with roots well established pre-*kiba*, is a good example:

Bjalanyana wa mmago Mpoyi	Beer of Mpoyi's mother
Ge o ntima, ntime	If you refuse me some, refuse me
Ge o nkgela, nkgele	If you give me some, give me
Ge o ntima wona	Even if you refuse me some
O tla mpona ge ke tagilwe.	You will see me drunk.
O setlatla seota	You are really a stupid one
Setlatla tena le go aga polata bodimo mahlong	The stupid one who builds a flat-roofed house
Thaka tša gago ba go jela bodimo mahlong.	Your friends are eating your sacred things in front of you.

These lyrics have a range of referents, including not only the older songs and known contexts from which snippets of them are drawn, but also the private associations they spark off in particular singers or listeners. On the surface, the song refers simply to a context in which people are drinking together, and in which the singer intends to drink whether or not she is offered beer by the hostess. Sexual infidelity appears as a hidden reference, however. The woman is mocked, not only because she built a flat-roofed house where a pitched roof would have been a sign of higher status, but also for her inability to see that her friend, 'eating your sacred things in front of you', is having an affair with her husband. He has been able to provide her neither with the outward trappings of material wealth nor with the security of sexual faithfulness.

Such inadequacies and infidelities, described in songs, give rise in turn to a variety of interpretations. These were sharply divided along gender lines in a case I witnessed where female *kiba* singers disagreed vehemently with a migrant man about the morality of an unfaithful husband described in a song. Reuben Malaka, listening to *Mokankanyane*, pointed out its parallel with the theme of another song:

Ge a tshika mmethe nko tše	Hit him on the nose when he is cheeky
A tswe mokola.	So that he can bleed.

He claimed indignantly that a wife often lays a trap for her husband, to prove him guilty of infidelity, by hiding on a plate some food which he did not eat the previous night. Having done this on three consecutive nights, on the fourth she will accuse him of sleeping away from home with a lover, strike him in the face, and then use the plate of uneaten food as evidence when the case is brought to court before his kinsmen. Three of the women who had been performing the song disagreed with this interpretation. Since husbands often stay away for the night with their lovers, they argued, the accusation against the husband in the song must have been well founded, and his wife was thus entitled to strike him.[15]

Lyrics describing domestic interactions between men and women may, then, contain veiled criticisms, with the true meanings of these being contested between male and female members of the audience. But however insistent female singers or female listeners may be about the inadequacies of male behaviour which songs are held to portray, the domestic situations they represent remain couched in the idiom of dependency. Similarly conventional-sounding epithets about proper relationships between men and women are expressed by migrant singers outside the *kiba* arena:

> I view it as a bad thing [that women come to town to work] because it is a known thing that husbands should work for their wives.[16]

The orthodoxies of marriage, thus endorsed despite the stated irrelevance of the institution in the lives of most of these singers, appear as a template held up to reality. *Kiba* lyrics generate a utopian vision of a 'traditional' family which serves as a platform for the appraisal, and denouncing of the inadequacies, of present-day kinship roles and relationships (Coplan 1987: 424; Vail and White 1991: 248–64).[17] Once again, as in the *kiba* lyrics discussed in Chapter 3, commentaries on present predicaments are contextualised and made meaningful by juxtaposing them with people's understandings of the past.

CONCLUSION

Expressed through *kiba* and through a redefinition of *sotho* kinship roles, migrant women singers' view of changing domestic relationships and changing gender roles is a complex and equivocal one. While they themselves appear to have stepped into social positions markedly masculine in their attributes and in their attendant duties, they continue to assess men's and women's interactions in terms of the criteria of conventional marital domesticity.

Migrant women's becoming more 'like men' can be seen in a review of the material presented in previous chapters. Chapter 2 contains a discussion of the way in which migrant women's acquisition of autonomy from 'home-boys' enabled them to group together as female migrants, within their own independent associations. In Chapter 3, the musical genre which gave them both the occasion for forming these clubs and the means for performing once thus united is shown as having been originally a male one. And migrant women's seeking-out of an apparently masculine identity by moving into the social roles normally occupied by brothers or sons is shown in the present chapter. But at the same time as assuming an apparently masculine identity, Northern Province migrant women continue to sing about the behaviour appropriate to women – and to the men on whom women rely – in the relational terms deriving from primarily marital domestic relationships.

If there is a challenge to conventional gender roles being articulated here, the idiom used is one which strongly endorses convention. On the one hand, there is the expected behaviour of a dutiful son or brother: on the other, there is the customary propriety which should operate between husband and wife. Both the new familial roles into which these migrant women have moved and which they validate in terms of kinship duties, and the old ones whose integrity they uphold in song, derive their authority from *sesotho*. Where Basotho women singers' performance is denied categorisation within the male-oriented definition of *sesotho* (Coplan 1991: 174; 1988: 348–9), these Northern Province migrant singers are laying claim to *sesotho* as a domain which includes them alongside men.

But *sesotho* is a concept with some adaptability, which can be invoked in a variety of ways by people of different sexes. It is used by migrant women, both by singing and by denoting a web of kinship obligation, to endorse their new domestic roles. But it is also operationalised by rurally resident and stay-at-home women who are thoroughly dependent on the earnings of men. While it appears in its use by migrant women as a validation of a position which straddles gender roles, its invoking by rural women performers denotes a wholly female enclave.

'I DRESS IN THIS FASHION': RURAL WOMEN SINGERS AND THE *SOTHO* LIFE-COURSE

Consciousness – and its 'colonisation' – have recently become issues of concern in the study of southern African society (Comaroff and Comaroff 1989; Bozzoli 1991). Although not expressed in quite the same terms, the processes by which such colonisation has been withstood have preoccupied scholars in southern Africa for somewhat longer (Mayer and Mayer 1971; Alverson 1978; McAllister 1980, 1991). While other writers have examined overt acts of resistance, anthropologists have concerned themselves with subtler means of defying domination, often through the reassertion of apparently traditional cultural forms, with effects sometimes perceptible no more widely than within local communities themselves.

Recent studies in this vein examine rural people's portrayal, through local knowledge, of their colonisation and their incorporation as an industrial proletariat within the capitalist world. This knowledge is seen as both enabling people to conceptualise their own history as dominated but resilient subjects (Comaroff and Comaroff 1987: 193) and, in parallel, facilitating the construction of group or individual identities by such people (Ferguson 1992; Thomas 1992).[1] The production of this local knowledge often involves the invoking of tradition (Coplan 1987, 1991), and often counterposes this with images of modernity, resulting in sets of opposed dualities: town/country, townsman/peasant, Christian/non-Christian, *setswana*/*sekgoa* (*tswana* ways/white ways) (Comaroff and Comaroff 1987; Roseberry 1989; Mayer and Mayer 1971).

Criticisms have been levelled at this writing. Spiegel, for example, disparages 'dualist approaches' for the inappropriateness of their search 'for persistences of a pre-industrial world view in the ways in which people order and perceive their contemporary relationships' (1990: 46). But the emerging contrast between, for example, *setswana* and *sekgoa* was not 'a confrontation between a primordial folk tradition and the modern world' (Comaroff and Comaroff 1987: 194–5). Rather, Tswana tradition came to be formulated largely through its complementary opposition to 'the ways of the European'. Roseberry suggests that the very images of a pre-industrial or pre-capitalist world which feed into the making of such dualities are products of people's encounter with the relationships and realities of the industrial or capitalist one (1989: 144, 201–3, *passim*).

Spiegel categorises the Comaroffs' work alongside that of McAllister, whose accounts of Transkei migrants show strongly bounded groups identifying consistently with 'Red' or 'traditional' values, and thereby resisting the inroads of the industrial world or the influence of Christian missionaries or neighbours. But the 'traditional' values of *sesotho* are not rigidly identified with a particular group of people. It is true that in some contexts they are thought of as aligned with *baditšhaba* (those of the nation; non-Christians), as I have outlined in the Introduction. As I will show here, however, the boundary between *majekane* (Christians) and *baditšhaba*, even in the heartland where it might be thought to be strongest, is fugitive and vague if one seeks for it in concrete terms. Both the contrast between *sesotho* and *sekgowa*, and that between *majekane* and *baditšhaba*, tend then to be used as conceptual tools rather than as labels for the actions or orientations of definite groups of people.[2]

The present chapter investigates these issues through a focus on rural women's *sotho* clothing, an important aspect of musical performance and a distinctive sign, alongside others, of whether or not such a performance qualifies as one of *mmino wa sesotho/setšo*. While migrant singers came from rural backgrounds where few had worn *sotho* clothes before arriving on the Reef, for village singers there are strong continuities between the clothing worn in everyday life within the village/domestic arena and that worn in the heightened context of musical performance. By adopting the clothes and performing the music of *sesotho* or *setšo*, migrant singers announced their newly forged identity as Northern Province female migrants. Village singers have remained within the domestic domain, dependent on men, through the stages of a female life-cycle viewed as typically *sotho*. Here, most wear *sotho* clothing both for singing *kiba* and when doing the normal tasks of domestic life.

Whether worn only for performance or every day, traditional *sotho* dress is not, however, static or unchanging. In a heartland Pedi village like Nchabeleng, the clothing identified with *sesotho* has progressively incorporated elements from the clothing of other groups and from that of *sekgowa* itself, in much the same way as *kiba* songs acquire new meanings or have new sections written for them by contemporary composers. The adoption of these new elements has often coincided with points of change in the life-cycle, after which they become adopted more generally. But, despite these changes, the clothing continues to be defined as belonging within the domain of *sesotho*, and is contrasted strongly with its opposite *sekgowa*.

In addition to the flexibility of the paired opposites of *sesotho* and *sekgowa*, there is another point which this chapter will stress. *Sesotho* and *sekgowa* are differentially adhered to and invoked by women and men, and the contrasts between the two sets of opposed terms are often thought of as aligned.

Village women can be identified through their clothing as having a *sotho* orientation. But due to the incorporation of new elements, introduced through a variety of channels but especially through schooling, the details of *sotho* dress have differed for each successive group of female initiates, as have the means of acquiring them. Older generations of women were given money to buy the clothes of adulthood by fathers, brothers or husbands, where their daughters spent short spells as farm workers to earn the money themselves. These stints of independence were followed, for women remaining single as for those who married, by a return to the sphere of motherhood, household work and subsistence agriculture. In contrast to *sotho*-clothed women, the earlier and more consistent involvement of village men in the worlds of school and work has meant that their clothing is invariably that of *sekgowa*.

But this opposition between male and female orientations and behaviours, as expressed in the outward and visible sign of clothing, is not consistently experienced or invoked. Indeed, in the context of particular women's domestic living circumstances with particular men, it may be absent altogether. It is on the occasion of musical performance, as the second part of the chapter shows, that *sesotho* is stressed through singing, dance, dress, and the consumption of sorghum beer. Through these means, performance provides for a dramatisation, partly through parody, of an overarching female identity in opposition to men.

SESOTHO OF SINGING, SESOTHO OF WEARING

In the village of Nchabeleng, situated in the Pedi heartland *Sekhukhune* not far from the seat of the Pedi paramountcy, there are several women's music groups. Each is based in a different part of the village, and draws its membership from this particular locality. The group whose members' experience forms the subject of this chapter, *Dithabaneng* (those from the place of the mountain), takes its name from the rocky hill around whose base its singers' houses are clustered.

The women of *Dithabaneng* can put a precise date on their origin as a group with this particular membership, clothing, and style of music and dance. They came together in 1976, having seen and been inspired by the new style – called *kiba* in an urban context, but referred to as *mpepetloane* or *lebowa* in a rural one – performed by women singers from *Mphahlele* some 70 km to the north-west.

Dithabaneng has many features shared by other groups which sing in this style. Members have elected a leader (*malokwane*) and a leader's deputy, whose function is to call the group together for practices and performances, to lead the singing, and to discipline latecomers or those inappropriately dressed. There is a variety of other personnel, including two 'police', who dress in khaki uniform with leather Sam Brownes and who levy fines upon male onlookers whom they arrest, and two nurses with epaulettes, who administer 'medicines' to the singers. In addition, members of the group have conceptualised and formulated a consistent policy which differentiates a range of different performance scenarios, from weddings, for which they charge a standard rate, through competitions, which they enter with a hope of winning, to dances at the houses of prominent group members, when they buy food and drink with their past earnings and, in the words of one member, 'We eat our money'.[3]

The members of *Dithabaneng* are drawn from a very small area, and many of them have played and sung together in the past. A succession of women's singing styles drew local singers – and before them their mothers and grandmothers, many of whom are no longer active in performance – together in a variety of groupings. Some of these were named, though none was characterised by such uniformity of dress as the present group.

As this generational continuity within a single village suggests, a number of women have remained in their natal village even after marriage. This is explained partly by the high rate of cousin-marriage among group members, even among women marrying as late as 1981.[4] Of the women singers I know, only one came to the village from a distant location (about one hour's drive away), a further three moved from nearby villages to marry, and the remainder were born in the village itself, some moving no further than a few doors away to set up house with or near their in-laws who were also their relatives.

The women in the group are thus connected by various ties of kinship, both consanguineal (including lineal and collateral relationships) and affinal. The group contains several pairs of sisters, several pairs of sisters-in-law, and one mother-and-daughter combination. A further linking factor, cross-cutting kinship to some degree, is that women of the same age-group born and raised in the village attended initiation and were formed into *mephato* (initiation regiments) together. The ties eventually formalised as membership of *Dithabaneng* thus had their origins in a range of previous and sometimes long-standing local connections, at least between the group's core members, from whom those more peripheral or recently arrived have taken their identity as singers.

Despite these close ties, the women do not normally regard themselves as equals. Even those as closely related as sisters are distinguished by their individual marriages, their widely differing levels of income and, consequently, their differing orientations to *sesotho*. They constitute an undifferentiated group only in the act of singing together, using a range of performance devices thought of as characteristically *sesotho*. It is the dance which forms the group.

One of these unifying motifs is the invocation of *tau* (the lion). By virtue of marriage if not of birth, all the people in the group – like most of those in the village – *bina tau* (dance the lion). In the context of performance, the

Table 5.1 Pedi clothing demarcating life-cycle stages (Mönnig 1967: 107, 123, 128).

	Male	Female
Pre-initiate	*Lekgeswa* skin loin-cloth	*Lebole* or *thetho* (short string apron in front around loins) *Ntepana* (triangular skin apron to cover buttocks) *Semabejane* (short cotton blouse just covering the breasts)
	Hair shaven close to head	*Leetse* (hair fashioned in long strings treated with fat and graphite)
Initiates	New loin-skins	*Lebole* or *thetho* (short string apron in front around loins *Ntepa*[5] (long back apron of married women) *Semabejane* (short cotton blouse just covering the breasts)
	Hair reshaven	*Tlopo* (hairstyle of marriageable and married women)

invocation *ditau* (lions) is used as an address to co-singers on occasions of heightened significance, or to assert some sense of overarching and symbolic local-political unity when performing in front of people from other villages or places.[6]

A further expression of group cohesion and uniformity is the clothing worn when singing. The entire performance, including *mmino* (dance) and *diaparo* (clothing), is characterised as *sesotho*.

'I DRESS IN THIS FASHION'

Dithabaneng's performances emphasise *sesotho* as an inviolate concept, but the actual orientation towards *sesotho* has been transformed over several generations. In addition, *sotho* clothing – albeit shabbier and less striking than the group's uniform – is worn by some singers all the time, while others, often due to the influence of their husbands, have made a move to the clothing of *sekgowa*, saving *sotho* clothes for performance only.

Neither the flexibility nor the variation of *sesotho* is visible in accounts of 'traditional' Pedi dress. In a classically static account of a rural lifestyle, Mönnig describes Pedi clothes as having been significant in demarcating the different phases of the life-cycle from one another, and simultaneously in providing for a gradually deepening distinction between the sexes. To substantiate this he gives information on the first two major phases of life (summarised in Table 5.1).

Mönnig comments, however, that:

> in practice, most [initiated] girls nowadays wear long, gaily-coloured cloths from their loins down to their feet, covering the traditional

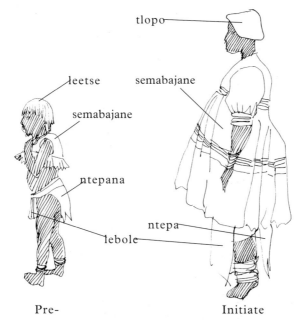

Figure 5.1 Female *sotho* dress of Pedi, showing *semabejane* or *gempe* in its pre-initiate and initiate form (James 1996).

clothing, while very few women wear the traditional hair-style, usually covering their heads with a head-cloth instead. (1967: 128)

He also indicates that *semabejane*, the short blouse worn by initiated and by older uninitiated girls, 'was introduced by missionaries, but has been adopted by all the Pedi, Christians and non-Christians alike' (*ibid.*).

This account, like many of its kind, sets up an idealised version of the traditional life-cycle with its accompanying clothing. If people adopt some western clothes, they are seen as treading a one-way path from tradition to modernity. In fact, the semiotics of dress, and its social concomitants, are more complex.

A good example of this complexity is the short smocked cotton garment Mönnig calls *semabejane*, and referred to by *Dithabaneng* women as *nyebelese* or *gempe* for initiates (from the Afrikaans *hemp* – shirt) or *gentswana* for non-initiates (little shirt). By the mid-1950s these garments, although certainly deriving in style and material from European influence, were items of clothing indicating a thoroughly *sotho* orientation, as the name given to one version of the garment – *sesothwana* (little *sesotho*) – suggests. An orientation towards the paired opposite, *sekgowa*, was shown by wearing clothes known as *roko* (dress; pl. *diroko*) or *khiba* (pinafore; pl. *dikhiba*). In the village, still

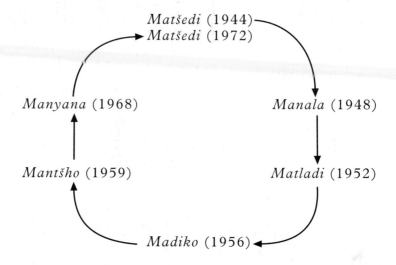

Figure 5.2 The cyclical succession of initiation regiments in Nchabeleng. Dates shown here are for girls' initiation, about two years later than those for boys in the same regiments.

cleft by a deep social and geographical divide between Christians and non-Christians, it was mostly the former who wore the clothes of *sekgowa*, while the latter wore *sotho* clothing.[7] In this instance, then, adherence to one or other polarity of the *sesotho/sekgowa* duality was associated with membership of definable social categories.

But *sotho* dress,[8] like its opposite, was to undergo continual transformation. Although *gempe* (*sotho* smocked shirt) and its accompanying *lebole* (string or leather apron) are still worn by returning initiates, in other contexts these garments have been supplanted by a new version of *sotho* dress. This has three main identifying features: a *lešela* (length of cloth) or *tuku* (from the Afrikaans *doek*) wrapped around the waist; a *šeše* (headscarf consisting of a large piece of fabric); and *maseka* (bangles). If these elements are present, the fourth element – a commercially made vest or 'skipper' (short-sleeved cotton knit shirt) – does not detract from the whole ensemble, but indeed becomes a part of it. This ensemble of clothes appears in various versions. For the performance of *kiba*, it is characterised by the use of striking colours and of materials thought to be particularly attractive. But in an everyday context, the materials used are often drab, and sometimes old and tattered.

It can be seen then that certain types of clothing deriving from mission influence, and named with words deriving from *sekgowa*, were nevertheless

Figure 5.3 Old *sotho* dress: Mmagopine dressed up in the garb she wore as an
initiate for rainmaking rites (Photo: Deborah James)

included within the definition of *sesotho*, and strongly contrasted with *sekgowa*, throughout. The *sesotho/sekgowa* contrast thus co-exists with an image of change within the category of *sesotho*. If, for these villagers, opposed polarities such as *sesotho/sekgowa* do enable a conceptualisation of historical change as the Comaroffs claim (1987: 193), the actual mechanism through which change occurs, and through which these categories are continuously replenished with new elements, is through life-cycle rituals, particularly initiation. The experience of successively initiated *mephato* orients these conceptions of change (Molepo 1984: 16–28). Thus, the life-cycle stages which in Mönnig's account provided for a static approach to understanding society in fact allow for a more dynamic self-perception, since each *mphato* (regiment) has a different experience of these stages.

The transformation of clothing, and of the *sotho* lifestyle, was prompted partly by a variety of what might crudely be called 'culture contacts'. For an older generation, these contacts were made through the presence of trading stores and through visits to husbands in town. But more pervasive for their daughters were the influences deriving from the proliferation of schools in the area after the 1950s. The means for purchasing the clothes defined as necessary to consecutive stages of the life-cycle had to be provided by wages earned beyond the domestic domain. For the older generation of women – the present grandmothers in *Dithabaneng* – this money was procured by men: by fathers and brothers in the case of initiates, and by husbands for their wives. A younger generation – *Dithabaneng's* present older mothers – followed the example of boys in leaving home to earn their own money on farms around the time of initiation. But in contrast to boys who then went off to work in contract labour in the urban areas, these girls, having earned enough money to buy the clothes appropriate to their new status of initiates, then returned to the domestic sphere to raise children and keep house. Here, they came again to depend on male earnings for clothing and other basic necessities, or in some cases were forced to subsist without these earnings.[9]

For the village-dwellers of *Dithabaneng*, then, the acquisition of clothing for different phases of life has necessitated links connecting them within their rural families to urban centres in white South Africa (referred to as *makgoweng*: the place of the whites). Although it became commonplace for women of an intermediate generation to make brief forays into employment at white farms (referred to as *mabaleng*: the place of the plains), these links have mostly been made by fathers, brothers and husbands.

MEN'S EARNINGS, WOMEN'S CLOTHES

The oldest of the group's singers, Makgolo wa Pine Khulwane,[10] was born around 1930 and initiated around 1944 in *Matšedi* regiment. For her co-initiates, as for older women whose activity as singers ceased some time ago and who never became members of *Dithabaneng*, the money for the

Figure 5.4 New *sotho* dress: Mmagopine in *šeše* (headscarf), vest and *dituku* (waistcloths): *Dithabaneng* in performance (Photo: Deborah James)

purchase of the clothes necessary to a proper *sotho* woman's lifestyle was earned by fathers, brothers and husbands in contract employment. Worn by a married woman, these clothes in turn, like the elaborate and heavy *gempe* (*sotho* smocked shirt) once worn by Mmagomathumasha Madibane and still stored by her in a trunk, became outward and visible signs of her husband's wealth. The more fabric used in the extensive smocking of these, and the more garments worn one over the other, the richer the provider was seen to be.[11] The clothes were thus worn with pride both on a woman's own and on her husband's behalf.

The lyrics of songs sung both by *Dithabaneng* and by older and now inactive singers reflect the dependence of this generation of women, and indeed of subsequent ones, on the earnings of men. In the song *Lebowa*, women sing: [12]

Lebowa la kgomo le motho	Lebowa of cattle and people
Pula-medupe yana Mohlakeng.	Stormy rain.
Lebona ge ke te kapere	Seeing me half-naked
Ke tšhonne ke hloboletše	I have no clothes to put on
Ke setse ka dibesete	Except a vest
Ke lebowa le kgomo le motho	It's Lebowa of cattle and people
Pula ya mamehlaka e yetla	A stormy rain is coming
Nke be ke na le kgaetsedi	I wish I had a brother
A nthekele onoroko.	Who would buy me a petticoat.
Re supa gore ga re sa šila.	We no longer grind our meal.

Like those of other *kiba* songs, these lyrics consist of a densely packed combination of themes, some surviving from older songs and others introduced by the current singers. Interpretations of these vary between different singers, and between different contexts in which the song is to be understood. One of these is the context of dancing itself: within this, the semi-nakedness of the woman in the song is interpreted as rendering her unable to dance with her fellows in *Dithabaneng*.[13] In more general terms, however, the theme of dependence on male earnings for clothing, and of deprivation without these, can be clearly heard. A similar theme occurs in the song *Marashiya* in which a woman bemoans the fact that her husband has failed to bring her necklaces, again making her unable to dance with her colleagues:

Ke reng ka hlaela pheta ye botse	I don't have a shiny necklace

Commenting on this line, Makgolo wa Pine Khulwane said:

> when other men have gone to town to work, he is always here at home not working, so I won't be able to dance as I have nothing to put on, no shiny necklaces.[14]

The dissatisfaction expressed here about men who have failed to provide new clothing might seem to indicate a greater desire for the fruits of an absent husband's labours than for his companionship in the household. Rather than being reflective of a callous desire for material gain, however, this theme co-exists with others to suggest an ambiguity about one of the central paradoxes of migrancy in southern Africa – the fact that spouses have been forced to live apart in order to ensure the well-being of their families (cf. Murray 1981: 102).[15] The song *Setimela*,[16] already cited in another context, bewails the absence of a brother who has become a *lekgolwa* (a person who leaves for the city and never returns):

Setimela sa Mmamarwale	Train of Mmamarwale
Nthshwanyama	Black carrier
Setimela nkabe se rwale buti bokgolwa	Train should carry my brother from *bokgolwa*
Buti e sa le a eya bokgolwa	My brother home from *bokgolwa* [i.e. the state of being a migrant who never returns]
Ngwana-mme o tla hwa ese ka mmona.	My mother's child would die without me seeing him.

Songs thus express sadness, not only about lazy men who have no employment, but also about those whose employment takes them away forever. On the other hand, the absence of a man who is working to send his wife money for clothes and basic necessities makes room for her to have affairs with other men who are present in the area, and it may be precisely those clothes bought by a woman's husband which she wears to make her look attractive to these other lovers:[17]

Wene o se nago lešira	You who have no headscarf
Makolone a tlogo feta	Those from the Cape will pass you by
Wene o se nago lešira	You who have no headscarf
O wa hlaka	You will suffer
Makolone a tlo go feta.	Those from the Cape will pass you by.

Those 'from the Cape' to whom this song refers were men who came to the bus depot in nearby Apel as drivers of railway buses, and who would spend the night with local women. As single men who went home only once a year and who 'saved all their money in an atchar tin', they were seen as rich and therefore as desirable lovers.[18]

For the present grandmothers of *Dithabaneng*, sources of contact with *sekgowa* were fairly limited. Since all were from *setšhabeng* (the place of non-Christians), none took any interest in church or went to school. They dressed in *gempe*. Although this was a missionary innovation, the garment had by the 1940s and 1950s already long been regarded as part of *sotho*

Figure 5.5 Mmagomathumasha Madibane with *digempe* she wore when first married (Photo: Deborah James)

apparel, and was definitely not a part of the dress of Christians. These women paid visits to their husbands in town, but these were sporadic and of short duration. Sometimes, as in the case of one singer who visited her husband in his Pimville, Soweto, shack for two weeks, the visits were made not only for the sake of general companionship but also for the specific purpose of falling pregnant:

> I waited long enough for him to give me 'a hairy man', then I returned home.[19]

When visiting town, the people these women met were not so much the white bearers of *sekgowa* as its black adherents from other parts of South Africa: an encounter for the most part equally alienating. For Makgolo wa Pine Khulwane, the speech of the Christian Xhosa people she met in about 1957 while visiting her husband in Springs, where he worked as a compound policeman, sounded so incomprehensible that she thought they were asking her to fetch water when in fact they were praying. But more alienating still was her experience when she left her daughter with them for some hours while running an errand and returned to find that they had taken off the child's skin garments and clothed her in *roko* (a dress):

> They took my child, undressed her and gave her a new style of dressing. I didn't like it, and as I didn't know what was going on, my

Figure 5.6 Woman with *mekamo* hairstyle, Apel, Sekhukhune (Photo: Deborah James)

> husband found me crying. He asked me what the matter was and I told
> him that these people want to *thopa* [capture] my child. They took
> away all that skin clothing and gave her a dress and had her hair cut.
> My husband told one old man about this, and he came and explained
> that they did this because they wanted the child to look like theirs and
> not to be different. Even if the children didn't understand each other,
> they should look the same. Upon realising that I was against this, the
> old man called the others after a few days to come and apologise for
> the mistake they had made.[20]

In this rather dramatic narrative, the use of the word *thopa*, normally used to
denote the taking of captives in war, illustrates the strength of Makgolo wa
Pine Khulwane's fears that her daughter would be taken from her and from
the nurturing bosom of *sesotho*, and lost to the world of *sekgowa* as
represented by these Xhosa Christians.

At the time of the visit, around 1957, Makgolo wa Pine Khulwane and
other married women of her original regiment were still wearing *gempe* and
mekamo (elaborately combed and greased hairstyles) similar to those
described by Mönnig. Certainly, the photo in Makgolo wa Pine Khulwane's
passbook, issued at around the same time, confirms that this was so.
Cognisance should be taken, however, of the fact that already at this time
the most *sotho* of clothes were being reserved for occasions of greatest
auspiciousness, and having one's photograph taken was one of these.
Although she wore *mekamo* for the photo, Makgolo wa Pine Khulwane was
by this time putting on *šeše* (a headscarf) for everyday wear.

WOMEN'S EARNINGS, WOMEN'S CLOTHES

There were a number of things demarcating the experience of this older
female regiment from those following it. One of these was that its members,
while firmly believing that brothers and prospective husbands should go off
to work on farms to prove their manhood, never worked on farms themselves,
whereas most of the women from subsequent regiments did. For a number
of male regiments, consisting of boys born from around the mid-1920s
onwards, farm work was an expected part of the life-cycle.[21] A large part of
the expectation placed on boys to work on farms – although to begin with
their departure was mostly without parents' consent – was as a kind of
second-tier initiation, proving adult male status and showing, especially to a
prospective wife, ability to work in more lucrative employment later on:

> To show that you will work in future, you will first run away from
> home to the farms. This showed that you were a man, and you would
> work for yourself.[22]

But a more immediate consideration for boys themselves was the necessity
to buy clothes.[23] This was likewise to be the main reason why girls in their

turn began running away from home to work on farms. Those born around 1940 and initiated in *Matladi* regiment in 1952 were among the first to do this. A possible reason why they had not done so earlier, apart from the greater restrictions placed on girls generally, is that the arduous journey on foot from *Sekhukhune* to white farming centres such as Marble Hall and Roedtan was seen as more easily undertaken by boys. By the time girls began to undertake this journey, they did so in the trucks sent by farmers right into the reserve areas to recruit labour.

Following in boys' footsteps into the world of labour at *mabaleng*, girls also imitated and adapted the songs they heard men singing. Mmagojane Kgalema, initiated in *Mantšho* in 1959, described such a song, which was sung while weeding on the farm: [24]

Owi owi owi	Owi owi owi
Eya tsena Neisele	The Nissan is coming
Ke ya ga khayi letebele Kekana	I am going there to the place of the Kekana Ndebele
Tlou letebele	Elephant Ndebele
Ngwana wa MmagoRaisibe	Child of Raisibe's mother
Mapeperesane	Truck with a large loading space
Pholo ya mpone tše pedi.	Ox with two side mirrors.

For a variety of reasons, parents were mostly not in favour of their daughters' working on farms, so most of the girls who did so departed from their homes with stealth and subterfuge, as Ramogohlo Diphofa, initiated around 1954 in nearby Mphanama, recounts:

> We didn't ask for permission from our parents, we ran away whilst they were away at their fields ... At times when they were around, you would just put your clothes and blankets over the wall of the yard without them seeing you.

> *If you asked for permission, wouldn't they allow you?*

> They would not allow us.

> *Were your parents and others upset about this?*

> In fact when we got on the truck, little boys would do so as well, but when the truck pulled off, they got off and we would ask them to tell our parents that we had left.[25]

Mmagopine Khulwane, from a regiment initiated about ten years later, tells a similar story:

> From my home, I met my father on the way ... He asked me where I was going and I lied, saying I'm going to fetch water. It was when I was next to the truck that I showed him the blanket and said, I'm going to the farms. My father told my mother about this.[26]

The reluctance of parents to let their daughters leave was in fact not always uniform: fathers were seen as most strongly disapproving while mothers were more ready to give permission, being unable to suggest any other means by which their daughters might acquire the clothes they wanted:

> Sometimes, if you find your mother is at home, you say, I'm going to the farms: 'Well, go, and buy yourself some clothes'.[27]

For girls as for boys, then, the main spur to this phase of mild defiance against parents was the need for clothes appropriate to the status of an initiate. Mmagoshower Debeila emphasised the necessity of this, since 'We would be thought naked if we continued to wear *ntepa*, *lebole* and *leetse*'.[28] She indicated that it was not her family's shortage of money which drove her to work at this stage, but rather the fact that she had seen older friends returning from work with clothes and was influenced by this, and by her co-initiates, to go. The departure for farms of Nchabeleng's adolescent girls, then, was similar to the phase spent working as domestics by young girls from Phokeng (Bozzoli 1991: 91–3): occurring at a phase of life when these women had not yet taken on broader familial responsibility, it was seen not as providing a contribution to general family finances but as facilitating the purchase of a specific set of goods for the girl herself.[29]

Despite this individual orientation, and despite the apparent rebelliousness of these girls, their departure for the world beyond the village was in a number of ways reincorporated into the life-cycle of the obedient daughter living out her life according to the tenets of *sesotho*. A contract lasted three months, and at the end of the first of these a daughter like Mmagoshower brought her wages – a total of R18 in around 1960 – back to her mother, who then used them to buy the vests and *dituku* (lengths of cloth) she needed.

By the time a girl went off on her second three-month stint as a farm labourer, after a break of about a month, her parents no longer protested at her departure. And for most, the third or fourth contract was the last, since it was at around this time that most of them prepared for marriage – 'we were being courted' as Mmagojunius Ramaila put it – and for building a home in the village.

While it is true, then, that *go tšhaba maburung* (to run away to the place of the Boers) signified in some sense a rebellion by groups of age-mates against control by the older generation, it is also true that the challenge to parental authority which this practice represented was soon co-opted and transformed as its perpetrators became, in turn, custodians of the domestic domain and of *sesotho*.[30] It must also be noted that the set of mores and practices rebelled against was based not on a monolithic and cohesive ideology, but on one deeply divided along gender lines. By the time the members of *Mantšho* were undergoing initiation in 1959, girls were rebelling not simply against the arduous duties defined as appropriate to them within the domestically defined boundaries of *sesotho* – child-care, fetching water, weeding and chasing the birds away from the crops, and helping to repair the house – but also against the emergent modern definition of a girl's role as scholar. Parents were frequently divided over which behaviour was most appropriate to a girl, and in some cases this division separated mothers as proponents of the conservative, domestic version of *sesotho* from fathers who, although not necessarily wishing to convert to Christianity, were keen to encourage their daughters to complete at least the primary levels of education and hence to engage in the world of *sekgowa* and *tlhabologo* (civilisation). This was so in the case of Mmagopine:

> My mother said that I should leave school and stay at home. ... If a girl could write a letter to her husband, that was just enough. ... She said that I should repair the wall with mud and do weeding in the fields. So I ran away to *mabaleng*.
>
> *So you were running away from duties at home?*
>
> I also didn't like going to school. I knew that after stopping school for a week when my mother told me to do so, my father would order me back to school again. So I realised that if I ran away to the farms I would spend three months there and during this time the teachers would take me off the school registers, knowing that I had gone to *mabaleng*.[31]

For this girl, her flight to the farms in order to escape conflicting sets of pressures from both parents nevertheless led her inexorably back home and back into the values and ways of *sesotho* when she returned to her mother's house to bear children and to become involved in domestic duties as a mother.

SCHOOL, CLOTHES, AND WOMEN'S LIFE-CYCLE

From around the 1960s it was school – whether attended or fled from – which was seen by people as playing a central role in transforming the attitudes, ways of dressing, and ways of behaving of men and women, and of older and younger people alike.

Makgolo wa Pine gives an account of this process. Having wept at the efforts of Christian Xhosa to dress her daughter in the clothes of *sekgowa* in 1957, a decade later she and her contemporaries were to welcome the new dressing style seen as emanating from school. They came to feel that the necklaces, bangles and many-layered *gempe* of earlier *sotho* clothing had been heavy and uncomfortable. When their daughters were encouraged by teachers to wash out the grease and graphite of the *leetse* hairstyle, they eventually followed suit by washing out the grease of the *mekamo* which till then had been thought appropriate to married women. Not wanting to be thought naked, however, they replaced this hairstyle with a small headscarf (*setlanyana*), 'then I saw those wearing a bigger one, and copied them', until eventually the bulky headscarf of contemporary wear (*šeše*) became the norm.

The change in headdress is an example demonstrating the full complexity of the transforming of *sesotho* dress. A generation of non-Christian women whose resistance to the idea of school for their daughters was so strong that they actively encouraged them to leave, in many cases successfully, nevertheless embraced some of the new stylistic trappings seen to accompany the activity of scholarship. Their incorporation of these trappings appears on the surface to have had something of the character of an acceptance of mission or colonial ideology.[32] From the point of view of the wearers, while representing on the one hand a wish to replace one kind of hair-covering with another, and thus to continue to express the respect required of a woman by her in-laws and by men in general, it signified on the other a transcending of the discomfort and restrictiveness of statically defined rural dress and a pleasure in the attractiveness of rapidly changing styles.[33]

Although this liberation from unnecessarily restrictive ways was rejoiced in, there is a sense of ambivalence about some of the changes for which school was seen as responsible. The proverb used by Makgolo wa Pine to describe the older generation's imitation of their children in adopting new ways shows that this process was not viewed entirely in a positive light.

> A cow will fall into a donga as it tries to follow its calf. This is the same with people. If your child is burning, you will go into the fire to fetch it out.[34]

School was seen by women of an older generation not only as having provided for changes in clothing styles, but also as having introduced transformations in behaviour – and indeed in the typical *sotho* life-cycle – which are viewed in a much more unambiguously negative light. Makgolo wa Pine offered the 'pencil' and the ability to write as a monocausal explanation for the ability of youth nowadays to evade parental authority, and for the associated decline in sexual morals:

> a boy may come and study with your daughter. The boy will take a pencil and write something for the girl to read. And if you as a parent suspect something and sit around with them to keep an eye on them, that wouldn't help. Because after the boy has written her something on the paper, she would also take her pencil and reply to him. All this happens in your presence, and when they do this, you will think that they are studying and that your daughter will pass at the end of the year because she has a friend who is helping her to study.[35]

But instead of engaging in diligent scholarship, what the couple would be doing, said Makgolo wa Pine, was taking advantage of the mother's inability to read in order to plan a clandestine liaison which would eventually lead to the pregnancy of the girl.

For some people, school and literacy appear as jointly responsible for having widened the generation gap between themselves and their children, and for having introduced a range of related ills. According to such a view, it is because girls no longer mix with other girls but rather form friendships with boys in class that girls began to fall pregnant at a younger age. This has caused the age at which children are initiated to decrease (from mid-adolescence to the age of six or eight years). Previously, when *re be re na la malao* (we had laws), a girl would leave for the farms, return without yet having become pregnant, and become initiated thereafter. But now children must undergo this ritual earlier, as 'We do not want to take a mother or father to be initiated'. In this account, the virtual disappearance of the phase of childhood prior to initiation – *bothumaša* for girls, *bošoboro* for boys – is seen as having come about because of education.

Schooling thus had a range of significances: it allowed for an incor-poration of new elements into the *sotho* lifestyle, but it also introduced lawlessness and indiscipline, seen as contrary to the principles of *sesotho*, or indeed to any code of morality. From yet another perspective, schooling appeared as a harbinger of *sekgowa*.

People's different orientations towards schooling were influenced by a range of factors. One was religious orientation: to Mmagomotala Mofele, who considers herself *moditšhaba* (one of the nation; a non-Christian), to go to school was foolishness: 'as we grew up we only knew that those going to school were children of *majekane* [Christians]', while *majekane* in turn would mock them, saying *ba tšhaba tlhabologo* (they're afraid of civilisation).[36] Another factor was age and/or position in the family: often older children did not attend school, or attended only for a few years, where their younger siblings acquired a fuller education as the necessity for this became more generally accepted. Place in the order of siblings played a part inasmuch as parents were sometimes able to send younger children to school once their older siblings had grown up and were contributing to the household finances. It was also sometimes the case that parents opposed to schooling for an older child had become accustomed to the idea when their younger children reached schoolgoing age. A further factor was individual motiv-ation. Mmagoviolet Phakwago, a member of *Matladi* regiment, was so keen to be a scholar that the teacher reached an agreement with her mother to let her stay home and tend children one day if she could come to school the next. Her younger sister, in contrast, ran away from school with friends to work on the farms. But it was gender which was perhaps the most important factor in influencing which children were sent to school and which were not, before a time when it became accepted that all children should attend school as far as possible.

According to Mmagoviolet Phakwago, when she was a child and people 'did not yet know the importance of education', old women thought it a waste to take a girl to school rather than having her come to help in the fields.[37] Mmagojane expressed the perceived differential needs for education thus:

> A girl will always be at home, but a boy needs to go to school so that he will be able to find employment. If he finds that he does not know even a single 'A', he will have to come back and stay at home.

> *So with a girl there is no problem [if she leaves school]?*

> No, there is no problem with a girl because a man will come and marry her and she will get support from him. Now, with a boy, who will support him?[38]

It was therefore expected that boys would be more particularly exposed to *sekgowa*, first at school itself, and then through the careers which took them off to the farms and then to work at centres of industrial employment. This is reflected in the clothes worn by boys and men. Although Mönnig's rather sketchy account of the differentiation of the male life-cycle by clothing describes initiated boys as dressing in 'new loin skins' (1967: 123), informants in *Dithabaneng* and elsewhere explained, in contrast, that from around the time of initiation – corresponding roughly with a boy's first trip to the farms for an older generation, or from the time of his first starting school for a younger one – he ceased wearing *lekgeswa* and began instead to put on trousers and shirts. There was in some cases an intermediate phase in which short trousers were worn during school hours to be replaced with *lekgeswa* for the rest of the day.[39] But in general, in contrast to girls, whose clothing throughout the life-cycle, although gradually acquiring new elements, was continually redefined as *sotho*, their brothers and cousins experienced a swift and decisive move from the *sotho* clothing of childhood to the clothing of *sekgowa* which defined their adolescence and adulthood.

For these men, working on the mines or in the cities, it was only during the performance of *kiba* both in town and during visits home that the clothes of *sesotho* could again be worn. In this domain there was, as with women's clothing, a redefinition of new elements, such as the Scottish kilt, as part of *sesotho* or *setšo*.

A similar differentiation of male and female clothing among reserve-dwellers is noted by Jean Comaroff in the case of the Tshidi Tswana:

> Indeed, male hair and clothing styles have been more closely regulated by the idioms of discipline and production than have those of females, reflecting the greater engagement of men in the world of industrial

capitalist production ... Women, on the other hand, remain closely associated with the domestic sphere. (1985: 224–5)

In Nchabeleng, as I mentioned earlier, the divide between the ways of *sesotho* and those of *sekgowa* was often thought of as aligning with that between two social groupings which, certainly for the first half of the twentieth century, were regarded as quite distinct: non-Christians (*baditshaba*) and Christians (*majekane*). But from the evidence presented here it can be seen how even within the social category *baditshaba*, and indeed even within a single family in that category, there are a number of further differentiating factors – age, place in the order of siblings, personal motivation, but especially gender – which align some members closer to one and some closer to the other side of the *sesotho/sekgowa* divide.

The present members of *Dithabaneng* have since childhood been identified more closely with home and with the domestic than have their brothers. The women have worked beyond the village only in rural employment and then only for short periods, while their brothers have spent years as labourers on the mines or in the city. The women have had little or no exposure to schooling, and always less than the male members of their families. From this series of comparisons, it is easy to see how women have had their role in the domestic domain identified closely with the idea of *sesotho*.

WOMEN, MARRIED AND UNMARRIED

I earlier suggested that *Dithabaneng*'s older members, as younger women, were dependent on male kin or affines to buy them the clothes necessary to the life of a proper *sotho* woman. As young married women, their adornment in heavy cotton smocking was an important means by which their husbands could display their wealth, derived both rurally and from contract employment. For the young women of later regiments, although their brief move into farm employment allowed them some independence and provided for the purchase of their own cloth, their return home was ideally a move towards economic dependence on a husband similar to that experienced by members of previous regiments. Indeed, it was the fact of 'being courted' and of preparing for marriage which made further stints of farm labour inappropriate, since it was thought that a married woman should not *bereka* (work for money).

For members of these younger regiments, however, this ideal did not always correspond with reality. Almost half of *Dithabaneng*'s members in this age-group, who became marriageable from about 1960 onwards, are now living their adult lives as unmarried mothers within their parents' or mothers' households, and dependent on the earnings of a brother or an uncle, or on a mother's pension. For the other half of this generation as represented within *Dithabaneng*, the return from farm work did result in marriage: to a cousin, in most cases.[40]

In Nchabeleng village and the broader area there are women who have spent periods working in town – mostly in domestic service – but none of the group's members, even unmarried ones, has done so. Although the presence or absence of a husband as a wage-earner is an important factor in economically differentiating *Dithabaneng*'s members on either side of the marital divide, the poverty of even those without husbands has never been sufficient to drive them to work in town. This is largely because all have remained ensconced within, and able to depend upon, broader agnatic structures.

Those members who are married and receiving regular remittances are, as were their older counterparts, dependent on their husbands for the purchase of clothes and other things. Such dependency also carries with it the obligation to listen to a husband's dictates about what to wear. Few husbands have much interest in influencing their wives' wish to wear the everyday contemporary *sotho* dress described earlier. But since husbands, even non-Christian ones, are often oriented more towards *sekgowa* than *sesotho*, wives' dependence on them sometimes entails a move towards a way of dressing, and of behaving, more in line with this orientation.

For Mmagoshower Debeila, the *malokwane* (leader) of *Dithabaneng*, such a change in style occurs only on particular occasions. She was married in a conventional western wedding dress, as a photograph on her wall testifies, and she wears *diroko* (dresses) when she spends some time staying in the location adjoining Premier Mine in order to visit her husband at his place of work.

In the rather unusual case of Mmagoviolet Phakwago, her husband's preferences overlaying certain tendencies in her own background have effected her transformation from a woman wearing *sotho* dress along with female siblings and cousins to a woman dressed in the clothes of *sekgowa*. It is only when dancing with *Dithabaneng* that she dresses in *sotho* style and sings *sotho* music. *Sesotho*, as I will show, serves in the context of musical performance to emphasise the equality of female kin and to offset the economic factors which in material terms differentiate these women from each other.

One of the things setting Mmagoviolet apart from her contemporaries, and indeed even from the sister born after her, is the fact that she knows the year of her birth – 1939. This is because her paternal uncles were Christians (*majekane*), and when she was born her parents were living with these uncles at their place. Although her father had not attended school, had been initiated, and so was not considered a proper Christian – the Lutherans originally forbade converts to become involved in this ritual – he lived amongst people who were literate. By the time her next sister, Mmagojunius, was born, her parents were 'no longer taking this [Christianity] seriously', and had moved away from these kin to the section of the village inhabited by non-Christians (*baditšhaba*), so the date of birth of this second child was not recorded.

It is hard to know whether it was this early influence from literate people which influenced Mmagoviolet in her later interest in schooling. Again, this was in contrast to her younger sister. Although both schooled only to Standard One, for Mmagoviolet it was a struggle to remain at school even for that long, where for Mmagojunius it was thought to be 'bad influences' which caused her to leave so early and run away to the farms: the idea of education which parents could not adjust to for the first daughter had become acceptable by the time the second was old enough to attend. For the older girl, attending school at all involved an elaborate negotiation between her mother, who wanted on the advice of some village women to have her tend the baby, and the teacher. Asked by the teacher to choose between school and home, and unable to relinquish what she desired – school – to do what she felt she ought to – child-minding – Mmagoviolet could not decide between the two. The teacher suggested a system of daily alternating, but domestic duties finally won out, causing her to leave school after three years. (Her youngest brother was eventually to be schooled right through to Standard Ten.)

The man Mmagoviolet was to marry came from a background in which there was a similar mixture of mission and anti-mission influences. His parents, too, had lived in 'the place of the Christians' (*majekaneng*), but although his father had been baptised his mother was 'one of the nation' (*moditšhaba*; a non-Christian), and they too moved back to 'the place of those of the nation' (*setšhabeng*) after some time. Having followed the normal trajectory for a youth from this section of the village, he was retrenched from his job as a factory worker and decided to establish a small rural trading-store, with various attendant enterprises such as picture-framing. His house is one of the few in *setšhabeng* with electricity and a television, and he likes to watch sport with his friends on a Saturday afternoon.

While he was at work on the Reef, he managed to procure a house in Tembisa. At an earlier stage in the family's development, his wife used to spend periods of several months at a time living there with him: now that he has left the Reef and moved back to Lebowa, his son in turn has settled in the family's Tembisa house. This pattern of procuring a secure place of urban residence as one of a rural family's assets is common in sections of the community with a long-standing history of migration, and often with a Christian background, and it is yet another feature marking off Mmagoviolet and her family from her contemporaries in *Dithabaneng*, whose husbands are all housed in compounds at their places of employment. In this family, however, a move towards the more modern and urban lifestyle described by the term *sekgowa* did not entail an affiliation to Christianity.

What the story of Mmagoviolet and her husband shows is that membership of social categories such as Christian or non-Christian, and affiliation to accompanying styles such as those of *sekgowa* or *sesotho*, were neither static nor historically pre-ordained. Within the life-course of one family, different members could be oriented in a variety of ways, or the same members oriented differently over a period of years, with respect to these major social and conceptual divides. Despite the ease of movement between these clearly distinguished and mutually exclusive categories, the history of this family still displays the basic pattern in which women and the domestic domain belong to *sesotho* while men are seen to connect them to and even pull them towards *sekgowa*. Mmagoviolet, although she wore dresses as her husband wanted her to, and went to town to be with and to keep house for him there, was far happier when she could return home where she had the help and support of her mother-in-law and the companionship of her female neighbours. The following section will explore the way in which, for her as for her less 'modern' sisters, cousins and co-singers, the occasions of *Dithabaneng*'s performance use the idiom of equality, subsistence agriculture and female *sotho* identity to express this sense of cohesive – albeit contested and only momentarily achieved – female companionship and bonding.

WOMEN, PERFORMANCE, AND THE CROPS OF *SESOTHO*

For a period after *Dithabaneng* was formed in order to sing the new *kiba* style of music, there was a wide range of performance contexts in which the group was involved. It took part in a number of local competitions, and was very much in demand to perform at weddings for a fee of around 'twenty pounds' (R40). More recently, however, their popularity has waned and live performance has been replaced at weddings by taped music played on a hired hi-fi system. The range of possible performances has thus shrunk to one main type: 'parties' held at the homes of individual members. These are ostensibly for enjoyment and pleasure alone, but in fact like many other such 'parties' in this reserve area they entail an aspect of *phasa* (ancestral propitiation).

A party at Mmagojane's

The preliminaries and preparations for the party, to be held at the house of Mmagojane Kgalema, one of the group's 'police', began in late July 1991. In an initial discussion between Mmagojane and her fellow group members on the one hand, and her husband on the other, he was informed that the group had designated her the host for the next of these parties. He expressed his surprise that this was the case and his reluctance to provide the food that he imagined would be required. He was assured that he would not be held liable for all costs, but would be asked to provide only a goat to be slaughtered and a tin of mealie meal. After some further protestations and expressions of dissatisfaction at not having been informed of this earlier, he finally agreed.

The next stage was for each member of the group to contribute a tin of sorghum from her year's crop, which was then made into beer by the hostess and some of her fellow-members. Indeed, it was said that August was the best month for such a party, since it came in the time between harvesting and planting when there was still some sorghum left for making beer.

On the night before the party the goat was slaughtered, leaving time for the meat to be cooked in black pots over a fire on the following day.

During the party itself, the sexes remained separate. The women of *Dithabaneng* performed in the open space in front of the yard, observed mostly by children and other women who stood or sat on the ground in a circle around the dancers.

During breaks in the performance, female members of the audience and singers drank home-made sorghum beer from calabashes. Mmagojane's husband and other men who were home from town sat on chairs under a tree some distance away from the performers, and drank bottled beer out of glasses. Men and women, in these separate areas, had their food served to them by the women of the house.

Occasionally one of the 'police' would approach the men in their separate circle and involve him in a mini-drama of mock arrest, with one of the 'police' making as if to handcuff him, asking aggressively for his pass, and eventually fining him some money before agreeing to let him go.

At the very end of the party, the skin of the goat which had been slaughtered was spread on the back of the woman who, the group had agreed, should host the next party. At the previous such event, held during December 1990 at the house of the other 'policeman', Mmagolina Sebei, a similar laying on of the skin had signified that this present party would be held at Mmagojane's house: 'We felt that, after one police, the other police should do the same thing'. Proposed future celebrations will be held at the homes of the leader and of her deputy, since it is thought that office-holders in the group should host these events.

To understand the significance of the different foodstuffs served at this party, it is necessary to examine the practice of – and the decline in – agriculture in the village and in the broader area of the reserve in which it is situated. All *Dithabaneng*'s married women acquired arable land from their in-laws when setting up house, and even its unmarried members work in the fields of their own parents.[41] As in reserve areas throughout southern Africa, the significant factor influencing agricultural output is not, however, the availability of land but rather the availability of cash.[42] The high cost of hiring traction makes it impossible to grow any food without an input from wages earned in urban employment. For married *Dithabaneng* women this comes from their husbands, while for those unmarried some money is paid out of a mother's pension or by a brother. In economic terms, then, the greater amount of money available for ploughing to married women receiving regular and fairly good remittances certainly ensures a higher return on this invest-ment: where Mathabathe Mokwale paid R50 to plough a section of her fields and reaped only one bag of sorghum worth R60, Raisibe Sebei paid R180 to plough a larger area and reaped five bags worth about R300 in total.

Even for those households with a more secure access to male wages, however, their fields are, and are regarded as, a supplementary rather than a primary source of food. This again is a common theme in studies of southern African reserve areas: indeed, in a more global view, it is the decline of these reserves which is seen as having caused their wholesale dependence on the sale of labour to the industrial centres of the Republic. In this area specifically, the factor of unremitting drought has been a further major impediment to agriculture: people who a few years ago reaped a reasonable harvest have found the returns on whatever cash they do invest in ploughing declining year after year. For some, the combination of a shortage of cash with the uncertainty of any return have made them plough smaller sections of their fields in each successive year.

Another factor which has led to the sense that field produce is supplementary rather than primary is that the land here, while able to be used for growing sorghum, has become incapable of sustaining the crop which has come to be regarded as a staple – maize or mealies. This food must be bought directly with money remitted by men, without the intervention of female agricultural activity to make it available.

An excerpt from a song sung by young women during the 1950s shows clearly how, at that stage when *mabele* (sorghum) was still a food eaten widely in the village as a whole, maize was becoming associated with migrant men, who both supplied it and demanded to be fed it: [43]

Mararankodi, taba tša le sego	Mararankodi, news of laughter
Moratiwa o tlile bošego ka tsoga kangwedi ka kgatla lehea	My lover came at night, at the time of moonlight, and I woke to grind maize
Moratiwa o tlile bosego rrago-ngwanaka ka kgatla lehea	My lover, the father of my child came in the night, I woke to grind maize
Ga a je mabele, ga a je leotša	He doesn't eat sorghum, he doesn't eat millet
Ke kgatla lehea.	I grind maize.

This rejection of earlier subsistence crops in favour of bought maize has since become commonplace. The sorghum which is still grown in varying amounts, having been assigned this marginal role, remains within women's sphere of control, and is used for two main purposes: as seed for the next planting, and to make beer. Although this sorghum beer provides a small income to unmarried women in some poorer households, such as Mmagomotala Mofele, the increasing rejection by men of sorghum beer, a signifier of backwardness, in favour of the bottled variety makes such an income negligible in comparison with that earned, for example, by Mmagoshower from the sale of commercial brands at her *sepoto* (from 'spot': informal bar).[44]

The main use of the beer made by *Dithabaneng* women from the sorghum they grow, then, is for the ritual and ceremonial purposes associated with *sesotho*. The fact that all members – despite fairly wide disparities in income deriving ultimately from differences in access to male earnings – can contribute some sorghum towards the beer which is to be drunk at a performance, and then consume the resulting brew together, stresses the links binding them together as equal participants and as kinswomen, and de-emphasises the economic differentiations which divide them and which link some to the ways of *sekgowa* through their links to particular wage-earning men.

Another aspect of the group's performance which dramatises the sisterly communality of women and the division – even antagonism – between them and men is that of the 'police' play-act. Although 'police' are not the only *dramatis personae* in *kiba* – *Dithabaneng* and other groups have a range of characters, including baboons and monkeys, *dingaka* (diviners), and doctors and nurses – the 'police' act has most impact since it involves members of the audience and even those outside the circle of onlookers. Its strong amusement value also derives from the fact that it involves transvestite dressing, and in this respect it is the reverse of some equally amusing pageants in male *kiba* groups in which men dress as women and engage in exaggeratedly female behaviour, including kissing and mock love-making. Here, the aspect of male behaviour and dress which is latched onto is that of intimidating uniformed authority.

There is an element of genuine crowd control in the function of these figures: in men's *kiba*, for example, 'police' do not dress in uniform, but are known merely for their use of a whip to keep extraneous people and onlookers from moving into the circle of dancers. For women's police, although they are thought of as having a similar controlling function, the limits on their authority, based partly perhaps on limited strength, have increased the play-acting component of their role:

> Some men force their way through because we are women. When arrested, they will refuse to pay and, just because we are women, we leave them.[45]

Mostly, then, women arrest unsuspecting men who they believe will comply with their demands for a fine rather than genuine troublemakers:

Do they arrest men only?

Yes, they don't arrest women.

Do they arrest those men who have done something wrong?

Its *papadi* [a play/game], they just arrest them even if they haven't done anything wrong.[46]

Sometimes an element of secrecy is necessary so that the 'police' can conceal her intentions from one of her innocent victims:

> As men are drinking there, we will go and arrest them. We will approach them as if we are dancing. ... You can't arrest them in a group because, if you arrest one, the others will try to run away. ... I will take him away and tell him, 'Why did you come to the dancing without your jacket, it is against the law?' He will take out some money, and then he is released. Whether he pays five cents or ten cents, there is no problem.[47]

But sometimes an arrested man might pay as much as R1. The fines are collected together, and counted up at the end of the day:

> after eating, just before we go home, someone would tell us how much we have raised: '*Batau* [lions], your money is so much.'[48]

In these dramatic interludes, a range of elements is compressed, including an obvious component of social commentary and satire about the arbitrariness and frequency of police intervention in black people's lives within broader South African society. But an equally important aspect – albeit of symbolic rather than material significance – is that of concerted female action to wrest from returnee migrants an amount of money which can be put into the dancers' collective fund and 'eaten' at a future party.

On a practical level, it would have been impossible to hold a party – despite the contributions in sorghum and female labour – without the pressure exerted by the collectivity of singers on Mmagojane's husband to donate a goat from his sphere of male-owned assets. In similar vein, but in the domain of *papadi* (play/game), women police, assuming the trappings of an authority normally denied them, make inroads into a source of wealth within the possession of men – cash – and incorporate this under their collective control within the domain of *sotho* performance, dress, and celebration.

SESOTHO AND THE DOMESTIC DOMAIN

Dithabaneng's stay-at-home wives and sisters are, then, associated with *sesotho* more strongly than are the men on whom they depend for a living. While often invisible or minimal in non-performative contexts, this association is foregrounded and dramatised especially through the use of *mmino wa*

Figure 5.7 Mmagojane Kgalema dressed in her 'police' outfit: *Dithabaneng* in performance (Photo: Deborah James)

sesotho (*sotho* song/dance). To appreciate why this association should exist at all, we must look at the connections between the domestic domain and *sesotho*, and at how the assigning of women to the former often entails their cloaking in the guise of the latter.

The role of women in providing for the continuity or reproduction of the household or domestic sphere is a common theme, in studies both of capitalism in the first world and of its intrusion into third-world contexts. There is some ambiguity as to whether this role should be seen as a sign of subordination and oppression, or as a source of social power, or perhaps as a mixture of both.

In some European peasant societies, for example, the domestic arena appears as a source of great influence to the women who occupy prime positions within it, where their menfolk, marginalised from power in the wider socio-political arena and denied any significant role in the family, are virtually without any influence at all (Rogers 1975; Gilmore 1980). In the case of southern African societies, there is a similar ambiguity about the assigning of women to the domestic sphere. It has been argued that the central dynamic of the pre-capitalist agricultural societies of the region arose from their ability to control women's productive and reproductive capacities within the homestead unit (Guy 1990). Later, the control of these capacities in turn lay at the basis of these societies' giving up of labour to the industrial centres of South Africa, while at the same time allowing them to escape full proletarianisation (Bozzoli 1983: 151). Indeed, according to one viewpoint, South African capitalism depended upon and even purposefully enforced the conservation of families in the reserves as systems of support and reciprocity, in order to be able to exploit the labour-power of their male members (Wolpe 1972: 108).

Some women were to escape from this realm of enforced and custom-bound domesticity, often under the rubric of alternative definitions of the domestic provided by Christianity or colonial ideology (Delius 1983; Comaroff 1985: 150; Bozzoli 1991: 15, 59–60). But those who remained as rural wives dependent on the earnings of male relatives continued to be seen as somehow responsible for the continuity of the household and the domestic domain. The ambiguity about the role of such women centres on whether this work has been assigned to them as unwitting dupes of the combined forces of pre-colonial patriarchal ideology and capitalism, or whether they have derived some power previously denied them by actively retaining and augmenting their part in sustaining household and village life as partly autonomous domains.

A rephrasing of this issue in local terms reveals that women's 'keeping house' amounts to doing the 'work of custom' (Murray 1981: 150). In the absence of migrant men from Lesotho, it was mainly women who, although subordinate and conceived of as inferior, played a major role in maintaining 'the ideas and practices which are recognized as "proper Sesotho"', and in using these to help 'reproduce social relations, between the living and the dead, between men and women, and between the generations' (*ibid.*: 149).

The claim that women have become responsible for the 'work of custom' is not one that derives only from the absence due to migrancy of males to do this work. In South Africa it has its genesis as well in other dislocations of the public socio-political domain which have been wrought by the *apartheid* regime. In an area north-west of *Sekhukhune* Hofmeyr (1994) shows how the genre of oral historical narrative, previously the domain of men and performed mainly in the central *kgoro* of a village, was unable to survive the destruction of this public space which occurred with the forced relocations of Betterment planning. Traditions of female storytelling, situated in the household all along, were in contrast transplanted successfully.

In *Sekhukhune*, as in Lesotho, what materialist approaches represent as women's role in reproduction is rendered in folk terms as women's role in enacting and behaving in the ways of *sesotho*. As with the more material tasks of reproduction, there is an ambiguity concerning the status with which this role is endowed. On the one hand, some of the most *sotho* of the things that a woman does – such as sitting on the floor while men sit on chairs – are thought of as part of the respect she should normally show to her husband and parents-in-law in particular, but also to men in general. In such a case, the upkeep of *sesotho* performed by a woman on behalf of others is synonymous with deference, and may appear as demeaning. On the other hand, *sotho* performance as described above empowers women: even those as dependent on their husbands and brothers as the village singers of *Dithabaneng*. In song and dance, they dramatise their unity as women and their mock antagonism to men.

CONCLUSION

Clothing, together with the total musical performance of which it often forms a part, is one of the most striking and visible markers of a *sotho* identity. In its differentiating of pre-initiates from initiates, men from women, and Christians from traditionalists, this clothing performs much the same signifying role as the Swazi dress discussed by Kuper in her seminal article (1973).

But neither the statuses thus distinguished nor the dress used to demarcate them are static and unchanging. Even in cases where *sotho* clothing delineates the membership of distinct groups, as in its frequent association with 'those of the nation' or non-Christians (*baditšhaba*), other contexts prompt alternative uses and alignments, such as its link with women in contrast to the link of western clothing with men. *Sotho* clothing does not, then, indicate a rigid adherence to the ways of the pre-colonial or primordial past any more than the clothing of *sekgowa* indicates a single-minded orientation towards modernity. Both are shifting markers rather than describing the permanent orientations of bounded groups of people; they are used as templates to order experience in a variety of different settings.

Like the social identities, the clothes used to designate them are also undergoing continual change. Even those women who regard themselves as most strongly bound by custom and convention have found an appeal in the rapid succession of changing styles. The variations of fashion, albeit generated from beyond the local arena, have lent themselves to a more effective expression of local identities (Heath 1992), rather than supplanting this expression with a slavish devotion to fashion as an end in itself, as in Kuper's account of the use of western dress by the middle classes of Swaziland (1973: 365).

If both the clothing which signifies and the statuses signified are undergoing transformation, there is a message which is nevertheless enunciated quite unambiguously in all of this. In women's performance contexts, *sotho* dress serves as an idiom of womanly equality and solidarity. As in the religious rituals described by Heath (1992: 26), dress underscores female sameness, and reiterates that all women in the dance group are equally able to contribute to and benefit from the celebration, even if the circumstances of their everyday lives serve to stratify them.

But, despite the differences which divide these rural singers, their use of *sesotho* expresses and dramatises some themes common to all of them: themes in strong contrast to those implied by *sesotho* in its use by migrant singers. One is their dependence on men, whether husbands, brothers, or uncles, for a livelihood. The other, linked to this dependence, is their occupying of the rurally based domestic arena usually associated with the stay-at-home female dependents of migrant men. For the wage-earning singers of *kiba*, in contrast, *sesotho* was something revived in adulthood after a set of life-stages and a youth spent in a rural context in which modernity and the things of *sekgowa* were much valued. Coming from disparate rural backgrounds, they grouped together to counter their experience of initial isolation as migrants by invoking the notion of a shared home to explain the strength of their commitment to each other. Chapter 6 presents something of the geographical and social disruption and flux which characterised their early lives.

6

DISLOCATIONS AND CONTINUITIES: DISRUPTED YOUTH AND ADOLESCENCE

The previous chapter showed how women singers from a heartland community succeeded through group performance in expressing a cohesiveness which countered in some measure their experience of the pressures of differentiation. Although all of them had lived through the massive changes wrought by migrancy, school and the collapse of the reserve economy, their experience of these, expressed in terms of the dichotomy between *sesotho* and *sekgowa*, provided for a sense of continuity in what was thought of as the *sotho* lifestyle.

The experiences of migrant women singers were very much more disparate. Their eventual sense of being people from one home and of sharing a common tradition represented a triumph over the diversities which initially divided them. Some of the women who were later to become urban *kiba* singers had lived with their families as labour tenants on white farms and later moved to the reserves; some had lived in reserve areas from birth; a few came from successful peasant families which had rented land outside the reserves and were producing plentiful grain for sale; and one grew up in Alexandra township and moved back to the country only at the age of ten. It was out of these very different experiences of childhood and adolescence, lived in a range of disparate areas, that urban *kiba* performers were painstakingly to build up a sense of cohesiveness.

Despite this miscellany of early rural experience, of which I shall try to present some kind of ordered picture in the present chapter, there were certain things which these singers did have in common. One was the fact that all of them came from *Leboa* (the north). It will be seen in the following pages that, in these northern areas, there was an earlier exposure to and even a seeking out of *sekgowa*; on freehold and white-owned farms, in rural towns such as Pietersburg and Tzaneen, and through missions, churches and schools. In such communities, although the basic conceptual division between *baditšhaba* and *majekane* existed, there was an even greater fluidity in people's affiliation to one or the other of these than in *Sekhukhune*. This often resulted from the movement of families during resettlement from areas in which one of these social categories held sway to those in which the other was dominant. Contemporary singers of women's urban *kiba* include *majekane* (Christians of long standing belonging to mainstream mission churches) and *baditšhaba* (non-Christians) who have recently affiliated to independent churches.[1] Some of these singers came from communities in which *sotho* clothes were worn and *sotho* music sung, whereas for others their joining of *kiba* represented their first exposure to this type of music and dress.

Despite the greater orientation in these northern areas towards the ways, dress and music of whites, and despite the greater fluidity between social categories based on acceptance of or rejection of Christianity, a division usually persisted between the sexes. Boys and men came into closer and earlier proximity to *sekgowa*, particularly through school, than did girls and women. When a small proportion of these women did migrate to the Reef to work, they did so with the built-in gendered disadvantage of little or no education, which together with other factors placed them squarely and inescapably within the low-paid sphere of domestic work, abandoned several decades previously by men from the same areas in favour of better-paid jobs in factories, dairies or the catering industry (Molepo 1984).

RESETTLEMENT AND CIVILISATION

The basic conceptual division between *Sekhukhune* and *Leboa* – coinciding with 'the distinction between those groups which had been subject to the Pedi Kingdom and those which had not' (Delius 1989: 588) – has been described in Chapter 1.[2] Certain fundamental contrasts between the communities of *Sekhukhune* and *Leboa* have also been spelt out. These include the contrasting degrees of pre-colonial political centralisation experienced in the two areas and, subsequently, the contrasting ways in which communities in these areas, decades after formally submitting to colonial control, reacted to the increasingly stringent restrictions which successive governments attempted to place on their lives and livelihoods. It was suggested that the less vigorous resistance to these state controls manifest in some northern communities was at least partly related to the disruptions of population resettlement. When the most stringent interferences with land and government were imposed, many of the people who were at that stage living in *Leboa*, in the north-western part of the Lebowa homeland, had spent most of their lives away from these areas, remote from any affiliation to the tribal chiefs who administered them. They thus lacked the strength of attachment to this land felt by their heartland counterparts in *Sekhukhune*,[3] and did not protest as vehemently against the imposition of fresh controls.

What had underlain the initial movement of these northern communities – from which urban *kiba* singers hailed – to places beyond the jurisdiction of their chiefs was not only the lack of farming land available in the officially designated 'reserves'. It was also the wish to farm as independent producers rather than under tribal tenure, and to involve themselves in the culture of church and school which often accompanies such a modernising orientation.

Thus it was that similar conditions of overcrowding and overgrazing in northern and southern reserve areas elicited somewhat different responses. Subjects of the Pedi chief were by the 1930s moving back into these areas rather than away from them; driven by a desire for freedom from white control which was expressed as a yearning for the glorious days of the Pedi chiefship: 'let us go back to Thulale, let us go back to the good old times.'[4] The traditionalism of this statement, although caricatured, nevertheless suggests a contrast with the individualism and desire for progress said to characterise those living in adjoining Pokwani and in the north-west, where many had grouped together to buy land, not under their chiefs as in the heartland but as 'pseudo-tribes' of people who were practising advanced agricultural techniques. But even for those *Leboa* residents who were working as labour tenants on white farms rather than ploughing independently, there was a strong desire to acquire schooling. Indeed, if people in these areas left the farms it was not so much from a desire to live under traditional chiefs but rather for the sake of children's education, and it was sometimes to towns rather than to reserve areas that they went.[5]

The twin themes of a desire for schooling and a wish to escape the strictures of farm labour run throughout the pages of evidence given to the Native Economic Commission at its sittings in these northern areas. While there were exceptional farmers who had schools on their lands or whose farms adjoined mission areas where schools were situated, and who could thus attract families to live and work on their lands, the life of labour tenancy or of 'squatting' on farms was seen in general as one which inhibited a child's chance of education. And while white farmers wished to implement farm apprenticeship schemes to bond youths to them in a kind of informal agricultural education which would destine them for a life as agricultural labourers, African urban representatives from Pietersburg were requesting more schools in the area precisely in order to avoid the possibility of boys' becoming farm labourers.[6]

It is true that there were reserve-dwellers in *Sekhukhune* as in *Leboa* for whom education had become an important issue, and for whom it was imperative that a compulsory state-subsidised education programme be set in motion as soon as possible to break the missionaries' stranglehold over schooling. Pleas were made by both constituencies that education – now beginning to be seen as necessary even by non-Christians – should not entail the alienation from families of their own children who would be taken 'to live at the Church' as had been the case with those accepting mission education for decades previously.[7] But the evidence in the northern area of extensive mission activity from early on, and of well-developed links between chiefs and townspeople, indicates that even reserve-dwellers in this area were more favourably oriented towards schooling and civilisation than were their heartland counterparts.[8]

There was then during the early decades of the twentieth century a broad contrast between people living on the freehold and white farms, and even the reserves, in the north-west, and people living in the Pedi heartland of the south-east, in attitudes to education and the things of *sekgowa*. Half a century later, the effects of this can be seen in the higher levels of education among urban *kiba* singers from *Leboa* than among their counterparts from *Sekhukhune*. In a sample of these singers whose average age is forty-five, the average level of education is Standard 2 (four years of school), where *Dithabaneng* with the same average age had an average educational level of Grade 1 (one year of school).[9] What this figure conceals is the fact that education and the things of *sekgowa* were differentially available to people involved in two very different kinds of landholding arrangement in *Leboa*: labour tenancy, and peasant farming on freehold or rented land. Whereas successful peasants were in many cases early adherents of one of the mainstream mission churches, people living on farms were more often *baditšhaba* whose eventual conversion, usually to an African independent church such as the Zionist Christian Church (ZCC),[10] took place more recently. It is true that the average educational level of urban *kiba* singers is inflated by its inclusion of some women from Christian peasant/freeholder backgrounds. But even if one ignores these and directs one's attention exclusively at women from this area who had grown up in reserves or on white farms, their educational level was significantly higher than that of their counterparts in *Sekhukhune*. *Sekgowa*, then, had been aspired to by, and had found its way into the lives of, a range of people from the northern areas: both those who considered themselves *baditšhaba* and those whose early Christian affiliations would have earned them the designation of *majekane*.

When the infamous 'population removals' of the 1960s, underlain by the imperative of ethnic consolidation, were carried out, their effect was to curb the freedom of both African independent farmers and African labour-tenants on white farms to live beyond the jurisdiction of their 'tribal chiefs'. But it was not only forced relocations which caused the movement of people within the *Leboa* area in this period. By the time coerced resettlements were occurring, there were other factors which led Africans off the land designated for whites and into the reserves which were now designated as ethnic homelands. One of these, which caused the movement of many future *kiba* singers' families off the farms, was the very same desire for schooling and progress towards modernity which had driven some beyond chiefly jurisdiction in the first place.

While one should not underestimate the disruptions caused by *apartheid* planners in the lives of the migrant women who became *kiba* singers, then, one should not ignore the extent to which individual choice, shaped as much by cultural as by purely economic factors, was possible in responding to broader processes apparently beyond the control of the individual.

Table 6.1 Categories of population relocation in South Africa (Maré 1980: ii)

1 Clearance of 'black spots'
2 Relocation due to the abolition of the labour tenant-system and 'squatting' on white-owned farms
3 Relocation through the operation of influx control legislation
4 Urban relocation
5 Relocations due to the institution of 'betterment schemes'
6 Relocation for strategic or infrastructural schemes
7 Relocation as resistance
8 Homeland consolidation

A glance at the categories of population relocation listed by analysts of *apartheid* indicates the types of landholding arrangement by Africans which these official relocations were designed to eliminate. Of these, future urban *kiba* singers' families were involved in freehold or mission-land farming and labour tenancy, destined for eradication by 'black spot' clearance (Category 1) and 'abolition of the labour tenant system' (Category 2) respectively (see Table 6.1).

'Black spots' included both African freehold farms such as Makgodu and Witfontein, where the Machaba and Lebogo families lived respectively, and mission farms such as Mara, where the family of Rosina Seshothi lived and farmed. In the 1960s, these families moved to a variety of homeland areas. Rosina Seshothi's family were relocated to the *Kgothama* section of the Venda homeland, and were subsequently dispersed as a family due to 'homeland consolidation' removals (Category 8) designed to separate members of disparate ethnic backgrounds. The different widows of the family head were relocated to three different homelands in accordance with their officially recognised ethnic groups. Labour-tenant families living on white farms in and around the Pietersburg district included the Dikotlo, Lelahana, Ledwaba, and Mohlomi families. In the mid-1950s (in one case) and in the 1960s, at around the time when such tenancies were being finally abolished in the Transvaal, these families all moved into nearby areas of Lebowa.

Relocations affecting families already living in reserve areas at this time were those resulting from 'betterment schemes' (Category 5). When the new arrivals, separated from their earlier homes, moved into already-crowded reserves or onto 'Trust' farms, room was made to accommodate them by forcibly relocating the existing residents – such as the Maleaka family of *Kgothama*, Venda, and the Monyela family of *Molepo*, Lebowa – from their previous homes and into the 'lines' of grid-planned villages. Although agricultural rationalisation was the stated reason for these removals, their primary effect here as elsewhere in South Africa was to make room for people resettled into the reserves.[11]

While for incoming families this betterment relocation provided space for them to take up residence, general overcrowding did mean a severe limitation on the size and availability of residential and farming land to which they could gain access. Even those families whose villages were not subjected to this replanning – as that of Anna Mei in *Kgothama*, Venda, and that of Fransina Monyela in *Molepo*, Lebowa – were indirectly affected by the population influx of the 1960s in that it caused especially their younger members to experience a severe shortage of land (see Map 1, p. 19).

But the families whose living arrangements prior to relocation have been briefly documented above were not all forcibly removed via one of the 'categories of resettlement'. Social planning of the magnitude, and involving the degree of dispossession, of that undertaken in the name of *apartheid* has been rightly condemned in many quarters. Its highest profile has been achieved both locally and internationally by such episodes as those of 'black spot' removal, in which African owners of freehold land (and their African tenants) have been summarily evicted from the farms which they have lawfully purchased, and dumped by government trucks in underequipped and inhospitable surroundings in the homelands. These dramatic and high profile events should not obscure the fact, however, that some of the movement of African people to the reserves during this era was due not so much to the direct interference of the South African state as to less visible and less sinister forces.[12]

In some cases – as in the movement of people from 'black spots' even before state intervention – these movements had their genesis in the conflicts between African landholders and their tenants (James 1983: 7–8). When the Machaba family left its tenancy in Makgodu village for GaKgare in Lebowa in 1957, preceding by several years the government's official removal of both the farm's African owners and their tenants to the homeland, it was tensions in the Machabas' relationship with their African landlords which prompted the move. In other cases – as in the departure by Sarah Motswi's family from the Reef to Lebowa – such moves were rooted in individuals' perception of the countryside as affording a greater degree of long-term security than the town. And in yet others – as in the departure by the Dikotlo, Lelahana, Ledwaba and Mohlomi families to the homeland from the white farms where they had lived as labour-tenants – one major factor had caused them to leave these farms before government legislation had made this imperative. This was the urgent desire to live under conditions less restricted and perceived as more civilised and modern.

PEASANT AND TENANT DAUGHTERS

The fluidity of social categories based on adherence to Christianity, and the ready blurring of these to produce an overall culture of modernising orientation with selective use of customary elements, was a function of the rapid population movements of this time, whether forced or voluntary. People from independent peasant backgrounds experienced the move as retrogressive on the whole, while those from labour-tenant backgrounds saw it as an advance on their previous conditions.

Those for whom their departure to the reserves represented a step towards a life which was *sekgalekgale* (old-fashioned) compared to that which they had been used to were those who had lived as independent culti-vators on freehold farms, such as the Machaba sisters, Salome and Andronica. They were born in the 1940s in Mmakgodu village, near Dendron, where their family rented land on a freehold farm cultivated by African owners. People in the village as a whole were Christians, and their mother's family who lived on the farm Uitkyk some distance away were staunch Lutherans. The girls' early upbringing then was one appropriate to a decent Christian family, involving regular attendance at school, the wearing of *diroko* (dresses) and the singing of the mission-influenced *koša ya dikhwaere* (choir songs).

The fact of belonging to one of these peasant families, however, was not sufficient in itself to guarantee that a daughter would be educated. The biases against sending a girl to school ran deep, especially in cases – like that of Rosina Seshothi's father who lived with his family at Mara – where the family's affiliation to the church served more as a guarantee of land on a mission farm than as a sign of fundamental commitment to an anti-traditional lifestyle. Although Rosina's father claimed Catholic affiliation, he did not have any of his children baptised, and he refused to send Rosina or any of her sisters to school:

> I don't even know which way the door of the school is facing. My father declared that girls will not attend school, only boys will attend. Boys attended and we remained at home looking after livestock.[13]

Here, despite the patriarch's apparent orientation to Christianity, his attitude to the education of his daughters reflected similar sentiments to those expressed by the heartland dwellers described in Chapter 5. Many *Leboa* families, indeed, despite a greater overall acceptance of or even desire for education, disadvantaged their daughters in this way:

> My father was not in favour of educating girls.
>
> *Why?*
>
> He said it was because he wanted us to be married and get cattle of *bohadi* [bridewealth].[14]

Beside some disparities in levels of and attitudes towards education, what girls from this kind of peasant background had in common was that, until they left these areas, their families had lived entirely from agriculture and animal husbandry, with no male migrant income whatsoever. In some cases, as in that of the Machaba family, theirs was a fairly modest output of around sixty bags of grain and beans plus vegetables, while in others such as that of the Seshothi family, whose male head had six wives, the family produced several hundred bags of grain for consumption and for sale.

What the removals of the 1960s entailed for girls from this background was both physical disruption – as in the case of Rosina Seshothi, whose half-siblings were relocated with their respective mothers to Venda while she and her mother were moved to Lebowa in the interests of 'homeland consolidation' – and a blurring of social and cultural categories, as in the case of the Machabas. When tensions in their relationship with their landlords caused them to move from Mmakgodu in 1957, a few years prior to the government's official 'black spot' removal of the farm's occupants to the homeland, they went to a village in the *Malebogo* district of Lebowa, GaKgare. Here, *sotho* ways were predominant. They found children wearing the leather *ntepa* and *thethwana* of Mönnig's account,[15] in contrast to the dresses they had always worn. Their attempt to lessen this cultural gap by attending *koma* (initiation) at their new home will be described in the next section of the chapter.

The people for whom the move to the reserves was a step forwards – away from what they saw as the stagnation of farm life and towards a life of convenience and progress – were those who had lived as labour-tenants on white farms. The backwardness from which they wished to escape, although characterised as *sesotho*, was not some primordial condition but rather a product of paternalist and patriarchal relationships established on the farms. In these northern areas, as elsewhere in the country, it appears that the authority of senior males within tenant families was intensified by the conditions of tenancy. This often made conditions unbearable, especially for the younger men of a family, who were expected by the farmer and by their fathers to render unpaid labour.[16] If the young men resisted this pressure to work, sometimes through the simple measure of deserting, the whole family would often be forced to leave. The family of Anna Dikotlo, for example, moved away from the farm Matjieskraal to the reserve area of *Molepo*, some 20 km away. Although a gradual trickle of families had preceded them as all were 'tired' of working on farms, what prompted the move in this specific case was that Anna's brother refused to work and so the family was evicted.[17]

Conditions of tenancy established in the early twentieth century had allowed varying degrees of freedom to different family members. In some cases the tenant's wife and all his sons and daughters-in-law were obliged to work as well, in others it was men only who worked for 90 days on the farm and then were free to go out to work in town, and in yet others there was the much more arduous and restrictive system of working two days out of every week in the year.[18] Increasing restrictions placed on the conditions of tenancy caused a movement off *Leboa* farms from the 1930s onwards, but for those families who remained on the farms until the 1960s, or who for some reason had to move to them after having lived elsewhere, their labour contracts became even more arduous.[19] A rejection of such conditions prompted the family of Anna's co-singer, Julia Lelahana, to move from the farm Bijlsteel to the *Moletši* reserve:

> women would work for a week without pay and they would work the following week for money, and it went on like that. In the case of men they worked three months for nothing and the following three months for money. That's why we ran away.[20]

Although white farmers regarded the labour of whole tenant families as bonded, the daughters of these families did not agree. They preferred to work on other farms during their school vacations for money. Like the girls already resident in the homeland areas to which they were to move they spent a period, after *koma* (initiation), of working on farms to earn an allowance. Julia Lelahana and her peers, though claimed as labourers by the farm owner at Bijlsteel, left stealthily (*go khukhuna* – to creep away) to work on a nearby potato farm at Mankgodi:

> We didn't want to work on the farm. We went outside to work for money. The older women were left behind, at work.[21]

The desire for a better life which acted as a spur for many families to move off the farms was expressed in other terms as well as those of escaping from arduous and unpaid labour. The backwardness of farm life included the entrenching of certain aspects of customary behaviour. As in similar situations elsewhere in the Transvaal, the farms had become sites not only of augmented patriarchal relationships within tenant families, but also of practices and rituals pronouncedly traditional in orientation (Delius 1989: 249–50). For people moving to the reserves in the 1960s, the contrast between farm and homeland was squarely identified as one between old-fashioned and civilised. It was on the farms that people wore *sotho* dress and danced *sotho* music. In some cases, it was back to the farms that children would be taken by their parents to attend *koma*, since the commitment to progress and the Christian way did not, for *baditšhaba* who converted more recently, exclude attendance at this important ritual.[22]

If backwardness, expressed in these terms, was a spur to leaving, then progress was thought of as an attraction of the places to which families were heading. For Flora Mohlomi, whose family had moved about a decade earlier than the Lelahana and Dikotlo families and under slightly less restrictive conditions, it was the wish for proximity to *tlhabologo* (civilisation), with its schools, shops and especially the ZCC church, which prompted the relocation from a white farm to Boyne, close to the ZCC headquarters Moria in the *Molepo* reserve. And although most *kiba* singers whose families had stayed on the farms until the 1960s had been able to attend school, it was a similar wish to have easier access to such facilities which acted as an important spur to the exodus from the farms.

Even before moving to the reserve, attendance at school was a feature of these girls' childhood. Most families recognised the necessity of schooling up to a certain age, although this age was lower for girls than for their brothers. This meant that farm labour, undertaken on their own or on adjoining farms, was combined with schooling rather than being allowed to interrupt or terminate it. Working on farms did not represent an escape from school as for the girls in *Sekhukhune*.

Both geographical and social disruption thus characterised the early lives of the women who later migrated and joined *kiba*. This was not simply the dislocation of forced resettlement, although the state's role in designating areas for African occupation and in moving people to these areas should not be underestimated. Much of the movement of population in which these girls' families were caught up was engendered, less brutally, through inextricably interwoven economic, social and cultural factors.

The cultural environment of the reserve villages in which these women – peasant and tenant daughters – were to live out their later childhood and adolescence was one which for some represented an advance and for others a retrogression. But this culture, mixing elements of custom like *koma* (initiation) and *go reta* (praising) with elements of modernity like clothes, church, and school, retained its overall orientation towards a life of *tlhabologo*.

INITIATION: CLOTHING, MUSIC, SCHOOL

In the context of this social and cultural flux, one childhood experience which all future urban singers of *kiba* from these areas did have in common was *koma*.[23] Their disparate backgrounds meant that their attendance at this ritual was prompted by widely differing, even contradictory impulses. Given this disparity, and given the experiences of dislocation which preceded involvement in *koma*, the ritual was not, for these girls, to have the same effect of binding age-mates together into solidary regiments as it did for the singers of *Dithabaneng*. Neither was its effect to entrench a commitment to a custom-bound lifestyle or to an outmoded social order, since the culture of post-initiation in which they engaged was to be one more oriented to church and school than to *sesotho*.[24] What the ritual did do, however, was to lay the basis for an identity which these girls, once working in town, were to revive and to enunciate as that of *sotho* or *setšo*. It also served as a site of transmission to them of some of the musical and performance practices which would become associated with such an identity.

The reasons for attendance at *koma* varied with these girls' social backgrounds. The peasant daughters who had moved from freehold farms, or girls who had moved from the Reef, were initiated because of pressure from peer groups encountered in their new homes, sometimes against the wishes of their parents. For the Machaba sisters from a family of *majekane*, rebellion against the authority of their father involved conformity – albeit motivated more out of desire to 'fit in' than out of a whole-hearted espousal of traditionalism – with the social mores of their age-group in the reserve. In the village of GaKgare to which they moved, where most children were dressed in skins in contrast to their dresses, they had felt isolated and conspicuous. After attending *koma*, they found that their status as initiates served to lessen the gap which had divided them from their age-mates. But although they felt less alienated after going to *koma*, the experience did not carry for them the same sense of unification and bonding as it had for the members of regiments in *Sekhukhune*.

Another family, which although not Christian had spent years in town and so was disinclined to send its children to initiation, reconciled itself to the idea:

I ran away to initiation, my parents did not send me.

What made you decide to run away?

I will say I was influenced by my peers to run away. Now the chief sent a message to our parents and informed them that we had run away to initiation in his village and our parents had to pay whatever fine we were fined.

So were your parents displeased that you went to initiation?

They were pleased because it is their *setšo* [tradition].[25]

For future singers of *kiba* who had grown up in the reserve areas, or for those who moved to these areas from tenancies on white farms, *koma* was not out of line either with peer-group or with parental expectation. These people were *baditšhaba*, recently converted to mostly independent churches, for whom Christian affiliation did not involve rejection of initiation as it had for those converted early by the Lutheran mission.

Seen as a stage or marker in the life-cycle, *koma* in these northern reserves demonstrates interesting contrasts with its equivalent among girls in the *Sekhukhune* heartland. As with members of *Dithabaneng* from *Sekhukhune*, initiation corresponded with the acquisition of clothes appropriate to *bokgarebe* (initiated girlhood). These were not, however, the *dituku* (cloths) worn by heartland girls, but rather *diroko* (dresses) or *dikhiba* (pinafores). The purchase of these clothes, although coinciding in some cases with the girls' experience of farm labour and even bought with the proceeds of this labour, was made in most cases by the girls' fathers. And where girls did work on the farms, as mentioned above, this was done not instead of but in combination with attendance at school.

Also indicating this overall orientation towards modernity, and of greatest interest in the context of my focus on performance, was the music which girls, reaching the status of *bokgarebe* (initiated girlhood), began to sing. This was a range of profoundly western influenced styles such as *dikoša tsa dikolo* (school songs), *dikoša tša dikhwaere* (choir songs), and *dikoša tša dikonsata* (concert songs), and also the more specifically Christian *mmino wa kereke* (church music).

The espousing of this school- and church-oriented culture did not, as might have been thought probable, signify an elimination of the differences between uninitiated and initiated children. Studies of 'traditional' rural music-making in southern Africa have placed great emphasis on the way in which musical performance differentiates gender and age roles from each other (Blacking 1967, 1969; Johnston 1971, 1975; Huskisson 1958). In such contexts, any broader category of music or song is eclipsed by smaller categories, each specific to a particular occasion and social status, and never sung outside of this (Merriam 1964: 262–70). The adopting of a mission-influenced musical culture has not been analysed in detailed terms as providing similar pointers to age or gender, but has, implicitly, been assumed to engulf all generations and sexes in its grip. But musical markers of status were important in *Leboa* communities, although they were not defined in the same terms as those used by heartland villagers. Age and initiated status were emphasised more strongly than sex.

The songs of pre-initiation for these *Leboa* girls, such as *dikoša tša go bapala* or *dikoša tša go raloka* (playing songs, for skipping and the like), were signifiers of childhood but not of *bothumaša* (uninitiated girlhood). This phase of life and its accompanying music were thought no longer to exist since 'there was now *tlhabologo*'.[26] This was in contrast with *Sekhukhune* where uninitiated girls of the same age were still singing the songs of *mathumaša* (uninitiated girls) – including a rain-making song crucial to the agricultural viability of society. For *Leboa* girls, the subsequent phase *bokgarebe* (initiated girlhood) was still designated by reference to sex and to initiation. But the songs and music whose performance marked it off, rather than being those of *sesotho*, were the songs of a mission culture which had become general to all social classes and categories in these north-western reserve areas. These songs were learned at school, through a mixture of oral and literate transmission, and performed by school choirs, especially in the context of competitions. The Machabas, for example, belonged to *mothetha*, a choir for both girls and girls under the leadership of a senior boy, which sang *dikoša tša dikolo*:

> We'd go with our school choir to visit other schools, and spend the night. We'd hear their songs, and learn them, and take them as our own.[27]

Various qualifications were given to the basic noun *dikoša* (songs) to describe the sub-styles of this music – *tša dikolo* (of school), *tša dikhwaere* (of choir), and *tša dikonsata* (of concerts). But all belonged to a genre described in the literature as *makwaya* (choir).

This musical genre first came into being as a result of the impact on local sung traditions in southern Africa of Christian hymnody, whose successful implanting in this context was probably due to the fact that: 'traditional music in the south is predominantly vocal, characterised by choral singing in complex, overlapping responsorial patterns' (Manuel 1988: 28–9). The impact of hymn-singing was profound: the imprint of its three-chord harmonic structure can be detected in a wide range of popular South African music not only including *makwaya* but also stretching from *marabi*, through *kwela* and *mbube*, to the mainly media-disseminated *mbaqanga* (*ibid.*: 86, 108). But even in the mission contexts where it initially took root in the nineteenth century, it provoked not so much the slavish imitation of which some writers have complained (Andersson 1981: 16) as the inventive and eclectic responses of such genres as *makwaya* (Manuel 1988: 107).

Most of what has been written about *makwaya* stresses its initial association with the nascent African middle class in both rural and urban contexts (Coplan 1985: 72, 118; Manuel 1988: 107). It was transmitted mainly through a medium available only to literate people – the tonic sol-fa system of notation – although the development of the genre in an urban context saw some choirmasters switch over to a way of teaching songs more oral in its focus, in which their choirs sang 'by heart' or 'out of their heads' (Coplan 1985: 117). The aspect of *makwaya* that has not been examined is that, simultaneous with its decline among the urbanising middle classes who began rather to favour jazz as an expression of their cultural aspirations (*ibid.*: 128), its popularity gradually increased in the rural districts of South Africa. Here, although in its strictly religious form as African hymnody it was sung only by church-goers, its most frequent performance occurred in schools by scholars on both sides of the Christian/traditionalist divide.[28] Although identified at its inception with the African middle class, its later developments took it across boundaries of income, occupation and status into the ranks of those who derived their income from unskilled migrant labour. In the areas of *Leboa* where urban *kiba* singers grew up, as in many other labour-sending areas of rural South Africa, this music became a major form of cultural expression for school-going children and adolescents.

The significance of initiation in *Leboa*, where urban *kiba* singers grew up, was thus a complex one. It was not, as it appeared to the girls of *Sekhukhune*, an opportunity for temporary freedom from domestic and agricultural obligations: these northern girls were committed to a vision of modernity in which the way forward lay in schooling rather than in 'running away'. Neither was it a mark of group identity which excluded those from other ethnic groups (La Fontaine 1969: 180–2) or from the ranks of non-traditionalists, since it incorporated Christians of long standing and of recent conversion alongside those who had never been church-goers. It did not mark a commitment to an outmoded social order. Indeed, while *koma* itself represented perhaps the most intense experience of *sesotho* and its ways yet undergone, especially for those of long-standing Christian affili-ation, it also heralded a phase in most girls' lives when the things of *sesotho* would be put behind them almost completely, at least temporarily. *Koma* did, though, lay the basis for proficient practice of *sotho* cultural forms when these girls, as women, began to sing *kiba* in town. The songs and music of *koma*, while secret and not supposed to be repeated outside of this strictly defined context, had a basic structure and style which were similar to those of present-day women's *kiba*. It was at *koma* that most informants, but especially those whose parents were Christian and so taught them no *sotho* music, learned through purely oral transmission to sing in a *sotho* style.

The theme of a general orientation towards modernity, which was to be followed much later by a selective revival of *sotho* culture when joining *kiba*, must be qualified in some important instances. The school culture which took root in these northern communities was not strongly differentiated by gender, as I have explained above. But girls were still required to perform more duties in the domestic domain, were still less free to move beyond this domain for long periods of time, and were still less likely than boys to be given anything further than a primary-school education. In some cases this meant that girls were thought of as 'more *sotho*' than their brothers. Their orientation to the domestic sphere often led to their acquisition of forms of musical or oral culture from mothers and grandmothers where boys, at school, were not in a position to acquire these. And it was these girls in particular, more *sotho* than boys and more *sotho* than some of the other women with whom they would later club together to sing in town, who would become the king-pins of *kiba* teaching and development in this urban context.

The life of Julia Lelahana, which was disrupted perhaps more than others portrayed here, is one example. She grew up on the farm Bijlsteel, about 30 km north-east of Pietersburg, 'ran away' to work on a nearby farm for money rather than yielding up her labour for nothing as her parents were compelled to do, and eventually moved with them to a betterment village in *Moletši*, Lebowa. This major move had not been the only one in Julia's life. When she was born her parents were living in a location adjoining the white town of Pietersburg. When this area, later called *Masoleng* (the place of the soldiers), was to be developed as an airforce base, they and others living there were evicted. Unable to acquire a stand in the officially designated township of Seshego, Julia's family moved to Bijlsteel farm where her paternal grandparents were living as labour-tenants. It was this move away from town which explained why Julia, the youngest of five children, had no education at all, while her older siblings, brothers and sisters alike, had schooled in the location up until the time the family left for the farm.

Growing up on this particular farm, she was remote from the school culture described above, but also from the gender-specific culture of heartland initiates. The songs she sang as a child were not the mixed choir songs of boys and girls, nor the *sotho* songs of *dikgarebe* (uninitiated girls), but the music of the herdboys with whom she worked and played. As a young girl she was sent to herd cattle together with boys her own age on the farm, and they taught her to make and play a string instrument called *botsorwane* or *setseketseke*. Perhaps with the hindsight of a migrant career, she observed:

> I was not shy and I had no problem in playing things that are *senna* [of men/meant for men]. I did this because I was a herdgirl.[29]

It was her lack of schooling which set this girl apart from all her older siblings. But the contrast she noted between herself as *motho wa sesotho* (a sotho person) and her brothers as *batho ba dikolo* (school people) was due not only to this educational disparity but also to her acquisition of an interest in *sotho* ways from her parents and older relatives. She learned *go reta* (praising) from her mother and grandparents, with whom she spent much time around the house. Another means by which she acquired a love of the ways of *sesotho* was through a kind of cultural inheritance from her father, who was a diviner, a maker of drums for spirit-possession drumming, and a player of men's *kiba*.[30]

Julia, with her exposure to and interest in *sotho* things beyond the boundaries of *koma* and despite her background in a generally mission-oriented area, was later to become a key figure in the development of urban *kiba*. She is the *malokwane* (leader) of *Maaparankwe*. Like Phina Komape and Joanna Maleaka, she leads the singing, teaches songs learned at home to her fellow-singers, embellishes existing songs with new words or actions, and can provide extensive interpretation of these words and actions if called upon to do so. Her relationship to the music contrasts with that of women like Anna Dikotlo and Margaret Ranku, who have learned all the songs from others, who mostly sing the chorus rather than the lead part, and who are hard-pressed to explain the significance of particular songs. Leading figures like Julia tend to be those who were exposed to some *sotho* ways in their own and in relatives' homes. Conversely, the musical followers are often those whose early exposure to this music was restricted to what they learned at *koma*.

The cultural background of the girls who spent their youth and adolescence on the farms and later in the reserve villages of *Leboa* was a complex one. A variety of inputs contributed to the overall culture of modernity to which they and their families aspired. These inputs were refracted through the lens of gender. Despite a strong desire for schooling, most were disadvantaged by the deployment of household resources in educating their brothers by preference. Although wanting the things of *sekgowa*, their role within the household gave some a leaning towards *sesotho*,

The place they occupied in relation to the men of their natal families, whether absent fathers or brothers in competition with them for crucial resources, was to prove formative in their adult lives. It was this situation within the family which drove many of them to leave home for work, and later influenced the way in which they came to see their roles as women once they had become breadwinners.

ADULTHOOD: DAUGHTERS, MOTHERS, MIGRANTS

The disruption of moving from the farms, whether freehold African- or white-owned, had consequences on a number of levels besides those documented above. One of these was the precipitation into migratory wage work of young women from communities and families whose daughters and wives had not previously migrated. Their entry into the labour market often followed hard upon the heels of a failure of paternal support, due to the desertion of a father also unaccustomed to working for a wage. Parental financial support also failed in the case of girls from reserve-dwelling communities in which migration had been a longer-term feature. In all cases besides those of the women who were called to town to join their husbands, migration commenced because of the need for a primary breadwinner who could act towards her natal family and parents 'like a son' in providing support, and eventually combine this with a role 'like a father' *vis-à-vis* her own children as well.

For those who had lived in the white areas of South Africa in peasant farming or labour-tenant families, their fathers' first move to town as work-seekers, and their families' first dependence on a migrant wage, occurred only after moving into the homeland.[31] The start of involvement in migrancy at this time confirms a claim made in the report of the Surplus People Project that relocation, especially from 'black spots' to settlements without agricultural land, often led to higher levels of migrancy within the population. The same report indicates that these relocated people newly entering the labour market often had to accept employment in the least skilled and worst-paid jobs, since they had not been involved in the gradual building up of urban networks known to those longer acquainted with migrant labour.[32]

One man who began to work only after leaving his original farm was the father of Flora Mohlomi. He took his family away from their tenancy at GaKgopa, and moved them to a new home in Boyne in *Molepo* district in 1953. His first migrant contract, after this move, took him to Port Elizabeth, which made visits to his family costly and thus infrequent.

In other cases it was not so much the father's initial departure to look for work that caused the disruption to the family, as his permanent absence from the family subsequent to this departure. For the father of Salome and Andronica Machaba, the family's move from their rented acres at Makgodu to GaKgare in the *Malebogo* district prompted his departure to look for work, but he never returned to his family:

> after he disappeared, that was the end of him. Even now we have forgotten what he looks like. Our children do not know him. They just hear us say 'you have a grandfather'.[33]

Other singers, especially those born late to older fathers like Mary Lebogo and Rosina Seshothi, had already lost their fathers at the time of the move to the homelands. And others, like Helen Matjila, had fathers who even in the face of dire need by their families were unwilling to travel to towns to look for employment after leaving the farms.

In contrast to these farm-dwelling girls, their counterparts already in the reserve areas came from families which had relied on migrant wages for at least one generation. But this did not necessarily mean a greater reliability on the part of the male providers of this income. Mary Kapa, born in the *Mašašane* district of the homeland, lost her father to the city just as the Machabas did. The father of Phina Komape from the *Moletši* district died when she was a child, leaving her family unsupported. And in the case of Fransina Monyela, from *Molepo*, her father became ill and so was unable to earn a living. For reserve-dwellers and former farm-dwellers alike the absence of a paternal income was to play a definitive role in causing these young women, in turn, to migrate.

But in most cases the future of progress and modernity to which they and their families had oriented themselves had not explicitly included the possibility of wage work. In only three instances, of families already in the reserves, had the mothers of these girls gone out to work before them. Two of these families were living in reserve areas directly adjacent to Pietersburg, and their mothers were working either in domestic service in the town itself, or taking in washing from townspeople to do at home. The other family, that of Joanna Maleaka, lived further north in the more remote *Kgothama* district of Venda, and her mother worked as a domestic servant in Pretoria. All the other mothers of *kiba* singers were stay-at-home wives or widows. As with the rural communities in Botswana studied by Izzard (1985: 278), the comparative recency of women's migration from these northern communities means that the first generation of female migrants is still mostly away in town, rather than retired in the countryside.

Migratory wage work was unusual, not only for the mothers of these women, but also for their contemporaries and their female relatives of the same generation. All *kiba* singers I know have sisters and sisters-in-law who remained at home as dutiful rural wives managing their absent husbands' households. And although each woman when questioned agreed that her area had become one from which women do now migrate to work in town, a good number of them preceded the wave of urban female migration by several years. Even if female migrancy later became more commonplace from these areas, then, it was unusual at the time the future singers of women's *kiba* first moved away from home: these women were unusual in both their families and their sending villages, in having become wage workers when they did. Given that 'a "need for cash" … is an almost universal "need" in the so-called "sending societies" from which *some* but not all individuals migrate' (Izzard 1985: 259), it must be asked why these particular women rather than others took the step into migrancy and thus away from expected female behaviour (*ibid.*; Moore 1988: 110–12, 114). In the case of Northern Province *kiba* singers, the answer lies in the interaction of a number of factors in the life of a migrant: the family history already explored above; and the place in the order of siblings, education and gender of the migrant. Linked to the social and economic disruptions of resettlement, and to the failure of a father's migrant income, was the disappointment of having to leave school early despite a strong desire to be educated. Most *kiba* singers I know were forced, by circumstances beyond their control, to leave school earlier than they would have liked.

Five of these left because of their fathers' inability to provide financial support for their families, which would later precipitate their entry into the labour market in turn. In other cases, these girls' leaving school was again due to discrimination against girls and in favour of boys: in families strapped for cash, their brothers had more schooling than they did. For some it was their place in the sibling order that underprivileged them educationally. As studies from elsewhere in the third world have shown, an early stage in the developmental cycle of a family entails a greater number of dependents than generators of income, making the family unable to afford to send its older children to school, whereas its later development with an altered ratio of providers to dependents may permit younger children a fuller education (Moore 1988: 110).

In many cases, these factors were interlinked, resulting in particularly severe educational disadvantage. The departure from school in Standard 6 of Helen Matjila, for example, was motivated not only by her parents' inability to pay her own school fees since her father was not working, but also by the need for her to earn a wage in town which would then enable her younger siblings to become further educated. Some of the brothers born after her were educated further than she was, and her youngest sister, born at an advanced stage of the family's developmental cycle, is presently studying for a teacher's diploma. In such a case, as Moore points out, an older child subsidises the education of her younger siblings, while allowing them to defer their entry into the labour force until their degree of schooling ensures them a more desirable and better-paid job (Moore 1988: 109–10).

Sometimes, given the rapid social mobility that characterises some areas of rural South Africa, the parental generation occupies a different position on the class/status ladder from that of its children. In a case like Helen's, the older sibling was placed in a mediatory position between these two generations. Helen's father was a farm labourer, her sister hopes to become a teacher, and her work in factories and in domestic service has bridged the gap between these polarities. Like female migrants from other parts of southern Africa, she has invested for younger family members in the education of which she was deprived, in an attempt to procure social mobility (Stichter 1985: 167; Bozzoli 1991: 238).

Arising in some cases from the disruptions of population resettlement, the failure of paternal support thus caused these daughters to take up the role of breadwinner, often curtailing their much-valued schooling to do so. Marriage and affinal ties featured only briefly or not at all, except for those migrants whose first trip to town was made to join a husband there.[34] For most *kiba* women, the preoccupations of adult life arising from the circumstances of their youth served to bind them ever closer, as responsible providers of support, to their natal families, and later to their children reared in these families. Their experience of domestic and gender relationships within these natal families, and their view of such relationships, have been spelt out in Chapter 4.

CONCLUSION

If we look again at the contrast between the rural *kiba* singers of *Dithabaneng* and the urban ones of groups like *Maaparankwe* and *Ditšhweu tša Malebogo*, we find substantial variations on the theme of rural-based *sotho* woman-hood. In both contexts, the security of marriage-based financial support is on the decline and is being replaced in importance by consanguineal relation-ships within the natal family or agnatic group. Rural singers remain in roles of dependence within these families, however, while their urban wage-earning counterparts are coming to play new, more central, and more male-like roles in ensuring the inter-generational continuity of their rural families.

The upbringing of these migrant women was in significant ways different from that of their brothers. In some cases this meant taking on roles which boys, moving closer to the things of school and *sekgowa*, had left behind them. In some cases it meant that girls, remaining within the domestic sphere, were better versed in the ways of *sesotho* with which this sphere was associated. And it will be shown in Chapter 7 how aspects of *sotho* custom associated with the realm of the spirits, as part of the cultural baggage being jettisoned by men, were seized upon by these migrant women and remade into a new statement of their own significance.

The revival of *sotho* cultural forms, both musical and spiritual, had its genesis not in a backward-looking but in a dynamic impulse, however. The move by urban *kiba* singers into the role of heir and breadwinner, normally thought of in *sotho* as the preserve of a son, represented the bold seizing of an initiative rather than merely the filling of a gap left empty by the absence of the normal incumbent. The same desire for advance which made almost all these women regretful that they had not gone further with schooling was manifest in their challenging of the accepted wisdom about appropriate female behaviour.

FAMILY GIFTS, FAMILY SPIRITS

Sesotho has provided an idiom for articulating women's new-found sense of themselves as migrants. Rural and urban sources of identity merged as the importance of sharing a common home became synonymous with the importance of sharing a set of experiences on the Reef. Interacting with this idea of belonging together with others from 'home' to a broader con-stituency of people subscribing to *sotho* ways was the sense of self which derived from a woman's place within particular rurally based households. For such a woman, conceptualising a position within her family involved not only the juggling of gender roles with a brother or the forming of bonds of co-operation with a mother, as discussed in Chapter 4. It also meant situating herself within a group of relatives having a deeper span: those no longer living. This was not the pre-ordained 'descent group' of functionalist anthropological theory, but rather a series of forebears from whose connections and continuities living *kiba* singers have constructed for themselves, in the midst of experiences of relocation and social dislocation, a sense of genealogical connectedness.

Deep-rooted family ties are evident in the influence of *badimo* (ancestral spirits) in the lives of their living descendants: through dreams and ancestral propitiation, and also through spirit-possession illness, its cure, and its conversion in some cases into the art of divination.

For urban singers, *sotho* music has not represented a continuation of the culture of girlhood, but has been grafted on to a youth spent in contexts where the cultural trappings of modernity, of *sekgowa* and of progress were things much sought after. But the invoking of this music in an urban context, although characterised by definite discontinuities, was not done through an entirely voluntary process of syncretism or bricolage. Their abandoning of the things of *sekgowa* was forced on some by possessing spirits who drove them inexorably into a world of *sesotho*. Here, praising, singing, propitiation and curing had the underlying logic deriving from affiliation to *badimo*. Even for those not summoned in this way, the sense of having 'inherited' or 'been given' certain gifts by those who preceded them provided an idiom whereby such women could position themselves in relation to the families within which they see themselves as so firmly ensconced.

FROM CHURCH TO *KIBA*

In Chapter 2 I gave an account of the gradual process which led to the founding of women's *kiba*. I mentioned that a number of women who became singers of the genre had previously belonged to mainstream or independent churches. Some had been raised in families of long-standing Christian affiliation called *majekane*, others were from families of *baditšhaba* who had joined more recently, and still others had converted when marrying (see Table 7.1). For the majority of these women, becoming members of *kiba* had meant a lessening or even an abandonment of their involvement in church activities. Of the seventeen women who have attended church at some point in their lives, only four out of seven *majekane*, and two out of ten *baditšhaba*, remain as active church-goers. This fading of the attraction of church for *kiba* singers, as I indicated earlier, raises some questions about the effectiveness of churches – particularly independent ones – as sources of migrant identity and as expressions of peasant/proletarian consciousness.

The popularity and success of independent churches have been accounted for by the fact that their members are drawn from among the 'poor' (Kiernan 1977) and more specifically from the ranks of peasant/ proletarians where the mainstream churches have tended to be associated rather with petty-bourgeois and bourgeois elements (Comaroff 1985: 188– 9, 192–3). To be even more specific, the Zionist Christian Church (ZCC) appears to have a particular appeal to workers themselves rather than to their rural-dwelling dependents: among the Tshidi, for example:

> the membership ... seems to have been drawn from roughly the same socio-economic stratum as the other Zionist groups, with one telling difference: it comprised more men and women in employment, especially female domestic workers, and contained fewer who were engaged in peasant production. (*ibid.*: 241)

The ZCC was certainly the most popular church among the proletarianising communities of *Leboa*: of the ten *baditšhaba* in the *kiba*-singing sample who were or became members of Zionist churches, six belonged to the ZCC. Their membership did not coincide with their entry into the labour market as Comaroff's point suggests, but rather preceded it, beginning in the rural areas during childhood, adolescence, or early married life. This was perhaps influenced by the fact that most of them spent their youth in areas very close to the headquarters of this church at Moria in the *Molepo* area. If their joining of the ZCC occurred before their move into the labour market, in all but the two cases of women who remain as ZCC members it was not to survive their arrival in town by many years. Those who had joined because of their husbands became involved with them in an intensive programme of church services, ZCC burial society meetings and social interaction with other church members. But rather than retain membership of the church in

Table 7.1 Church membership: *baditšhaba* and *majekane*

Church membership	Attend church today	Do not attend church today	Total
Majekane	4	3	7
Baditšhaba			
Never joined	0	2	2
Raised from childhood	1	2	3
Joined in adolescence	1	4	5
Joined when marrying	1	2	3
TOTAL	7	13	20

their own right, these women upon becoming widows allowed their membership to lapse and transferred their affiliation to *kiba*. Other former church-goers followed a similar course of action. This suggests, as I have said before, that the ZCC appealed more to migrant men (and to the women attached to them) than to the particular group of unattached migrant women who became singers.[1]

In my earlier account of the abandonment of church by migrant women who became involved in *kiba*, I suggested that this decision was part of a move away from dependence on men in general – husbands, brothers or uncles, and home boys – and towards a more autonomous form of migrant association generated by women independently of men. This suggestion is supported by accounts which stress the central and dominant role of male preachers in these churches and the subordinate role of their largely female congregations. But if we shift our attention from the social structuring of such churches, we may find other reasons why *kiba* women ceased to participate in them.

One important factor was the paucity of leisure time for these women in domestic service, and the number of activities between which this time had to be divided. Only one singer, who did 'piece jobs' rather than being a live-in domestic servant, had the whole weekend off. For others, arrangements varied between having every Sunday free through the more restrictive scenarios of 'every second Sunday' or 'Sunday afternoons only'. Considering the difficulty of fitting into this limited monthly leisure time attendance at both a burial society meeting and *mohodišano*, and a visit home, as well as the regular weekly dancing practice and various 'away' performances, an additional commitment to attendance at church required a considerable sacrifice of time and/or money. Some of those who managed to combine church with *kiba* did so by going to church one week and singing the next, while others attended church early, in one place, and had to pay the extra taxi fare to arrive at *kiba* on time. But most have simply chosen to leave attendance at church out of their weekly schedule altogether.

This opting out of one Sunday activity in favour of another should not, though, be taken as an indication that the two are irreconcilably opposed. For some of the women who have abandoned formal Christian worship for the singing and dancing of *kiba*, these are rather alternative ways of realising the same principles. Compatibilities in cosmological beliefs, according to some writers, have allowed for a merging of the Christian and traditionalist notions of 'spirit', and thus paved the way for the emergence of a variety of syncretic religions whose divergence from 'traditional' religion is not nearly as marked as was that of the mainstream churches (Schutte 1972, 1974; Sundkler 1961: 238–94; West 1975). The very emergence of the independent churches is seen as having been based on this spiritual merging.[2] It is against this background that one might understand the affiliation to *kiba* of Flora Mohlomi. She was raised in the ZCC, later became a Methodist when she married a Xhosa-speaker she met in town, and now no longer attends church at all: 'My church is *Maaparankwe*'.[3] A singer who expressed similar sentiments is Anna Dikotlo. As a child, she accompanied her family every Sunday on their journey from the white farm where they lived to the Roman Catholic church in the neighbouring *Molepo* location. At present, although she sees no contradiction between church and *kiba* and acknowledges that there are members who combine membership of both, she stated that:

> Now, I mostly go for dancing. I can't mix the two [church and dancing]. … Even in the Bible, in Psalm 130, they say, you can please God by dancing *dinaka* [pipes], *makope*, *metato* [one-stringed musical instruments], so there is a connection.[4]

There is a certain irony in Anna's use of this biblical reference to justify her leaving the church. The use of vernacular terms to translate the musical instruments of David's famous psalm was part of a well-meaning missionary endeavour to make Christianity accessible to the heathens by couching it in an indigenous idiom (Comaroff and Comaroff 1989: 282–8), but here it becomes an indication that the ends of religion may be served as well by 'traditional' as by Christian music and affiliation. The boundary between Christian and pagan belief and practice is seen in this case to be permeable in both directions.

But for certain *kiba* women there is a distinct opposition between the spiritual forces underlying church membership and those seen as reconcilable with *kiba* performance. These are the women who were driven away from church by the *malopo* possessing spirits. Of the five women interviewed who experienced the illness which these spirits inflict, two continued to attend church without any apparent ill-effects, but the other three were informed by diviners or by church leaders that the spirits would not allow them to combine their affliction with attendance at church. Other urban singers, on whom I have less comprehensive life-history information, had a similar experience.

One of these afflicted people was Joanna Maleaka. Before beginning her career as a labour migrant, she became sick as a young woman of twenty, at her home in *Kgothama*. She suffered from swollen feet and neck, and from blurred vision and occasional black-outs. Although she joined the ZCC in search of a cure, the healing offered by this church was ineffective. The sickness became worse after she began to work in Johannesburg, and she was told after consulting a ZCC prophet that she must leave the church and do as her ancestors wished: the church could not cure the sickness of the ancestors. She then went to a *ngaka* (diviner) who confirmed that her illness was due to possession by *badimo* (ancestral spirits), whose complaint was that Joanna had forgotten them and no longer did anything for them. Her cure entailed her training, in turn, as a *ngaka*, and her avoidance of church:

> I no longer go to church because they will complain, saying, 'Why am I moving away from them? Why am I in conflict with them?'[5]

Whereas Joanna relied on intermediaries for the interpretation of her symptoms, another sufferer, Mary Kapa, was more conscious of the message being conveyed to her by her forebears. Raised in a family which attended the ZCC, she began at the age of thirteen to suffer feelings of strangulation and to have dreams in which *ditaola* (diviners' bones) featured strongly. Again, the prophets were unable to offer a cure, and told her, 'This is your own people who are doing this to you. Your people want you: they want you to do something'. When she consulted a *ngaka*, the diagnosis was confirmed: 'The ancestors want you, and you are defying their laws'. She, too, trained as a *ngaka*, and ceased going to church.[6]

The *kiba* women who left the church, then, were advised to do so by spiritual leaders, both within and outside of Christianity. These leaders diagnosed an illness ancestrally caused, whose cure lay in the recognition that the sufferers were being summoned by their ancestors to the profession of *ngaka*, and in their being trained to assume this profession. Before being called by their ancestors in this way, both Mary Kapa and Joanna Maleaka belonged to the ZCC. This was a church whose appeal lay not only in its providing of an identity to proletarianising communities like those from which these women came, but also in its ability to heal. In my earlier experience in southern Lebowa, it was, indeed, often through a failure to become healed of illness by 'traditional' diviners that sufferers had made the decision to join the ZCC. But the illness from which these women suffered proved untreatable by the methods of this church.

To some *kiba* women, then, the ZCC proved inadequate not only in terms of the social constituency to which it introduced its members in town, but also in terms of its inability to contain particular kinds of ancestral affliction. The route into *bongaka* (divining) which they subsequently followed provided them with a source not only of specific ancestrally given identity, but also of professional status, which the church could not have given them. For these two women, and for three others called in the same way, the prestige they acquired as ancestrally appointed diviners paralleled the independence they were achieving as major breadwinners, and the autonomy they were gradually acquiring as *kiba* singers within a female-dominated group.

Women's entry into the previously male-dominated role of diviner, expressed in the idiom of spirit-possession, is believed to entail the direct influence of the dead upon their living descendants. The implication of strong continuities between the generations in this process will be seen to underlie the devolution, not only of this particular role, but also of a range of other abilities, skills and behaviours to be discussed in this chapter. But, like *kiba* singing itself, the practice of *bongaka* and other inherited arts is very different for relatively independent women in an urban context, such as the singers of *Maaparankwe*, and for dependent rural householders in a rural one, like the singers of *Dithabaneng*. In the case of healing, first, the phenomenon of women's possession in a rural context has led to such a proliferation of diviners that the profession has become somewhat devalued. Migrant women called to this profession and practising it in an urban context, on the other hand, enjoy an enhanced status. In the case of other qualities – especially negative ones – thought to be transmitted or passed down within the family, there is a sense for dependent rural householders that these must be passively accepted. For independent migrants, in contrast, the idea of acting on one's situation – often by appealing to or propitiating ancestors, or by praising them – provides a way of transcending their 'given' situations. The theme of independence and autonomy, gained by these migrants on material and social levels, is once again paralleled on the level of spiritually guided identity.

MALOPO: ILLNESS OR VOCATION

Let us deal first with the question of possession illness and divining. My argument, stated briefly, runs like this. The role of diviner, according to the literature and to informants, was one previously reserved for men. It was a spiritual gift to them, mostly given through dreams, from their fathers and grandfathers (Mönnig 1967: 95). The illness associated with *malopo*, although also ancestrally caused, was in contrast usually suffered by women (Krige and Krige 1943: 248; Mönnig 1967: 87; van der Hooft 1979: 148). In rural society as documented by these writers, the cure of *malopo* led its sufferers not to the acquisition of an important role in mainstream ancestral religion, such as that of *ngaka*, but rather into membership of a 'peripheral' or 'marginal' cult. Presently, however, among stay-at-home women and in migrant constituencies alike, it is acknowledged that a woman possessed in this way may be receiving the diviner's calling from her own male forebears.

This recognition is by no means an uncontested one. In rural circles particularly, the rate of spirit illnesses has reached the proportions of an epidemic, and some of the diviners who receive their calling as a result, and who then become trained, are thought to have had their illnesses wrongly diagnosed. Even in the urban situation, male migrants speak of this women's illness with the combined embarrassment and dismissiveness characteristic of the way in which maladies such as premenstrual tension have been seen in Europe. But, although the acknowledgement of *malopo* as a means to becoming a mainstream diviner is neither universal nor uncontested, some of the migrant *kiba* singers who have acquired the art of divining through this route have derived definite status and recognition from its practice.

Any approach which posits that ritual and healing practice are undergoing change must challenge the accepted wisdoms about the tenacity of entrenched ritual practices. This is particularly strongly entrenched in the literature on spirit-possession, in which a fundamental separation is posited between societies where spirit-induced dissociation is central to mainstream religion and those where it is peripheral (Lewis 1971; Firth 1969; Douglas 1973). Cults in the former type of society are dubbed 'central' cults involving 'mediumship', while those in the latter type are characterised as 'peripheral' and as involving 'possession'. Possession in this latter sense has been documented as a feature of societies or of segments of society which experience deprivation. Women, in particular, have been found to suffer disproportionately from possession sickness. Their doing so has been interpreted as a semi- or sub-conscious ploy which enables them to advance their interests (Lewis 1971: 31–4).

Working with this conceptual dichotomy, some authors have attempted to understand the relationship between mainstream ancestral religion and peripheral possession cults in a southern African context (Sibisi 1975; Hammond-Tooke 1986). In an overview of existing ethnography, Hammond-Tooke indicates that cults involving 'spirits of affliction' have arisen in Africa south of the Limpopo during the last eighty years, originating probably among the Shona of Zimbabwe. He describes the possessing spirits as foreign in origin rather than ancestral, and as being dealt with by exorcism rather than through communicative incorporation. He concludes that these mostly female cults are 'a response to fundamental social change in African society' (*ibid.*: 164). The dangers of being afflicted by an alien spirit are expressive of, or in parallel to, the confusing and potentially harmful intrusion of alien people – whites, Indians, or simply people from other tribes – 'into the family life of the indigenous peoples' (Sibisi 1975: 54).

The view of these writers is that, when possessing spirits intrude, they do so in a way which is unconnected to the mainstream religion. Like a coda hurriedly added to an integrated musical composition, such spirits fail to interfere with the internally consistent world view engendered within such religions.

But, although possession cults may have been foreign in origin as these writers claim, they have been in some instances integrated with ancestral cults. As long ago as the 1940s, the *malopo* possessing spirits of the Lovedu in the Northern Province were written of as being those of the ancestors, with a cure which involved not exorcism but the acknowledgement of the ancestor and his/her demands (Krige and Krige 1943: 241–9). Of similar provenance were the *malopo* spirits afflicting Pedi-speakers (Mönnig 1967: 87; van der Hooft 1979: 149, 151).

The insistence on rigid classifications by writers on religion and on spirit beliefs is thus misleading. Both the distinction between 'mediumship' and 'possession', and that between mainstream ancestral cults and fringe spirit-possession cults, can be seen to impose 'a conceptual rigidity that distorts the essential fluidity of interpretation and consequent ... articulation of the phenomena [of possession]' (Crapanzano 1977: 9; see also Boddy 1994). The main problem with a conceptual rigidity of this kind is that it obscures the possibility of processual or historical change. Altered circumstances in the Northern Province have generated the transformation of a peripheral cult into one through which the deities of mainstream religion begin to communicate, and in which – as cause or consequence – the sufferers have moved from the sidelines to take up a position closer to centre stage.

In the process, the distinction between possession as a peripheral cult whose sufferers are treated by drumming and by entry into the possession cult, and possession as a route to mainstream divining, has become blurred. For some women suffering possession, the normal cure of having to *leletšwe moropa* (go though drumming), and perhaps of joining the cult of *malopo* dancers, is sufficient. But for others who continue to be troubled the diagnosis or their own persistent dreams about *ditaola* or *dipheko* (diviner's bones) indicate that an ancestor is calling them to take up the art of healing: not as a marginal *malopo* or *mapale* doctor, but as a mainstream *ngaka*. Possession has begun to replace the older style of inheritance as a means of entering this profession, and women have begun to outnumber men as *dingaka*.

This process is recounted by some of the rural women singers of *Dithabaneng*:

> *Would you say that there are more male or female doctors today?*

> Most of them are female *dingaka* today. ... It's because they are the ones who are mostly troubled by *malopo*.[7]

Older people are uneasy in the face of the change:

Would you say most of the dingaka *in the past were women?*

Most of them were men, women were afraid of becoming *dingaka* in the past. You would hear people saying, so-and-so refuses to accept *dipheko* [diviner's bones], saying, she is still young, she can't manage. ...

Is there one of your family members who suffered from this?

Yes, there is one.

What did she do to get cured?

She had *malopo* and she went to *thwasiša* [get cured], a goat was slaughtered, ... and she began to dance *malopo* every day. ... As this person was dancing, later on she told us that so-and-so has given her some *dipheko* ... so it was felt that a goat is needed so that we can ask *badimo* to leave her. And, after slaughtering the goat and telling them, they left her for some time and we thought it was over. We asked them to leave her, telling them that it's because she is a woman, a woman can't manage as a *ngaka*, this needs a man. There was peace for some time ... but they visited her again and told her that she is a *ngaka* ... there was no alternative, and finally she became one.[8]

Although there are still *dingaka* who receive their calling from ancestors without possession, and although there is a clear distinction between the two alternative styles of calling, the end result is the same:

Are there different types of dingaka or are they the same?

They are different because some have to dance *malopo* to become doctors and others don't have to do this, they are born given *bongaka* [the ability to divine]. You will sometimes hear people saying that so-and-so has gone somewhere to 'drink' divining bones [i.e. to train as a *ngaka*] and one day you will see him/her divining. ... Both of these have got divining bones but had these given to them differently. One got them whilst dancing *malopo* and the other one whilst being cured [i.e. undergoing training].[9]

While some sufferers receive clear communications in dreams or during possession itself about the nature of their affliction and thus about its cure, others experience their symptoms as inexplicable, and must rely on the interpretation of diviners. The extensiveness of *malopo* affliction in recent times, and the fact, linked to this, of the huge proliferation of diviners in the present day, are thus in part dependent on the diagnosis of illness by other diviners. While citing as proof of the veracity of *malopo* the case of a teacher who was called away from his profession to practise as a healer, one Christian informant nevertheless laid the blame for the almost epidemic proportions of *malopo* at present on the existence of fraudulent healers. A healer interested only in financial rewards, he claimed, would be inclined to diagnose illness as being due to possession rather than to some simpler cause, since he could receive a higher payment for the ensuing treatment.[10] In a view such as this one, the increase in the number of diviners is both cause and effect of an increase in sufferers of *malopo*.

While not necessarily analysing the problem at this level, other people share the same critical perception of diviners' motives. In contrast to *dingaka* of the past, who would wait until the efficacy of their treatment was proved before receiving payment, those of the present are disparaged for demanding money in advance. The lack of this verifying mechanism of withheld payment is in turn seen as buttressing and making unassailable the position of fraudulent *dingaka*, called *gadikgone* (those who cannot):

> They won't tell you that they are incapable, this is because they want *ntadiyana* [money]. They will just say, let's try, and you hope that it will work out. You will keep on waiting but nothing will take place. But money is gone: you shall have parted with some money by this time.[11]

In the opinion of many – including some women – it is the healers who have undergone training in recent times as a result of *malopo* possession who are the most suspect. But there are also those – especially women – who claim that they prefer to consult a female *ngaka* since it gives them more freedom to explain their secrets and troubles. One result of the recent increase in the number of healers, then, appears to be that it allows for a wider choice (and, one might argue, for a kind of 'fair competition on an open market').[12]

Overall, then, in a village context there is a sense in which *malopo* possession, and the status of healer to which it may lead, appears to have escalated out of control and at the same time to have become devalued. It should be borne in mind, however, that not all sufferers of possession go beyond the state of *thwasiša* (being cured) to become diviners in their turn. This lengthy process may involve an initial *leletšwe meropa* (going through drumming), future involvement in *malopo* drumming and dancing for the benefit of other sufferers, and a stay of months or even years at the home of the diviner who has diagnosed the sufferer's illness and who is effecting the cure. The rural group *Dithabaneng*, for example, counts among its members four women who have suffered possession at some point in their lives, but none of these has been called to become a healer. While some of them, whose cures are complete and who seldom engage in *malopo* dancing, are no different in appearance from their neighbours, others can be identified, by their apparel and their frequent engagement in *malopo* dancing sessions, as belonging to the ranks of cured possession-sufferers (now known by the borrowed Nguni term *sangoma*). For such people, possession does still appear to denote a seeking for recognition, in a domain beyond the mainstream, by marginal figures (Lewis 1971: 30–6).

In the case of urban migrant women who sing *kiba*, possessing ancestors did not stop short at the point of demarcating their sufferers as members of a marginal group, but took them further, leading them towards mainstream *ngaka* status. Out of the five women I interviewed who have *malopo*, two are fully trained diviners holding certificates from a training centre in Hammanskraal north of Pretoria, while a further two are undergoing training intermittently during visits home.

One of these certificate-holding and practising healers is Helen Matjila. The illness which began some years after her first coming to the Reef to find employment was diagnosed by an old family friend as caused by her being *etelwa* (visited) by her father's paternal grandfather, who had been a *ngaka* and who was handing on his craft to her as *mpho* (a gift). She found time after the end of one domestic job and before beginning to look for another to spend three months undergoing training in Hammanskraal. Her entry into the diviner's profession, apart from facilitating the cure of her possession illness, has also had material benefits. It brought her luck in finding a better-paid domestic job, she says, and gave her a way to supplement her earnings with the money she is paid by patients: she may earn as much as R500 extra a month. When prompted by her great-grandfather in dreams, she travels to *Thaba ya Badimo* (the mountain of the ancestors) near Nylstroom to gather the herbs needed for her practice. The only real difficulty of her situation is that her employer, who regards the terms 'witchdoctor' and 'witchcraft' as synonymous, must be kept ignorant of Helen's profession: a sometimes tricky operation given the numbers of people who make their way into her small domestic servant's quarters to have her consult her bones on their behalf, or who enter her minuscule backyard bathroom to be given ritual cleansings. Aside from this minor obstacle, however, Helen's experience of her role as healer has been a positive and rewarding one, and has enhanced her status in the eyes of everybody except the woman who pays her monthly salary.[13]

From the story of Helen Matjila, as from that of the other possessed women mentioned earlier, it is clear that entry into the divining profession has proved generally beneficial. But even for these migrant healers in an urban context, their status as women who have been called to the profession through the *malopo* route is not unequivocally prestigious, particularly among men. I saw an illustration of male dismissiveness towards *malopo* sickness during one of *Maaparankwe*'s weekends performing in a rural area. Mary Kapa, a *malopo* sufferer who has already undergone training as a diviner, manifested the characteristic falling-down behaviour typical of *malopo* possession. Several other *malopo* women, almost as if by contagion, fell down in turn. The unaffected members of the women's group put great effort – by singing snatches of song and by speaking directly to the spirits in quiet and urgent tones – into making them 'cool down' and cease troubling their descendants. It was because the group's *malopo* sufferers had failed to perform a suitable *phasa* (ancestral propitiation) informing their possessing ancestors that they were to travel to a faraway place, and asking them not to give trouble during this absence, that the unexpected attack of *malopo* sickness was thought to have occurred. Throughout the procedure of bringing the afflicting spirits under control, the male members of *Maaparankwe* sat around, half-amused and half-embarrassed at this public display of possession illness in a strange place and amongst strangers. In response to my concerned enquiries about whether the women, apparently in a dead faint, needed to be rushed to a doctor, the leader of the men's group laughed, and indicated that these women were 'not sick'.

The incident illustrated a clear difference of response between the group's men, who scoffed at and dismissed *malopo* sickness as something old-fashioned and womanly, and its women, who rallied round to provide support and to administer a cure through singing. It is precisely this access to a group of women who understand the nature of the sickness and can help to treat it which in part explains the appeal of *kiba* to *malopo* sufferers. Some migrant women joined a singing club in town because they saw it as a sort of substitute for the therapeutic dancing and drumming of the rural *malopo* cults. This is especially necessary in an urban environment, in which strangers might be unable to understand the cause of the illness, as I was told by Andronica Machaba:

> Let's say I'm with some people, and these people don't know anything about this *setšo* thing – *malopo* – and should it happen, they will be frightened and call my employers, who will then take me to hospital. I tell you, I won't get cured at the hospital, and the other thing is that I'm not actually sick, it's just *malopo*. At the hospital, when seeing this, they might think I'm mad. But if this happens while people like Joanna Maleaka and Phina [fellow *kiba* singers] are around me ... they won't call the whites. Instead they will try to talk to the *badimo* to cool down.[14]

Other singers are less ready to posit a link between the drumming and singing of *malopo* and that of *kiba*. They acknowledge only the connection that *badimo* like and approve of this music, since they once danced it themselves. Yet others deny any connection between *kiba*, which is 'just a play', and *malopo* dancing, which is 'a serious matter'.[15] But despite these different interpretations, all the women singers proved ready to rally round and help in the cooling of the troubling ancestors.

The definition of *malopo* as a woman's illness, and of the calling to *bongaka* which results from it as somehow different from that of a male diviner, is, then, still prevalent among male migrants. Even for the sufferers of this possession in my urban *kiba*-singing sample, there may thus be some truth in the theory that possession provides a route to recognition by the disenfranchised (Lewis 1971). Although they have achieved some independence and autonomy, these singers do experience the irksomeness of subjection to male and patriarchal authority at both the urban and rural poles of their existence,[16] and so might be thought to gain a degree of leverage over men from a veiled expression of protest.

More convincing, however, is the view which sees migrant diviners as acquiring the prestige previously reserved for a role played by men, even if the perception of this prestige is restricted to the ranks of fellow migrant women and does not extend to their male counterparts. Of perhaps greatest importance, though, *malopo* is a channel of ancestrally given identity. It is women's own grandparents or great-grandparents who speak to or through them, and who pass on to them the ancestrally inherited 'gift' of healing. Whereas this gift was previously passed down through males from grandfather to grandson by means more normal and less vividly and dramatically experienced, the disruptiveness of its transference to granddaughters appears to necessitate a direct and physical intervention of the ancestors in the lives of their descendants.

Two ways were cited earlier in which a person may 'get divining bones' (become a diviner). One was through being given the ability to divine at birth, and the other was through dancing *malopo*. A decline in the number of male healers, who were thought of as born with this ability, has been accompanied by an increase in the number of female healers, who enter the diviner's status through *malopo*. Possession by the ancestor bequeathing the divining gift has become the idiom in which inheritance is couched, as it switches from patrilineal inheritance by males to a flexible inheritance by females.

Malopo is thus concerned with the construction of an identity by a woman out of characteristics acquired from her forebears. Taking up recent suggestions that the idea of the 'self' in many non-western cultures is not necessarily that of a bounded, rationally motivated and unified entity, Crapanzano claims that 'the spirit idiom ... provides a means of 'self-articulation' that may well be radically different from the self-articulation of the Westerner', and that 'much of what is articulated in the West as within the individual may be articulated as outside the individual in those societies in which the spirit idiom is current' (1977: 11–12). If the ability to play a significant and high-status role in relation to the sacred world is still conceived of as properly part of the male domain, and as couched in the idiom of patrilineal succession, then its transfer to the granddaughters rather than to the grandsons of families requires the radical externalising, and then incorporation, of this male principle into the identity of the female self.

LUCK, SUFFERING, PROPITIATION AND PRAISING

Possession, then, is most fruitfully understood as one of the many ways in which *badimo* (ancestors) communicate with, or bequeath things to, their living descendants. The transference of a special ability or talent like that of healing (*bongaka*) is described by the use of the word *go fa* (to give), and the ability thus transferred is thought of as *mphu* (a gift), using a term surprisingly close to the English one for the same idea.[17]

It is tempting in this context to use the English term 'inheritance', since this encodes a range of processes whereby members of a senior generation – living or dead – confer certain assets or qualities upon family members junior to them. But this term should be used with caution, since it imputes conceptual unity to a series of separate phenomena. A youngest son's acquisition of the rights to his parents' residential plot and their field, for example, is called *go šala lapeng* (to stay in the family yard), which carries the same sense of continuity as the word 'inheritance' without the implication of transferred material assets.[18]

The word in *sesotho* which does approximate the English 'inheritance' most closely is one which refers to the transfer of personal qualities – *leabela*, with its associated verb *go abela* in the active form (to confer in inheritance) and its passive form *go abelwa* (to receive in inheritance). A variety of physical features or flaws is thought of as being acquired through this means, such as *hlogo ya seopi* (a congenital headache) or the propensity to suffer from toothache, as well as less material qualities such as *botho* (humanity or kindness) and *bokelema* (from the Afrikaans word 'skelm': the quality of being bad, like a 'tsotsi' or gangster). Another thing which is spoken of using the word *go abela* (to inherit) is luck, both in its negative sense as *mahlatse madimabe* (bad luck) or *mahloko* (suffering) and in its positive sense as *mahlatse mahlogonolo* or *mahlogo* (good luck).

Older rural women, like the grandmothers of *Dithabaneng*, use a discourse which conveys a sense of unavoidable destiny in the transfer of qualities from parents or grandparents to their children or grandchildren. An example can be seen in the lyrics of the song *Marashiya*:

Ke reng ka hlaela pheta ye botse	I don't have a shiny necklace
O se ke wa ntelela mohlako	You who are looking at me, you see suffering
Ke gore bjale ke ago kgalema wene o ntelelago	Don't scold me or feel pity for me
Ge e le mohlako ke leabela	Suffering is an inheritance
Nna ke abetse mmane	I inherited it from my mother
Mme o abetse makgolo.	She inherited it from her mother.

In explaining this song, the singers of *Dithabaneng* showed a remarkable degree of consensus in their acknowledgement that luck is something *o wa tswalelwa* (one is born with), and that there is little one can do to change it. The woman in the song is complaining about her husband's failure to provide her with the womanly attire she desires, but in attributing this suffering to inheritance rather than to his inadequacies she is resigning herself to her situation:

> She says that, despite the suffering, she won't part with him, but will console herself saying that maybe she has inherited it from her mother and ... from her grandmother.
> If you are born into it [suffering], you may try to change it, you may have money but misuse it. You may buy a car and people might think you are getting better, but after a short while the car breaks, you spend a lot of money trying to fix it, but all in vain. The car will then be towed into the yard and stay there.[19]

There was less agreement within the group about the ultimate origins of this luck: for some its source lay no deeper than with one's own forebears whereas for others it was attributable to *modimo* (God), conceived of less as the biblical patriarch and more as a being senior to *badimo* but operating through their mediation.[20]

Only members of the younger generation feel that suffering, being *ka boomo* (self-made), can be avoided by their own efforts, according to the older rural women who discussed this issue with me. The girl in the song who was not given a shiny necklace was experiencing a bad luck specific to stay-at-home women. Such women are dependent on men's earnings both for a livelihood and for clothing and adornment. Revealing this perception, *Dithabaneng* singers suggested that the way in which a younger woman could sidestep or escape her destined allocation of bad luck would be by attaching herself to another man – perhaps a teacher – in the hope that he might provide for her more adequately than her husband had done:

> she won't depend on the head of the family. She will say, 'this means that I am going to inherit suffering', and in order to avoid this, she will have an affair with someone and get some food so that when her real husband comes home he will find some food. He will think that she got this from her parents. That's why we say that a young person never suffers.[21]

In the idiom presented here, the inevitable destiny of being 'born into' a position of misfortune is conceptualised in terms of descent. Although younger women are said to be less passively resigned to this fate than their elders, it is suggested here that the only means by which such a woman may actively transform her situation is through transferring her dependence on her parents or husband to a different man, conceived of as alternative provider.

This rather touchingly idealised version of the Cinderella story appears, in purely material terms, to express a faith in the possibilities offered by hypergamy – a romantic link to a teacher! – for overcoming the poverty of a woman's life in the labour reserve. But it belies the fact that marriage or its variants have proved far less durable than the structures of agnation for providing dependent rural women with support. The singers of *Dithabaneng*, whose husbands or lovers have failed to sustain their needs for cash, have had to rely on brothers or uncles for the sustenance necessary to insulate them against the necessity of going out to work.

The singers from *Leboa* who lacked such insulation explained their fortune in rather different terms. The notion of 'luck' does to some extent hold sway among these migrants. It was used, for example, by Anna Dikotlo when expressing her uncertainty about her future as a childless woman who would one day retire to her rural home without the assurance of a source of wage income. Asked whether the nephews and nieces to whose support and education she is presently contributing financially would support her in retirement, she replied that she was unable to answer this question, since it was a matter of *mahlatse* (luck). The use of this idiom by urban *kiba* singers I have spoken to, however, tends to focus less on the inevitability of inherited suffering or bad luck than on the possibility of asking their ancestors to send good or better luck.

This is done through an informally constructed system of *phasa* (ancestral propitiation), which lays especial emphasis on the communication between a single individual and the spirit of a particular forebear. In the rural context, individual ancestral visitation or crisis on the one hand, and family misfortune or thanksgiving on the other, give rise respectively to more private and personal, and more strongly group-oriented, versions of *phasa*. The latter usually involve the slaughter of a beast and the making and offering of beer, whereas the former may be accomplished by a person on his/her own, with a simple mixture of water and snuff.

It is this simpler and more solitary version of *phasa* which has become current among *kiba* singers in an urban context. Living in cramped servants' quarters in the back yards of white suburban residences, they choose a special spot just outside the door of the room, pour on the ground the water-and-snuff mixture, and speak to the ancestral spirit in question. According to Anna Dikotlo:

> when I am asleep, if I dream of my father, the following day I will take snuff and water and *phasa*, even if I'm here in town.[22]

A similar account was given by Flora Mohlomi:

> If I do not *hwetša bophelo* [find life] I will consult *dingaka* [diviners]. They will tell me that my grandmother wants something from me. ... I should take snuff and some water and then go to a particular corner outside here, and pour them out, and speak to her.[23]

In the lives of these women whose circumstances and personal qualities led them to become major providers for their rural families, their very departure to town to find work was accompanied by individualised *phasa*:

> You will have to take some water and snuff, then go outside and tell them that you are going away to *makgoweng* [the place of the whites] to look for employment, ask them to be with you, and give you some *mahlatse* so that you can find some work.[24]
>
> You should tell them by way of *phasa* ... that you are leaving for town to work for your children.[25]

The sense of acquiring ancestrally given good fortune was most marked in the case of those *kiba* singers who had actually experienced ancestral intervention in its most direct form, through possession. Some are undergoing training as a *ngaka*, like Joanna Maleaka and Phina Komape. Another, Helen Matjila, was already certificated as a *ngaka*. For all, the diagnosis of their possession illness and the onset of its successful remedy are seen as having marked a turning point of fortune in their migrant careers. But even those engaging with the spirits in the more 'mainstream' mode of dreams and ensuing propitiation do so with an awareness that it is thus possible actively to transform their circumstances.

There is a clear parallel between the material and social situation of these people and the way they think about invoking the spirit world in the pursuit of good fortune. These are single women who visualise themselves as situated primarily within the context of their own natal families. By becoming major breadwinners for their parents, siblings and eventually children, they have demonstrated their capacity to act on and change rather than resign themselves to their rural situation. Although marriage and its attendant status as dependent wife became a possibility for some of these women at an earlier point in the life-cycle, none was in a position to continue deriving security from this status, or to see it as the primary means of escape from the circumstances in which they found themselves in their own families. Even those who eventually contracted marriages or became involved in informal conjugal partnerships in town did so in ways which were not fundamentally to affect, and certainly not to derogate from, their primary responsibilities to their rural families of origin.

The single status of most urban *kiba* singers has another important implication for the link between migrant women, their kin and their ancestors. In customary family ritual, an important role was played by the *kgadi* (senior father's sister, or woman of a senior generation belonging to the family group by birth rather than marriage).[26] Although a senior man would attend to the slaughter of a sacrificed beast, it was the *kgadi* who officiated and performed the ritually more significant tasks, such as ensuring that the blood was spilled correctly onto the grave, placing the pots of beer appropriately, and returning to fetch them when the spirits had had their fill. If a *kgadi* were married, her role would have been an ambivalent one: although ritually crucial to her own family and even featuring as an ancestor within it, she was ritually of little significance to the family in which she was married and in which she spent most of her time (Mönnig 1967: 56–7; Krige and Krige 1943: 235).

For most urban *kiba* singers, who have not married or whose marriage has not endured, and who see their only responsibility as being towards their family of birth, the role of *kgadi*, in which most singers are positioned in relation to these families, becomes less ambiguous. It is true that in terms of authority and material resources the non-married status of these women does place them in a situation of potential conflict with their younger brothers, whose right to be the heir or the one officially designated to *šala lapeng* (stay in the family yard) is still enshrined by 'traditional law'.[27] But this same unmarried status operates to buttress the strength of their ritual position. The assumption of this crucial ritual role by singers such as Helen Matjila, Anna Dikotlo and Andronica Machaba in relation to their rural families is seen by them to have occurred with the death or absence of female agnates of a generation senior to them. But it can also be seen as a reflection on a ritual level of the social status they have achieved, as members of the urban work force and as supporters of their families. Public ancestral ritual at their homes, either cyclical like the harvest thanksgiving or occasioned by some particular incident or misfortune, cannot take place without their involvement.

In some cases they are called upon to perform this role even in an urban context. In addition to the private version of *go phasa* (propitiation) described earlier in this chapter, Andronica Machaba, the oldest daughter in her family, has on two occasions had to *phasa* on behalf of her siblings who like her are working in Johannesburg. On one of these, her younger sister Salome was troubled by eerie noises in her room at night, and was told by the diviner she consulted that, since this was due not to witchcraft but to neglect of her ancestors, a sacrifice was required. On another, her brother was experiencing problems, and was given the same advice by the leader of the Apostolic Church to which he belongs. On neither of these occasions would a private propitiation have been sufficient. The younger sister Salome could not simply have sacrificed on her own behalf:

> *Why didn't you just* phasa *at your place?*

> It's because Andronica is the eldest, she is older than me ... and so she is the one whom the ancestors would listen to. I cannot face them on my own and do this personally, no.

So the ritual was performed instead in the context of a family gathering, with Andronica officiating:

It was good timing, because all my mother's children were here. ... Salome and my sister came very early in the morning, and my brother John also left Baragwanath [near Soweto] very early in the morning, and before the sun rose, we were all together here. We took the bucket of *mabele* [sorghum beer] and did *phasa* with it, and we took that chicken, killed it, and did *phasa* with the blood. ... Then we took that chicken and cooked it, and ate it. Then my brother was fine after that.

On the occasion of the first sacrifice a measure of judicious management was required to ensure that Andronica's employers did not become aware of the ritual taking place in their backyard, but on that of the second they were fortunately away on holiday, having left the house in Andronica's care:

They were not there, that's why we enjoyed it, and had a nice time.[28]

It is not only an older sister acting on behalf of her junior siblings, but also an older *kiba* singer acting for her group as a whole, who may play the role of *kgadi* in an urban context. Since the club contains many unrelated men and women, communication with *badimo* is here conducted in the most generalised of terms. The logistics of urban accommodation exclude female members from certain rituals performed by a *kiba* group, such as the slaughter of a beast for the annual year-end and year-beginning parties. This is because, in order to leave time for the skinning, cutting up, and cooking of the beast, it must be slaughtered in the township during the Saturday night before the Sunday when women arrive from the suburbs to attend the party. But other parties are organised on the initiative of women, and involve them in a central role. At the child's birthday party described in Chapter 1, Flora Mohlomi was the hostess and prime mover during the festivities. Being the oldest female member of *Maaparankwe*, she was seen as *kgadi* in relation to her fellow-performers as a whole:

Mokete wa matswala a ngwana (child's birthday party)
After the women had danced into the performing space in the street from Jan Seašane's back yard, carrying the child and his birthday presents, Flora gave a welcoming speech and invocation couched in the formalistic language of *go reta* (praising), the form of oratory in which so many singers excel:

Le a mmona, le a mmona naa?	Do you see him, do you see him?
Ke sello	He is Weeping [proper name]
Sello sa masetha le pelo.	The weeping that will make one feel heartbroken.

She then addressed the ancestors – again in a generalised sense, on behalf of the child and the group as a whole – directly:

Bagolo tsogang	Great people rise up
Ke ya ngwana wa lena	Here is your child
A le a mmona, a le a mmona naa?	Do you see him, do you see him?

This was followed by the singing of a song about the child, by a ceremonial giving of presents, and later by a performance of the group's general repertoire.

A party like this one was a voluntary event, unsanctioned by rural ritual practice except through the remotest relation to the customary three-month hair-cutting ceremony (Mönnig 1967: 102). It appears as secular in nature, with its spirit of cultural revivalism in an urban context, and its inventive combining of ancestral invocation by a senior woman with music, praising, and present-giving. But whether primarily or only at one remove concerned with the actual presence and influence of the ancestors, such a performance demonstrates how these forms of oratory and performance associated with *sesotho* or *setšo* appear to derive their central logic from a connection to the deceased forebears of their living practitioners.

At this party Flora's role as *kgadi* involved no formal *phasa* but rather a generalised invoking of the ancestral presence through *direto* (praises). The ability to praise (*go reta*) is one which is frequently associated with ancestral invocation, both in this more general sense and in its more ritually specific one:

> Through *phasa* one can learn to do a *sereto* [praise] because she will be listening to someone talking to a particular person and say a lot of things about that particular ancestor, and from there switch over to others as well. To *phasa* and to *reta* is nearly the same thing.[29]

Praising is centrally concerned with, and is propagated through, the continuity of the family. Especially in the domestic sphere, it is practised largely by women, who have learned the art from their mothers and grandmothers. Often, as in the case of Andronica Machaba, the same older sister who has assumed the role of *kgadi* also specialises in *go reta*.

Besides the manner of its transfer from the older to the younger generation, and its association with occasions on which the living communicate with their dead forebears, *go reta* (praising) is linked to family continuity and inheritance in another important way. Through its elaborate stanzas and chant-like incantations, a practitioner of this art reiterates the descent lines and affinal ties which underlie her own existence. Bilateral rather than unilineal, the unique combination of these which characterise every new generation must be mastered and skilfully merged by the praiser. In Andronica's case, for example, although she spent more time with and so learned more praises from her maternal grandmother when growing up, she also picked up some of the praises appropriate to her father's side of the family from his mother. The result, in which both are 'put together', provides a lengthy but rapidly recited account of Andronica's forebears on both sides of the family, each addressed ceremoniously via his/her animal 'totem'[30] rather than individually, as the following excerpt demonstrates:

> We are the people of Machaba and Maraba,
> The ones who shine among the clouds in the sky,
> Those who get food for themselves;
> You who swears and curses the Baupo people,
> Where will you get a brother-in-law?
> We are the grandchildren of Ranyalwa and Selaelo of the Lions,
> And Mosibudi and Lekgaphola of the Leopards,
> We are the grandchildren of Motlatso of Nkgaru and the Hare,
> Those who don't die the death of a dog, but who die only if killed by
>   a hunting stick
> If you strike me I won't feel the pain, the pain will be felt by the
>   heart,
> We are the grandchildren of the milk that overflows from a bucket,
> I'm Motlhaloga, the cousin of Mmapoo, the one of the black
>   mountain from which you can see Bokgatla Makotong,
> People of the spear that pierces, the one which has pierced the sister
>   to Mathakgale of Matloga,
> Matloga the son of Malesela,
> The people who, when they are hungry, get angry,
> Who are used to being bellyful.[31]

For women of Andronica's generation, the experience of resettlement and the resulting social dislocation made it more difficult to reconstruct these histories, owing to the interrupted contact with the older female family members from which such praises were learned. But these experiences also made the reconstruction of histories easier, since they established conditions which made the creative articulation of a family-based identity perhaps more crucial than it would have been under circumstances less disrupted.

Sotho activities like praising and possession, in which urban *kiba* singers are to a greater or lesser extent involved, do not occupy a fixed place in an unchanging universe of coherently connected cultural forms. Just as *malopo* suffering is handled inventively by these singers, so the art of praising is flexibly reinterpreted in new ways by them, and made to overlap and interact with other genres.[32] In addition to its fully fledged performance by a practitioner such as Andronica Machaba, mentioned above, it is imaginatively incorporated into *kiba* songs by singers such as Joanna Maleaka, or by Julia Lelahana, who prefers to reserve praising proper for performance at home with her family. Andronica Machaba and Joanna

Maleaka, acknowledging that home is the proper place for praising in its complete form, have found an ingenious way to straddle the distance: they have made cassette recordings of themselves praising, and sent them back to their mothers to play.

Whether in the unabridged form associated more strongly with rural performance, or in one of a number of urban permutations, praising facilitates the expression of identity. Women such as Andronica Machaba and Julia Lelahana, despite the social dislocations which accompanied their early childhood and those which brought them to town as young women, root themselves through praising in the context of an orally transmitted tradition of the perpetuation of the family. What *malopo* possession achieves through the direct and unmediated intrusion of spirits into the bodies of their female descendants, then, the art of *go reta* accomplishes through conscious learning, artifice and skill. For a woman involved in either or both of these activities, her actions and words provide a 'screen on which are projected, in condensed form, her family history and her own biography' (Zempleni 1977, cited by Crapanzano 1977: 26).

CONCLUSION

Migrant women from the Trust and reserve areas of *Leboa* in the Northern Province were not seeking in *kiba* simply the security of a 'voluntary organisation', as the overly functionalist accounts of adaptive urbanisation by writers of the 1950s and 1960s might lead us to believe. Participation in *kiba* provided not just a cohesive group of fellows with whom the tribulations and successes of migrancy could be shared, but also an environment in which a number of activities, conceived of collectively as those of *sesotho*, could be carried out. The pursuit of these activities played a crucial role in providing for a sense of migrant female identity.

Such activities – the propitiation of and in some cases possession by ancestral spirits, divination, and praising, all combined in an urban context under the rubric of the weekly *kiba* practice or performance – had been first experienced or engaged in by these women during childhood.[33] In most cases, however, *sesotho* had represented a weak strain of girlhood culture, culminating in the experience of *koma* (initiation) but soon overtaken by an adolescent culture more oriented to school, to *tlhabologo* (civilisation) and to the things of *sekgowa* (white ways).

Their intensive reinvolvement in this world of *sesotho* as mature women, some years after beginning to work in town, could be accurately characterised as having the appearance of a selective cultural revival, since its adherents did abandon those aspects of *tlhabologo* still thought to be beneficial. What such a characterisation would overlook, however, would be the rootedness of *sotho* singing, praising, divining and ancestral invocation in the idiom of family permanence and continuity.

Many of these women had previously been members of independent churches, especially the ZCC. This might suggest that they had already, before singing *kiba* in town, established attachments to sources of group-oriented healing and support as solutions to the problems of individually experienced affliction and misfortune. But most were disinclined to maintain their church membership after they had ceased being linked to the churches through their husbands. This suggests that the idiom and message of such churches were better suited to the expression of male migrant identity and consciousness than they were to that of these women – first-generation female migrants, whose departure for the Reef was generated out of a strong sense of responsibility and connection to their families of birth.

For these women, the range of performative genres associated with *sesotho* uses the idiom of kinship, bilateral descent, and the concern of forebears in the affairs of their living progeny. Through these means, *sesotho* provides for the expression of a specifically female migrant identity.

CONCLUSION

This book has been an investigation of the use of 'traditional music' by a range of people involved in, or affected by, Northern Province migrancy. Methodologically it represents a re-exploration of a number of terrains which, although they have been traversed by other writers, have not previously been mapped to highlight the features which appear prominent in this study. Nor have they been laid over each other or seen as intersecting as they appear in this context.

Migrant labour has been an issue of great interest and concern to anthropologists, not only in South Africa, but also in West and East Africa, and on the Zambian Copperbelt. One aspect of the study of rural–urban migration has been an interest in regional or ethnic associations during the 1950s and 1960s and, in more recent years, in ethnicity more broadly. A contemporary trend has been to re-explore the same issues in different terms: through looking at the use of real and imagined space in orienting people's worlds and conceptions of their worlds, and the aligning of different places with values which go beyond the merely spatial or geographical. In my own study, this has become manifest as an interest in the significance of migrants' ideas about home. Home, more than just a geographical locality, is a source of orientation and identification created by migrants using materials drawn from pre- and post-colonial history.

Here, the anthropology of migration has intersected with the anthropology of music: it is partly through musical performance that images of home are created. Southern African studies in ethnomusicology have attempted to document, in advance of other studies, the culture and consciousness of town- and country-dwelling Africans. But this approach, while giving due attention to culture, tended to underplay the importance of the material and socio-political circumstances of particular constituencies of musicians and their audiences. The people who played or listened to music appeared to belong to broad and relatively homogeneous categories, and little information was given about the significance of songs or dances in the context of particular lives or life-experiences.

A marrying of the anthropology of migration with the anthropology of music required the acknowledgement that life-experience and musical performance overlapped in fundamental ways. Migrants' music and dance are not merely passive reflectors of already-constituted social relationships and identities, but play a role in formulating and cementing these. Songs labelled 'traditional' sung by migrants in town are not anachronistic survivals from a rural home, but building-blocks in the creation of home and identity in an urban setting.

Exploring the convergence between music and migrant experience became an exercise in understanding the particular and the subjective. From a political economy perspective, migrancy is often understood as a product of broad processes occurring on the level of the capitalist economy and the state. But the migrants whose life-histories I recorded and whose performance I observed and documented were not the passive victims of such processes. Rather, they were actors, drawing on both personal and cultural resources to shape their choices and to structure their lives. A focus on migrant performance allowed me to look at the 'local knowledge' in terms of which broad processes of rural dispossession and of proletarian-isation were understood and dealt with.

The anthropology of women and gender was a third major area of interest. This, too, was a terrain previously traversed. But its intersections with migration and performance had not yet been mapped. In discussions of migration and of ethnic associations, women have often been assumed to be appendages of men. But the migrant women who came to constitute the major focus of my study were making their own choices about the creation and affirmation of a sense of home. For them, perhaps more than for men, musical performance was a crucial means by which this home was created. Given that the intersection of music and migrancy had directed my attention to the particularities of subjective experience, it was one of my concerns to understand what it was that made women migrants, apparently coming from the same areas of the country and using the same broad set of symbols as men, view 'home' and 'tradition' in such unique ways.

In so doing, it became necessary to challenge the standard opposition between Christian and pagan/traditionalist which has structured so many studies of South African migrancy and also of South African music. The women migrant singers of my study are mostly former Christians. Their adoption of a style of music normally viewed as the preserve of pagan or traditionalist men represents a transcendence of the rigid dichotomies – of religious orientation as well as of gender – which have characterised much of the literature.

Rather than being limited by the behaviour associated with given social categories, the migrant women singers of *kiba* have thus drawn eclectically on the materials of tradition and modernity, of manhood and womanhood, in constructing a sense of shared home and of identity. It is to this process of identity formation, in which the substance of *setšo* (origin or tradition) is paradoxically used in concocting something which emphasises autonomy and emancipation, that I wish to turn in the last few pages of this study.

ORIGIN AND IDENTITY

Sometimes replacing and sometimes used as an alternative to *sesotho*, the word *setšo* denotes a series of values, experiences, places and relationships which is drawn on as a resource by various migrant constituencies in the Northern Province. Music and dance are one major means through which this is achieved. Migrant men and migrant women on the Reef, and stay-at-home women in the villages of Lebowa, group together for regular practices and performances of a music/dance defined by reference to origin or tradition.

The structures and rhythms of this music show little evidence of change, but the lyrics, particularly those of women's music, provide a space and an opportunity for extensive commentary on present-day situations and predicaments. *Kiba* integrates topical comment by contemporary composers with accounts of the experience of composers from previous generations, and places these within a marked-off arena of heightened expectation and attention. It is this capacity for combining the new with the old which makes the performance of *kiba* ideally suited to articulating *setšo* or *sesotho*.

As this suggests, neither *setšo* nor the musical genre which it defines is immutable and unchanging. Its use in particular social contexts is what imbues it with specific significance. Male migrants in compounded employment and in hostels and shacks have utilised it to activate and elaborate a sense of a rural 'home'. In the contemporary *kiba* performance of these migrants, events from different regions' contrasting pre-colonial and colonial histories are selectively invoked, with those from the south favouring imagery which celebrates the nineteenth century Pedi polity while those from the north stress specific, often totemic, local identities. The performance of the female version of the same genre by stay-at-home women articulates and dramatises – sometimes in an exaggerated fashion – their domestic, dependent status, and their position within a separately defined, female realm.

But this study has been mostly concerned with a social context in which *setšo* appears in its most shifting and innovative and least immutable forms: the associations formed around musical performance by groups of Northern Province migrant women. In this context, the suitability of music to articulating the values of *setšo* – in its most innovative and changeable form – becomes particularly clear. In the experience of women newly arrived in the Reef as migrants, things of home or origin were at first narrowly defined by reference to a particular home area. It was through the evolution of a broad, encompassing and homogeneous style of dance/music/lyrics out of a series of area-specific local ones that the development of a broader home or place of origin was largely achieved. Here, a development on the level of a 'traditional' musical style was the means through which an urban-based grouping of autonomous wage-earning women came to claim a common home, as manifestation of the common experiences which bound them together on the Reef.

These women's common experiences as migrants on the Reef were laid over a series of earlier rural experiences characterised by high degrees of social dislocation on the one hand, and aspirations to live in a civilised way on the other: both features in strong contrast to the lives of the stay-at-home heartland singers of Chapter 5. Against this backdrop, 'origin' has come to have uses and significances different from those which it has in its use both by male migrants and by stay-at-home women. The identity which migrant women have assembled using *setšo* or *sesotho* – expressed mainly through its musical manifestation, but also using the other ideas, contexts and values associated with it – is a strikingly modern one.

Tradition, and particularly the music associated with it, has frequently been used as a means to modernity (Erlmann 1991: 11), or as an idiom through which to articulate modernist aspirations (Ranger 1975, cited in Vail and White 1991: 50). As Waterman notes of the immensely popular *juju* style in Nigeria, 'modernity and tradition may be mutually dependent, rather than opposed processes ... images of deep cultural identity may be articulated and negotiated through cosmopolitan syncretic forms' (1990: 146–7). It may, indeed, be precisely the claim to authentic traditional status which lies at the basis of a music's claim to be popular and modern (*ibid.*: 82–6). Ranger's acclaimed observations about the essential flexibility of pre-colonial African custom can thus be seen to be true of indigenous 'traditions' in the contemporary era as well. Links with custom and continuity serve not to make for something static and unchanging as in the European 'invented' version of African tradition, but to maintain a sense of identity despite the changes and adaptations for which tradition allows (Ranger 1983: 247–8).

The case of migrant women singers of *kiba*, and their use of the music and things of *setšo* as the cornerstone of an identity as autonomous wage-earning women beyond the domestic domain, is not, then, as paradoxical as it might at first appear. But is it not perhaps a distortion to single out and stress as central the strand of modernity in the identity which these singers assembled from the materials provided by *setšo*? The backgrounds and communities from which they came were not, after all, uniformly oriented towards *tlhabologo* (civilisation) or away from a custom-bound way of living. The very dislocations of the resettlement era served to juxtapose with unprecedented immediacy those from progressive Christian backgrounds with those from traditionalist ones, often leading the former to adopt customary practices such as initiation where they would not otherwise have done so. And even in those families with an apparently wholehearted commitment to the modern way, gender made for an uneven texture in the fabric of this commitment. Boys had the edge in becoming educated, and thus in being integrated into the industrial labour force under relatively favourable conditions. Girls had less education, which was eventually to put them at a disadvantage when they began to work. They spent more time around the house with grandmothers and aunts, often acquiring the elements of a 'weak' strain of *sesotho* in this way, despite the overall modernising orientation of their families.

The trajectories followed by the lives and careers of these Northern Province migrant women, like the 'life strategies' of the women of Phokeng who came from a more uniformly Christian or Christianising background, were thus a mixture of 'assertiveness and conformity' (Bozzoli 1991: 237). They belonged to communities of people who had sought freedom from the strictures of a custom-bound or patriarchally controlled existence, but their place as girls within the household had made for their acquisition of some of the culture and values of *sesotho* which they were later to draw upon when formulating an identity as migrants.

It was, then, a mixed bag of background influences and experiences, both within and beyond the household, which formed the background to these women's adult lives. Within this framework, their assumption of new roles conceived of as similar to those of men, their ability to exist as relatively autonomous breadwinners, and their aspirations to educate themselves or at least their younger siblings and children do indeed appear as emancipated. The stressing of the importance of 'the tradition of our home people' by migrant *kiba* singers does not contradict or outweigh, but rather complements and gives shape to, the equally emphatic stressing of the importance of *tlhabologo* and the modern way.

The asserting of a broadly defined home by these women, through the medium of a music 'of origin', should thus be understood not as a sign of nostalgia but as a project of social advancement. This is easiest to grasp if one thinks of the relationship between tradition and modernity, not as the stark contrast between a past of docile obedience to customary ways and a present of liberation and freedom (Berman 1982: 25), but rather as a contradictory combination of the 'desire to be rooted in a stable and coherent personal and social past, and [the] insatiable desire for growth' (*ibid.*: 35). To be a part of the modern world is to be involved in a process 'that destroys both the physical and social landscapes of our past and our emotional links with those lost worlds' but simultaneously to seek allegiance 'to ethnic, national, class and sexual groups which we hope will give us a firm identity' (*ibid.*).[1]

It is the search for such an 'identity' which thus motivates the use of images of origin and tradition in the lives of Northern Province women migrant singers. Since these are images associated with *sesotho*, which is contrasted implicitly or explicitly with the ways of other cultures, their invoking by these women does appear to suggest the seeking of an allegiance to a group defining itself in ethnic terms. The idea of ethnicity and that of identity have, in fact, occasionally been used interchangeably in recent writings in the social sciences.[2] But although they are linked, they refer to two different processes. If ethnicity describes the way in which a group comes to develop a 'sense of otherness and distinctiveness' (Maddock 1991b: 10), then investigating identity should make us focus on how particular selves come to regard themselves as part of such a broader group. Identity 'unites a sense of self with a sense of belonging' and so comprehends elements of both personal and collective psychology (*ibid.*: 11).

Both the strongly emphasised quality of a group's boundaries, and the strength of an individual's commitment to such a group, appear as highly contingent and situational in the light of recent writings about the 'construction of identity'. Individuals may be 'born into', and even socialised within, particular social circumstances, but it is the process by which they activate this birthright, or – for those not included by virtue of birth – the process by which they claim or legitimise their group membership through some other means, which is of interest from a constructivist standpoint.

For migrant women, scattered in the suburbs as domestic workers, there was a variety of materials available for the assembling of a migrant identity. One was the exposure to *sesotho* which some acquired during girlhood. Another was the model for association provided by male dancing groups, around which their groups were later to form. But, in constructing an identity from these elements, women were to overcome both the under-valuing and ghettoisation of female *sotho* culture in a rural context, and the limitations both on autonomy and on the extent of actual geographical 'homes' which would have put them at a disadvantage in the strictly male-dominated clubs in town. Neither of these ingredients would have served, on its own, to define a broad-based association which would eventually accommodate not only women speaking northern Sotho, but also those from Ndebele-, Tswana- and Venda-speaking communities and families. Alignment with a group and a musical culture which defined itself as *sotho*, for these 'outsider' women perhaps more than for their counterparts whose socialisation gave them some basic components of *sotho*-ness, involved them as active subjects choosing a position in the world.

But the group identities which people construct or with which they align themselves are not only ethnic ones. Between an individual and a group defined by reference to the usual trappings of ethnic identity – shared blood, common origins, ancestral land, and the like – there may be smaller groups within which an individual positions him/herself. For the migrant singers of *kiba*, identification with the smaller unit has perhaps been a means through which an individual identified herself, or reinforced her identification, with the larger. *Kiba* singers' allegiance with *sesotho/setšo* occurred not only in public through their performance of music and dance, but also within the domestic sphere. This is evident in their taking up of positions in the family normally occupied by brothers or sons. It can also be seen in the transformation of ideas about the inter-generational devolution of gifts and spiritual qualities within the family. Certain migrant women have been possessed by male ancestors, even in some cases receiving the gift of divination from their fathers or grandfathers, and have been in subtle ways empowered by their assumption of a role once reserved for men. In both the shouldering of new male-like roles of support and responsibility, and the assuming of inherited spiritual traits previously the preserve of men, the notion of *sesotho* has served as a validating motif. Behaving in accord with the dictates of *sesotho* within the sphere of the family, and enunciating the values of *sesotho* in the broader realm of urban migrant life, thus appear as closely linked processes.

In seeking out a space for themselves within the legitimating precincts of *sesotho*, the women of kiba have begun to sing in a male style in a public domain previously reserved for males, have taken on male roles within the family, and have become inheritors and practitioners of male spiritual arts. Is the identity of *sesotho/setšo* which these women are constructing for themselves, then, an essentially masculine one?

Anthropological writings on ethnicity have mostly posited male subjects. Ethnic identities emerge around the control of resources – access to urban employment or housing, or rural land – which have been assumed to be of importance primarily to men. Indeed, women have been seen more often as belonging among the resources controlled by ethnic, tribal or regional associations than as belonging among the ranks of the potential controllers. And where women do align themselves emphatically with the ways or traditions of a particular group, they have been seen as acting in defence of a threatened way of life, and as resisting 'the destruction of their culture' (Etienne and Leacock 1980: 21). Thus, while the claiming of a primordial identity by men was seen as articulating situationally evoked struggles over scarce resources, the claiming of a similar identity by women appeared, where it was discussed at all, as a wholehearted and unmediated alignment to roots and to a culture of origin.

But for women to align or identify themselves unconditionally with a specific ethnic identity in this way would be an undertaking of uncertain and ambivalent value. Male identity is likely to be valued more highly than female within a group identity that has developed around the control of resources including subordinate or dependent women. Under these circumstances, it is easier for a male subject to identify himself squarely and unequivocally with the predominant image of male-appropriate behaviour within a given culture or ethnic identity than for a woman to identify herself with the predominant image of the female.[3] For rural dependent wives and sisters in the Northern Province, for example, *sesotho* represents ambivalent values. It is the locus of family continuity and of the positive values associated with this. But at the same time, seen from the perspective of 'the male-dominated dominant discourse' (Moore 1994: 8), it is marginal, and hierarchically inferior, to male *sotho*ness.

Alignment with *sesotho* in this sense might indeed, in the case of rurally based women, represent the defence of a domain of domestic and customary values against encroachment and ultimate destruction by the ways of *sekgowa*. At the same time, however, it signifies identification with a sphere which is marginal and undervalued. But alignment with *sesotho* by migrant women seeking independence represents a bold step beyond the sphere of custom and domesticity. Their version of *sesotho*, unlike that of rural women singers, does not allow for them to be 'pathologized' (*ibid.*) by having their songs labelled as less important than men's. Like men who perform the music of *sesotho* or *setšo*, they have the authority to comment publicly. But the necessity to remain autonomous of men prevents a whole-hearted alignment with male images of *sesotho*. Migrant women performers of *mmino wa setšo* have created an identity by selecting and interweaving elements from the shifting terrains of *sotho* manhood and womanhood.

APPENDIX 1: LISTS OF DISCUSSIONS AND INTERPRETERS

Tapes and written transcriptions of discussions are housed in the M.M. Molepo Oral History Collection, Institute for Advanced Social Research, University of the Witwatersrand, Johannesburg. The names marked with an asterisk are those of the women on whom I recorded comprehensive life-history information.

MIGRANT WOMEN

Name	Date	Place
Esther Rapetswa	1/3/90	Alexandra
Joanna Maleaka	24/3/90	Johannesburg*
Dora Mashaba, M. Sabati, Mary Lebogo and Reuben Malaka (man)	7/4/90	Alexandra*
Rosina Seshothi	21/4/90	Johannesburg*
Andronica and Salome Machaba	13/5/90	Johannesburg**
Martina Ledwaba	20/5/90	Johannesburg*
Phina Komape	31/5/90	Johannesburg*
Anna Phetla	20/6/90	Soweto
Elsie Lekgotwane	18/8/90	Johannesburg*
Mary Lebogo	25/8/90	Johannesburg*
Fransina Monyela	20/9/90	Johannesburg*
Joyce Ledwaba	21/9/90	Johannesburg*
Margaret Ranku	22/9/90	Johannesburg*
Sarah Motswi	19/10/90	Johannesburg*
Anna Mei	10/11/90	Johannesburg*
Julia Lelahana	4/5/91	Johannesburg*
Helen Matjila	8/7/91	Johannesburg
Flora Mohlomi	11/8/91	Johannesburg*
Anna Dikotlo	17/8/91	Johannesburg*
Anna Dikotlo	5/9/91	Johannesburg

Name	*Date*	*Place*
Salome Machaba	7/9/91	Johannesburg
Paulina Mphoka	2/10/91	Johannesburg*
Joanna Maleaka	5/10/91	Johannesburg
Julia Lelahana	13/10/91	Johannesburg*
Salome and Andronica		
Machaba	19/10/91	Johannesburg
Mary Kapa	23/10/91	Johannesburg*

MIGRANT MEN

Mr K. J. Nalane	27/10/89	Johannesburg
Lucas Sefoka	27/2/90	Johannesburg
Maleka & Co	11/3/90	Alexandra
Lucas Sefoka	2/5/90	Johannesburg
Alfred Thobejane	30/6/90	Johannesburg
Piet Makola	7/7/90	Edenvale
Sam Nchabeleng	29/7/90	Johannesburg
Lucas Masemola	28/10/90	Johannesburg
Frans Sefoka	1/12/90	Alexandra
Jan Seašane	24/3/91	Tembisa
Pieter Thobejane	24/3/91	Tembisa
Prince Seroka	6/4/91	Tembisa
Reuben Malaka	10/4/91	Johannesburg
Prince Seroka	21/4/91	Malebitsa, Moutse

RURAL MEN AND WOMEN

Mmagomathumasha		
Madibane	25/1/89	Sephaku
Eva Mogosa	27/1/89	Sephaku
Mathumasha Madibane	2/11/89	Sephaku
Magobaby Lerobane	2/11/89	Sephaku
Magoouma Mashiane	2/11/89	Sephaku
Dipalela Tlala	3/11/89	Sephaku
Lucas Kgole	3/11/89	Sephaku
Kutupu	3/11/89	Lukau Mission
Norah Sekonya	18/8/90	GaNkwana
Mpe Sebei	7/9/90	Nchabaleng
Ramogohlo Diphofa	20/12/90	Mphanama
Mmagojane Kgalema	29/12/90	Nchabeleng
Mathabathe Mokwale	29/12/90	Nchabeleng
Raisibe Sebei	29/12/90	Nchabeleng
Ramadimetse	30/12/90	Madibong
M. Kgobalale	8/1/91	Madibong

Name	*Date*	*Place*
Mmagolain Sebei	13/7/91	Nchabeleng
Motlatle Sebei	14/7/91	Nchabeleng
Jackson Shaku	14/7/91	Nchabeleng
Dithabaneng	14/7/91	Nchabeleng
Johannes Mokgwadi	16/7/91	GaMasha
M. Phakwago	17/7/91	Nchabeleng
Mathabathe Mokwale	17/7/91	Nchabeleng
Makgolo wa Pine Khulwane and Dithabaneng	19/7/91	Nchabeleng
Makgolo wa Pine Khulwane and Dithabaneng	28/7/91	Nchabeleng
Singers of Mararankodi	28/7/91	Nchabeleng
Maribulle Ramaila	16/12/91	Nchabeleng
Hutama Debeila	16/12/91	Nchabeleng
Mmagojane Kgalema	20/12/91	Nchabeleng
Ramogohlo Diphofa	23/12/91	Mphanama
Makgolo wa Pine	24/12/91	Nchabeleng
Rangwane Jane	29/12/91	Nchabeleng

UNRECORDED DISCUSSIONS REFERRED TO IN THE TEXT

Thapedi Lerobane	24/1/89	Sephaku
Nkapile Hlakola	24/1/89	Sephaku
Bafedi Madihlaba	25/1/89	Sephaku
Mogopi Madibane	25/1/89	Sephaku
Magomadripana Makeke	2/11/89	Sephaku
Magomadereka Lerobane	5/2/89	Sephaku
Mmagoshower Debeila	16/7/91	Nchabeleng
Mmagomotala Mofele	17/7/91	Nchabeleng
Mr Makgaleng	19/7/91	Apel
Lebopo household	19/7/91	Nchabeleng
Maaparankwe	27/7/91	GaSelepe
James Makola	8/9/91	Johannesburg
Mr Kgalema (education spokesperson for NUM)	8/11/91	Johannesburg
Modderfontein dancers	11/11/91	Modderfontein
Mmagoshower Debeila	16/12/91	Nchabeleng

ABBREVIATED NAMES OF INTERPRETERS WHO ASSISTED
WITH DISCUSSIONS AND WITH TRANSCRIPTIONS:

AM	Anna Madihlaba
MTN	Malete Thomas Nkadimeng
PM	Philip Mnisi
PMb	Philip Mbiba
NP	Neo Phakathi

APPENDIX 2: LIST OF *KIBA* PERFORMANCES

This list excludes all regular practices, which take place on Sundays (usually excluding the last Sunday of the month, when many migrants return home to visit their families). It is not an exhaustive list, but it gives an idea of the variety of venues and occasions at which groups performed during the period 1990–92. I either attended or was given information about these performances.

5/2/89   *Dipalela Tlala* performed at a party at their leader's house.

26/11/89 A variety of groups from the Reef performed at the Second Annual Traditional Dance and Attire Competition, organised by Sabikwa Arts Society incorporating Daveyton Cultural Foundation, at Sinaba Stadium, Daveyton.

18/3/90   *SK Alex* annual party in Alexandra township, featuring performances by *SK Alex*, *Bapedi Champions* and *Ditšhweu tša Malebogo*.

22/7/90   *Kiba* competition at the Funda Centre, Soweto, organised by Pete Makola and the Lebowa Mmino wa Setšo Association. Won by *Ditšhweu tša Malebogo* (women's section) and *Bapedi Champions* (men's section).

22/7/90   Rally at Phokwane, Nebo district, to welcome John Nkadimeng, returned ANC exile, back to Lebowa; featuring Manganeng rural woman's group. Debate about whether these women's groups should become ANC-affiliated.

3-8/9/90 *Kiba* competition at the Lebowakgomo show, featuring numerous groups of rural women singers and of young men and women of school-going age.

1/11/90   *SK Alex* trip to Masemola village, to perform at the wedding of the younger sister of group member Lucas Masemola.

30/12/90 *Dithabaneng* performed at the house of one of its 'policemen', Magolina Sebei, in Nchabeleng.

24/2/91   *Ditšhweu tša Malebogo* and *Mašašane Alex* group performed at a party in 4th Ave, Alexandra. *TV3* (from Potgietersrus) performed at a party in 11th Ave, Alexandra.

2/3/91   *SK Alex* performed at a wedding in Potgietersrus. The *Matlala Alex* group performed at a party in the Malebogo area.

9/3/91   *SK Alex* performed at a party at a group member's home in Dennilton.

28/3/91   *Maaparankwe* spent the Easter weekend performing at the opening of a bottle store and bar/lounge belonging to Nelson Ramodikwe, the Chief Minister of Lebowa, in Lenyenye, Naphuno district.

21/4/91   *Maaparankwe* performed at Malebitsa, Moutse district, at a party for an old man, a *kiba* enthusiast and former dancer, arranged by his daughter.

21/4/91   *Maaparankwe* performed for the birthday party of Maradona Maroka, the grandchild of the group's leader Jan Seašane.

5/5/91   *Maaparankwe* performed at a Tribal Dancing festival organised by Eskom at the Standard Bank Arena, Johannesburg.

27/7/91   *Maaparankwe* performed at GaSelepe, Sekhukhune district, at a party held by the wife of a group member.

17/8/91   *Dithabaneng* performed at the house of another of its 'policemen', Mmagojane Kgalema, in Nchabeleng.

8/9/91   *Ditšhweu tša Malebogo* performed at a meeting of a *mohodisano* consisting of group members, held in the backyard room of Salome Machaba, in Johannesburg.

20/10/91   *Maaparankwe* performed for the birthday party of the grandchild of Julia Lelahana, a group member, in Tembisa.

1/12/91   *Maaparankwe* performed at their own end-of-year party in Tembisa.

16/2/92   *Maaparankwe* performed at their own opening party '*go bula modiro*' (to open the business/work) in Tembisa.

APPENDIX 3: SELECT DISCOGRAPHY

This list was kindly compiled for me by Rob Allingham, both from records in his own private collection and from records and master tapes in the Archive at Gallo Africa. Dates are rough estimates, since no record of exact dates was kept.

EMI RECORDS
Bakxaga Singers (Composer Credit: J. Shai)

MV JP126	Dikgaka	OAS 565-1	c. 1952
	Mmapula	OAS 566-1	
HMV JP127	Moyakhakga	OAS 567-1	c. 1952
	Nama Lemphaka	OAS 568-1	
HMV JP2009	Samphephethu	OAS 569-1	c. 1952
	Mashekane	OAS 570-1	

Elizabeth Radzaga (Composer Credit: Radzaga)

HMV JP2001	Matimba	OAS 1006B	c. 1953
	Mathinya	OAS 1007B	

Dipela Tsabapedi (Composer Credit: J. Mashelane)

HMV JP2052	Thsusu	OAS 909	c. 1953
	Kxetsi	OAS 910	

Vesha Dinaka (Composer Credit: Traditional)

HMV JP 2070	Lexalani	OAS 968	c. 1953
	Lexowa	OAS 969	

Dipela Tsabapedi (Composer Credit: Dipela Tsabapedi)

HMV JP542	Sewelewele	OAS 1227	c. late 1950s
	Sekonkwani	OAS 1228	
HMV JP561	Skinkbord	OAS 1289	
	Kakapan	OAS 1290	
HMV JP624	Matjid	OAS 941	c. 1953
	Mmaijele	OAS 946	

HMV JP693	Bothakga	OAS 1567	*c.* late 1950s
	Mogobo	OAS 1568	
HMV JP718	Moria	OAS 1709-1	*c.* late 1960s
	Mmutla	OAS 1719-1	

TROUBADOUR RECORDS
Mmatou Rammutla

B2 1218	Setata	AD 493	*c.* mid-1950s
	Dithakaume	AD 494	

Johannes Marera

B2 1342	Sekutupu	AD 742	*c.* mid-1950s
	Maphere	AD 743	

Dinaka

B2 1379	Mathavhagomo	AD 816	*c.* mid-1950s
	Mutshaini	AD 817	
	Linotsi	AD 818	
	Visa	AD 819	

Malopo Aba Thokwa

B2 1418	Makole	AB 894	*c.* mid-1950s
	Doropong	AB 895	

Marara Chewe

B2 1502	Dinotshe	ADB 198	*c.* mid-1950s

SK Skukuland (Composer Credit: Jack Sloane)

	Monte		*c.* 1954
	Keba		
Frans Ncha			
	Mamarupini		*c.* 1956
	Maleriya		

Evans Ncha and the three girls

	Mahlalela		*c.* 1960
	Sebedubedu		
	Shuru		
	Mnamutsumi		
	Adiyo jaxo kxaja Nkwe		

Mapedi a Pietersburg (Composer Credit: Daniel Rankofi)

	Pesha Latshoene		*c.* 1960
	Lekoapa		

GALLO TAPES

Makgagkasa	Dikgwari tsa rena Lebowa (compilation) 1988
BC647	Makgakgasa (J. Mohlala)
	Kgoparara (J. Mohlala)
	Setla ka masa (S. M. Malapela)
	Difofora (J. Mokgwadi)
	Tshisthi (J. Mohlala)
	Marashiya (E. Ntobeng)
	Tsodio No. 2 (J. Mokgwadi)
	Shibale Barwele (L .Kgole)
	Mpoho (J. Mohlala)
	Mmabaledi (L. Kgole)
	Terone No. 2 (J. Mohlala)
	Sebiletsa (J. Mohlala/E. Mohlala)
	Lepelele (F. Matseke/E. Maila)

NOTES

INTRODUCTION

1. The area was, at the time of research, in the northern part of the Transvaal Province. It has since been designated as one of the nine new provinces of post-*apartheid* South Africa, and renamed the Northern Province. I will refer to it as the Northern Privince throughout the book.

2. Where Sotho denotes a language or some other feature attributed to a group by outside analysts, it is spelt with a capital letter and is not underlined. But where, as with the noun *sesotho* or the adjective *sotho*, it denotes a state of being, a way of life or a set of qualities which informants have enunciated or commented upon, it is italicised and spelt without a capital. See Comaroff and Comaroff (1989: 276–96) for a similar usage.

3. Contemporary informants accounted for the origins of this term in various ways: one said it derived from the missionaries' insistence that women cover their breasts by wearing jackets, while another claimed that it came from the Afrikaans *'ja, maar kan nie'* (yes, but [I] can't), a derogatory reference to Christian converts' inability to stick to the stern tenets of their faith.

4. Similar social and conceptual divisions were established through mission activity in a number of other southern African areas, particularly the Eastern Cape (see Hammond-Tooke 1962: 63–5; Hunter 1936: 351; Mayer and Mayer 1971: 20–41, 1980) and Natal (Clegg 1981; Meintjies 1991; Reader 1966: 338–42). The division appears to be particularly pronounced among *sotho* communities in the Northern Province, perhaps because of the Lutheran missionaries' insistence on their converts' total, almost feudal, subordination (Delius 1983: 160–78), and on their abandoning of all aspects of 'indigenous culture' (Pauw 1974: 427).

5. Lucas Sefoka, recorded discussion with the author (hereafter DJ) and Malete Thomas Nkadimeng (hereafter MTN), Johannesburg, 2/5/90.

6. I am grateful to the late David Webster for making newspaper clippings available to me.

7. There is a common belief that the media manipulates the populace at large. Critics of mass culture, from widely differing political perspectives, have emphasised its commodity nature, and its passive consumption by audiences no longer able to choose a cultural expression more immediately suited and relevant to their way of life (see Manuel 1988: 11–12; Frith 1978: 191–6, for summaries of this approach). Hamm's approach is more in line with an alternative view which points to the ability of consumers to appropriate these commodities and integrate them into 'subjectively motivated social practice' (Middleton 1990: 139), or to have an influence on the nature of the commodities produced.

8. See also Ferguson (1990) for a critique of 'modernist narratives' which portray

urbanisation on the Copperbelt as an even and continuous process, and Bonner (1995) for a nuanced account of the second generation of urban-dwellers on the Reef.

CHAPTER 1

1. *Sekhukhune* or *GaSekhukhune* is the local appellation, which does not recognise the limits of the magisterial district Sekhukhune, but extends its boundaries to most south-eastern parts of the northern Sotho homeland of Lebowa, and even to much of the white farming area beyond. I have used *Sekhukhune* to approximate this historically derived area, and Sekhukhune for the officially imposed magisterial district. In similar vein, *Leboa* is the name for the northern areas as locally imagined, where Lebowa is the official name for the homeland as a whole.
2. Notable exceptions are McNamara (1978, 1985) and Pearson (1978).
3. In similar vein, the ethnically organised welfare and recreational associations of Ouagadougou were transformed into political parties (Skinner 1974: 211–17): a trajectory predicted for other such associations throughout Africa as well (Wallerstein 1963).
4. These overall trends and patterns might appear oversimplified. In fact there was a range of possible ways, between the option of perpetual oscillation from town to country and back again, and that of settling with wife and children in a secure urban dwelling, in which a man from a northern country area could arrange to stay on the Reef. One of the material factors influencing this choice was the time when members of the family first began to migrate, and the availability of accommodation at that time. The Introduction describes how another, less concrete, of these factors which acted to influence the trajectory followed was that of orientation to or away from mission Christianity. This orientation provided a conceptual dichotomy, between *baditšhaba* and *majekane*, in terms of which the difference between migrants and those who have become more permanent urban-dwellers is often described.
5. Lucas Sefoka, recorded discussion with DJ and MTN, Johannesburg, 2/5/90.
6. For a discussion of some of the problems of the dependency-theory version of this approach in South Africa, see Kuper (1987: 1–10).
7. The names of these reserves have been italicised, like *Sekhukhune*, to convey the sense that they exist, as named thus, in local conceptualisations rather than in official nomenclature. Although the original locations did bear the names of these chiefs, they have now been subsumed under magisterial districts with different names.
8. This sense of a unifying connection to a symbolic animal has been translated as 'totemism' and as involving membership of a 'fairly loose association of agnatic kin' (Mönnig 1967: 234). But Kuper argues that these were not kinship groups or clans (1982: 46–8), and according to Hoernle 'there is no special native term' for such a grouping (1937: 91–2).
9. As with *Sekhukhune* and *Leboa*, I have italicised these area names to indicate local terms not used in official parlance.
10. See Delius (1983: 12, 48–59) for detail on these strategies. Women from the ruling family were sent as wives to the leaders of subordinate, local groupings, which were then inescapably locked into these alliances through the practice of matrilateral cross-cousin marriage. The practice of marriage with close kin is regarded as a typically Sotho feature (Wilson 1982: 59; Kuper 1975, 1982). But its strictest enforcement was in its use as strategy by ruling groups to augment their power.

11. See Delius (1983: 15, 19–30, 83–104, 239–46).

12. Paragraph based on Minutes of Evidence of the Eastern Transvaal Natives Land Committee (hereafter E TVL) UG 32-1918, p. 9, evidence of Sequati, p. 14; evidence of Maserumo, p. 15; James (1990a: 45–7).

13. E TVL, evidence of Wedepohl, p. 95, Masasane, p. 98, Maraba, p. 98; evidence of the Native Economic Commission (hereafter NEC), 1930–2, evidence of Nicholson, pp. 100–4, Mamabulo, p. 109, Senthumula, pp. 78–9 (modern orthography has altered this spelling of the chief's name).

14. Paragraph based on NEC, evidence of Hunt, p. 658, 706, Kirsten, pp. 258–64, urban location representatives, p. 90, Daneel, pp. 193–7.

15. See Chapter 6. Some of these removals were occasioned more by 'free market forces' or by people's desire for education or civilisation than by the grand plans of *apartheid*'s architects.

16. See Delius (1980: 356, 1989: 605–15); James (1987: 191–2); Sansom (1970: 38–43, 53–5).

17. While it would be inaccurate to claim that the actions of betterment planners were accepted passively and without protest anywhere in the 'homelands', there is evidence that, in heartland communities long attached to their land, resistance to betterment was more uncompromising than in more marginal – often more recently settled 'Trust' – areas (Surplus People Project 1983: Vol. 5, 195; Hofmeyr 1994: 120–5; Yawitch 1982: 23–4, 55, 62, 71–9).

18. Burial societies do sometimes bear the names of particular villages in the region, but the symbolic use of totemic animals is restricted to village contexts rather than finding its way into the discourse of *Sekhukhune* migrants on the Reef. See Chapter 5, p. 29.

19. *Serokolo* may be translated literally as the name of a foul-smelling herb used by healers in the *Sekhukhune* area to cure various ailments. The proverb *serokolo se se nyane se e kokotša ka monkgo* (the small herb can magnify itself by emitting a foul smell) suggests that a person's achievement and ability to lead are not restricted by his inborn qualities. The term thus stresses achieved rather than ascribed qualities (Sam Nchabeleng, personal communication).

20. This and the following two paragraphs based on Jan Seašane, recorded discussion with MTN, Tembisa, 24/3/91.

21. See *SAIRR Survey* (1966: 194) for an outline of the plan to remove all Africans in the East Rand area from the older townships to one of the following: Tembisa, Daveyton, Natalspruit or KwaThema.

22. Prince Seroka, recorded discussion with MTN, Tembisa, 6/4/91.

23. *Ibid.*

24. Lucas Sefoka, recorded discussion with DJ and MTN, Johannesburg, 27/2/90.

25. Mitchell attempts to analyse the content of the *kalela* dance. But his claim that it represents a thinly veiled expression of middle-class aspirations has been criticised (see Argyle 1991). Locally, recent studies by Thomas (1988) and Clegg (1982, 1984) on Zulu migrant performance have analysed the lyrics of songs and the symbolic import of the dance.

26. Mr Kgalema, education spokesperson for the National Union of Mineworkers (NUM), discussion with DJ, Johannesburg, 8/11/91; see also Andersson (1981).

27. See Chapter 3.

28. See Finnegan (1989: 273–93) for an account of remarkably similar attitudes and practices in amateur musical groups in an English town.

29. See Thomas (1988, cited in Argyle 1991: 82) for an account of similar hosted visits home by Zulu migrant dancers. See Figure 3.10 for pictures of migrant performers on 'home' visits.

30. See Chapter 3.
31. *Malokwane* is also used to refer to a football referee and to the leader of a girl's initiation regiment.
32. This relatively recent date of arrival does not hold true for all women who have left rural homes in the northern Transvaal in order to find work in the city: there are women from mission backgrounds who have lived in freehold houses in Alexandra for decades, and have worked and raised families there.
33. In 1970 domestic service was the second largest occupational category – after agriculture – for African women, engaging 38 per cent of all employed black women (Cock 1980: 250, cited in Moore 1988: 87). See also Gaitskell *et al.* (1983: 86–108).
34. The census merely lists those men and women from particular areas who are employed, and gives no details about where this employment is situated. It does not, then, strictly speaking record female migrancy. The figures were obtained by taking the rurally-based female population of each district, and looking at the low-paid sectors of employment – service, production and unskilled work, together with 'workers not classifiable' since this seemed likely to describe low-paid rather than middle-class or professional occupations. Although theoretically these workers could all be employed within the district in which these women reside, this is unlikely since there is an extreme scarcity of jobs in the homeland areas for both men and for women. Calculating the numbers of female migrants is made even more complex by the fact that boundaries of the magisterial districts in South Africa have been changed. This makes data from earlier censuses incompatible with later ones. The earlier magisterial district boundaries cut across what would later be designated as 'homeland' boundaries.
35. See Chapter 6 for details.
36. Neither the experience of living on farms as independent farmers or as labour tenants, nor that of resettlement from these farms into the reserves, was unique to communities living north of Pietersburg. But it was from northern communities who underwent these experiences that the migrant women singers of *kiba* were drawn.

CHAPTER 2

1. See also Izzard (1985: 271) for a criticism of Little's depiction of migrant women as motivated primarily by a desire for independence.
2. Brydon (1987: 167) writes of West Africa that a common cause of female migration prior to 1970 was coming to town to join a husband: Parkin (1975b: 40) says that most East African migrant women at the time of his study were still dependent wives. Similar dependence accounts for female migrancy elsewhere in Africa, but to a variable degree: in Kenya and Tanzania, for example, there was a period during the inter-war years when more women migrated independently than motivated out of a desire to join their husbands (Robertson 1984: 40). But Stichter, in her overview of African migrancy, insists that most women in Africa have migrated, not to join their husbands, but because of directly economic or family-crisis-related reasons (1985: 151).
3. Chapter 6 gives an account of the circumstances which led some migrant *kiba* women to see themselves in this way.
4. The fact of rurally derived church membership was one of the important factors differentiating *Leboa* migrant women performers from the stay-at-home women performers in *Sekhukhune*. See Chapters 3 and 4 for more detail.

5. See Chapter 7 for more detail.
6. This information was gleaned from recorded discussions with Joanna Maleaka, DJ and MTN, Johannesburg, 24/3/90; Andronica and Salome Machaba, DJ and MTN, Johannesburg, 13/5/90; and from my attendance at the meeting of the *Kwena Moloto* Burial Society in Alexandra, 3/11/92.
7. My thanks to Eleanor Preston-Whyte for suggesting this line of research to me, based on her own work among domestic servants in Natal. See *SAIRR Survey*, (1985: 233–5, 1986: 209–13, 1987–8: 93–8).
8. See Chapter 6 for details.
9. Elsie Lekgotwane, recorded discussion with DJ and MTN, Johannesburg, 18/8/90.
10. Rosina Seshothi, recorded discussion with DJ and MTN, Johannesburg, 21/4/90.
11. A 1987 poll showed that the average monthly income for a domestic worker was highest (R149) in English-speaking urban homes and lowest (R59) in Afrikaans-speaking lower-income homes. The average monthly wage in the Transvaal in 1987 was R110 (*SAIRR Survey* 1987–8: 324). The monthly wage of live-in domestic servants in South Africa usually excludes board and lodging, which are expected to be provided by employers as payment in kind. The improvement in conditions of service described here was, of course, highly relative: by comparison with any other form of labour in the same area at the same time this was still an appallingly low wage.
12. It is not my intention in this book to document in any detail these women's experiences of exploitation at work, apart from looking at the impact these have had in structuring their 'leisure' (that is, outside-of-work) time. For the earlier history of domestic service in Johannesburg see van Onselen (1982); for theoretical overviews of domestic service in South African see Cock (1980: 5–15 and *passim*), Gaitskell *et al.* (1983); for an excellent account of how domestic service fitted into the lives of a female migrant constituency, see Bozzoli (1991: 91–105).
13. There were in fact important areas of overlap between these two constituencies, despite the clear conceptual boundaries between them on which informants insist. See Introduction.
14. Phina Komape, recorded discussion with DJ and MTN, Johannesburg, 31/5/90; Joanna Maleaka, recorded discussion with DJ and MTN, Johannesburg, 24/3/90, gave a similar account.
15. Fransina Monyela, recorded discussion with DJ and MTN, Johannesburg, 20/9/90.
16. A park in the white suburbs of Johannesburg.
17. Joanna Maleaka, recorded discussion with MTN, Johannesburg, 24/3/90.
18. See Kuper and Kaplan (1944) for an account of *mahodisana* (*sic*) and other voluntary associations among urban residents of Western Native Township during the 1940s: see Kurtz (1973) on rotating credit associations as mechanisms of adaptation to poverty, and Parkin (1966) on the same associations as ways of adapting to urban life.
19. Alfred Thobejane, recorded discussion with DJ and MTN, Johannesburg, 30/6/90.
20. Rosina Msina, recorded discussion with DJ and MTN, Johannesburg, 21/4/90; Salome and Andronica Machaba, recorded discussion with DJ and MTN, Johannesburg, 13/5/90; Sarah Motswi, recorded discussion with DJ and MTN, Johannesburg, 19/10/90.
21. I am grateful to John Argyle for reading and commenting on this chapter. He suggested that the founding of women's *kiba* was no different from that of any

other migrant association, quoting a colleague saying 'The trouble with women is that they are too much like men.' I still disagree with him.

22. See Chapter 1 for a discussion of this point.

23. See Chapter 1.

24. See Chapter 6 for a detailed account of the youth and adolescence of these women.

25. See Guy and Thabane (1987) for a similar concept, also situationally and flexibly invoked, among migrant members of the *Marashea* (Russian gang) from Lesotho.

26. Flora Mohlomi, recorded discussion with DJ and Philip Mnisi (hereafter PM), Johannesburg, 11/8/91; Julia Lelahana, recorded discussion with DJ and PM, Johannesburg, 13/10/91.

27. Flora Mohlomi, recorded discussion with DJ and PM, Johannesburg, 11/8/91.

28. The male-initiated burial societies had been based on an extension of this idea: the notion of taking the body back home for burial. See Delius (1989: 589–9).

29. Julia Lelahana, recorded discussion with DJ and PM, Johannesburg, 13/10/91.

30. This process, for both men's and women's music, will be further explored in the next chapter.

31. See also Introduction for an account of the use of this music to symbolise the 'national' unity of Lebowa. See Figure 3.10 for urban groups on 'home' visits.

32. Until the violence of early 1991, drums were normally kept in the men's hostel during the week, and brought out on Sundays for practices (see Figure 3.2).

33. Joanna Maleaka, recorded discussion with DJ and MTN, 24/3/90; Salome and Andronica Machaba, recorded discussion with DJ and MTN, 13/5/90; Rosina Msina, recorded discussion with DJ and MTN, 21/4/90: all in Johannesburg.

34. Phina Komape, recorded discussion with DJ and MTN, Johannesburg, 31/5/90.

35. Joanna Maleaka, recorded discussion with DJ and MTN, Johannesburg, 24/3/90; and recorded discussion with DJ and PM, Johannesburg, 5/10/91. For background on Trust areas, see Chapter 1.

36. Anna Dikotlo, recorded discussion with DJ and PM, Johannesburg, 17/8/91; Prince Seroka, recorded discussion with MTN, Tembisa, 6/4/91.

37. See Chapter 1.

38. See Chapter 4 for details.

CHAPTER 3

1. The tendency of *kiba* to retain these features may be explained in the light of an observation made by Blacking: that of all systems of symbolic representation musical symbols are the most resistant to change (1977, cited in Erlmann 1991: 11). But this would not of course account for the cases in which, like *marabi*, a transformed and highly syncretic style has arisen in a very short time span. I am grateful to Rob Allingham of Gallo for making available to me the early recordings of *kiba* in his extensive record collection. See Appendix 3.

2. See, for example, Johnston (1975); Blacking (1956, 1964). The exception, for both Johnston and Blacking, was in discussing the music of imported spirit-possession cults whose charismatic leaders attracted a substantial following. See Johnston (1973, 1974); Blacking (1964: 64, 333–4). Here, musical change was seen as linked to a fluid social setting which allowed for individual charisma: the links between social structure and musical form still gave rise to a logical and invariant stylistic consistency.

3. Bafedi Madihlaba, discussion with DJ and Anna Madihlaba (hereafter AM), Sephaku, 25/1/89; Eva Mogosa, recorded discussion with DJ and AM, Sephaku,

27/1/89; Mr Makgaleng, discussion with DJ, Apel, 19/7/91; see also Huskisson (1958: 101–5; 133–6, 140).

4. A preoccupation with the origins and diffusions of musical styles was typical of an early phase of ethnomusicology. Kirby speculated extensively about the spread of this and other pipe dances (1934: 147, 155, 162–7).

5. For detail on the Venda *tshikona* national reed pipe dance, see Blacking (1962). It is interesting to note that this dance, although occasionally performed by migrants, has not undergone a transformation into a migrant cultural form comparable to *kiba*.

6. For details on the substantial Pedi involvement in World War II, see Delius (1989: 596–7).

7. *Makgakgasa* is an onomatopoeic word describing the sound made by the stamping of women's feet with shakers attached. In some parts of the northern Transvaal countryside, *makgakgasa* has not yet been replaced by *kiba*.

8. From the original few *kiba* songs documented by Kirby in the early 1930s, there appears to have been a proliferation as indigenous songs were included into the genre, resulting in a standard core repertoire which, in contemporary performance as at the time when Huskisson did her research in the 1950s, varies little even between distant areas (Kirby 1934; Huskisson 1958).

9. Women were acquainted with the drumming patterns of men's *kiba*, and in other contexts than those of compounded labour were often the principle drummers for this genre. But the performers for whom they drummed were male.

10. See Chapter 1.

11. See Delius (1989: 589–92).

12. Members of the Lebopo household, discussion with DJ and PM, Nchabeleng, 19/7/91.

13. Prince Seroka, recorded discussion with PM, Malebitša (Moutse), 21/4/91.

14. I have been unable to establish with any certainty where this name originates. One suggestion is that it comes from the name of Montgomery of Alamein, thus referring, like a number of other *kiba* motifs, to Pedi soldiers' experience of World War II. It could also refer to 'the full monty', which was a three-piece suit issued to World War II soldiers upon discharge.

15. Prince Seroka, recorded discussion with PM, Malebitša (Moutse), 21/4/91. *Mogobo* denotes both a regimental song of war (the meaning used here by Prince Seroka) and a song sung by initiates who have undergone and 'conquered' the hardships of initiation.

16. Informal discussions with a variety of informants; and Johannes Mokgwadi, recorded discussion with DJ and PM, GaMasha, 16/7/91.

17. Members of *Maaparankwe*, discussion with DJ and PM, GaSelepe, 27/7/91.

18. Orlando Pirates and Kaiser Chiefs, the two most popular South African football teams.

19. Lucas Kgole, recorded discussion with DJ and Neo Phakathi (hereafter NP), Sephaku, 3/11/89. *Lebowa* is the mostly rurally used name for the women's equivalent of the men's song *kiba* from which the entire genre takes its name. The popular recording artist and herbalist Johannes Mokgwadi, in recorded discussion with DJ and PM, GaMasha, 16/7/91, gave a similar account of the origins of women's involvement in *kiba*.

20. *Dithabaneng*, recorded discussion with DJ and PM, Nchabeleng, 14/7/91. The name *marashiya* (or *marashea*) probably comes from the name given to the 'Russian' gangsters from Lesotho, whom northern Transvaal migrants encountered on the Reef (Sam Nchabeleng, personal communication).

21. See Kuper (1987: 187). I am grateful to Adam Kuper for suggesting this line of investigation to me.
22. Vail and White have borrowed this term from Tracey to describe, with more precision than the term's normal use in English, the satiric or critical content of much southern African oral poetry (Vail and White 1991: 42–5).
23. Lyrics and interpretation from Nkapile Hlakola, discussion with DJ and AM, Sephaku, 24/1/89. It is common for women to express their dissatisfaction with men who hold positions of authority in this veiled manner (Sam Nchabeleng, personal communication). See also Vail and White (1991: 248–9). For further information on the co-op, see James (1987, 1990b).
24. Lyrics and interpretation from women of *Dithabaneng*, recorded discussion with DJ and PM, Nchabeleng, 14/7/91.
25. See Chapter 5.
26. Lyrics from Paulina Mphoka, recorded discussion with DJ and PM, Johannesburg, 2/10/91.
27. See Chapter 5 for a more detailed account of the role of these 'police' in performance.
28. Lyrics and interpretation from *Dithabaneng*, recorded discussion with DJ and PM, Nchabeleng, 14/7/91.
29. Lyrics and interpretation from Julia Lelahana, recorded discussion with DJ and PM, Johannesburg, 13/10/91.
30. In certain contexts, *lekwapa* refers to Nguni speakers in general, in others, to speakers of the Shangaan/Tsonga language. These people lived in areas of the northern Transvaal adjacent to, and even the same as, those inhabited by northern Sotho speakers. *Apartheid* removals attempted, not always successfully, to separate members of the two language groups into their respective 'homelands'.
31. Lyrics and interpretation from Julia Lelahana, recorded discussion with DJ and PM, Johannesburg, 13/10/91.
32. See Chapter 5.

CHAPTER 4

1. Makgolo wa Pine Khulwane, recorded discussion with DJ and PM, Nchabeleng, 28/7/91.
2. See Chapter 5.
3. Lyrics and interpretation from *Dithabaneng*, recorded discussion with DJ and PM, Nchabeleng, 19/7/91.
4. Lyrics from singers of *Mararankodi*, Nchabeleng.
5. Lyrics from Makgolo wa Pine Khulwane, recorded discussion with DJ and PM, Nchabeleng, 28/7/91.
6. See Chapter 5 for songs which express a sister's dependence on a brother for affection and for the purchase of clothes, and which lament his absconding as a migrant.
7. See Chapter 7 for a fuller discussion of this point.
8. A number of these women had their access to the household's educational budget curtailed in favour of their brothers' schooling: see Chapter 6.
9. Helen Matjila, recorded discussion with DJ and PM, Johannesburg, 8/7/91.
10. Prince Seroka, recorded discussion with MTN, Tembisa, 6/4/91.
11. Sarah Motswi, recorded discussion with DJ and MTN, Johannesburg, 19/10/90.
12. Julia Lelahana, recorded discussion with DJ and PM, Johannesburg, 13/10/91; Joanna Maleaka, recorded discussion with MTN, Johannesburg, 24/3/90.

13. Lyrics and interpretation from *Ditšhweu tša Malebogo*.
14. See Chapter 2, p. 66.
15. Both sets of lyrics, and interpretation, from Reuben Malaka, Dora Mashaba, Maggie Sebati and Mary Lebogo, recorded discussion with DJ and MTN, Johannesburg, 7/4/90.
16. Rosina Seshothi, recorded discussion with DJ and MTN, Johannesburg, 21/4/90.
17. Women poets from Lesotho give utterance to two apparently opposed perspectives on marriage: one rejects it as restrictive while the other enshrines it as a worthy, if unattainable, ideal (Coplan 1987: 424).

CHAPTER 5

1. The 'construction of identity' is frequently discussed in contemporary studies, but has in fact been of concern to anthropologists since Barth (1969b) and Cohen (1969b) published their influential pieces on ethnicity/retribalisation. The debate about 'the construction of ethnic identity' has occurred in parallel with, but only recently in explicit conversation with, that about 'constructed identities'. See below. For recent studies on southern African ethnic identity, see for example Vail (1989b); Harries (1989); Webster (1991).
2. See Introduction for a discussion of the origin and meaning of the *majekane/baditšhaba* contrast.
3. Mmagojane Kgalema, recorded discussion with DJ and PM, Nchabeleng, 29/12/90.
4. Evidence suggests that this practice has been more persistent in heartland than in Trust contexts. Bothma's research in Nchabeleng in the late 1950s showed that 'almost all the marriages were contracted between relatives of some sort, because hardly anybody is not in some way related to everybody else' (1962: 46), while my own work in a Trust village peripheral to the reserve (James 1988: 37) shows the decline of cousin-marriage in such a context.
5. Mönnig spells this word, and its diminutive version, wrongly as *ntepha/ntephana*.
6. See Chapter 1 for a discussion of 'totemic' animals in northern Transvaal society.
7. Members of *Dithabaneng*, recorded discussion with DJ and PM, 19/7/91, Nchabeleng; dates calculated according to when members of particular regiments were initiated. The geographical divide in the village was reflected in terminology: *majekaneng* was 'the place of the Christians' while *setšhabeng* was 'the place of those of the nation'.
8. Lit. '*sesotho* of wearing' (*sesotho sa go apara*). This is distinguished from *sesotho* of speaking (*sesotho sa go bolela*) and from various other forms of *sesotho*.
9. The money earned was used to buy cloth, and to pay a village seamstress using a treadle or manual sewing machine to make up the garment.
10. Rural women singers address each other as 'the mother of so-and-so' or 'the grandmother of so-and-so', rather than by the names given to them at birth or at initiation. Thus, Makgolo wa Pine translates as 'Pine's grandmother', Mmagopine as 'Pine's mother', Mmagoviolet as 'Violet's mother', and so on. Migrant women singers, in contrast, address each other not with *sotho* names at all, but with English, often biblically derived ones – Salome, Mary, Joanna.
11. Mmagomathumasha Madibane, recorded discussion with DJ and AM, Sephaku, 25/1/89.
12. Lyrics from Mathabathe Mokwale, recorded discussion with PM, Nchabeleng, 29/12/90.

13. Members of *Dithabaneng*, recorded discussion with DJ and PM, Nchabeleng, 14/7/91; for more detail on the reinterpretation of lyrics as referring to the context of dance itself, see Chapter 3, pp. 92–3.
14. Makgolo wa Pine Khulwane, recorded discussion with DJ and PM, Nchabeleng, 28/7/91.
15. Vail and White document a similar ambiguity on the part of Tumbuka wives about labour migration, similarly expressed in terms of the clothes it can provide or the lack of clothes if a migrant neglects his duties to his far-off family (1991: 258–9).
16. *Dithabaneng*, recorded discussion with DJ and PM, Nchabeleng, 14/7/91.
17. In the Molepo district further north, when male migrants began to use privately owned taxis rather than buses to return home, these became known as *mmethisa [wa mathari]* (those which cause young married women to be beaten), since these brought husbands home at unexpected times and enabled them to walk in on their wives' illicit affairs (Molepo 1983: 77).
18. Song and comment recorded in writing during discussion with members of *Dithabaneng*, Nchabeleng, 28/7/91.
19. Singers of Mararankodi, recorded discussion with DJ and PM, Nchabeleng, 28/7/91.
20. Makgolo wa Pine Khulwane, recorded discussion with DJ and PM, Nchabeleng, 19/7/91.
21. Lucas Sefoka, recorded discussion with DJ and MTN, Johannesburg, 27/2/90; NEC, Evidence of Neethling, p. 8–11, 31. Delius (1989: 595–6) claims that even traditionalist communities in *Sekhukhune* were changing their attitudes to education and beginning to send their sons to school from around the 1930s, and that a number of 'tribal schools' were established in the 1940s. But judging from life-histories of migrant men from *Sekhukhune*, it was only in the 1960s and 1970s that schooling for boys gained acceptance so widely, for non-Christians as much as for Christians, that it eclipsed or supplanted the period of work on the farms, or displaced this into the period of school holidays.
22. Mmagojane Kgalema, during recorded discussion with members of *Dithabaneng*, Nchabeleng, 19/7/91.
23. This reason given by men for first leaving home to work is reflected by other accounts from the Transvaal: Niehaus (1993); Molepo (1984: 16); NEC, evidence of Neethling, pp. 31, 50, Gilbertson, p. 50, Mareli, p. 333, Fuller, p. 412.
24. Members of *Dithabaneng*, recorded discussion with DJ and PM, Nchabeleng, 19/7/91.
25. Ramogohlo Diphofa, recorded discussion with PM, Mphanama, 20/12/90.
26. Members of *Dithabaneng*, recorded discussion with DJ and PM, Nchabeleng, 19/7/91.
27. Mmagojane Kgalema, recorded discussion with PM, Nchabeleng, 29/12/90.
28. Mmagoshower Debeila, discussion with DJ and PM, Nchabeleng, 16/7/91.
29. In the case of Phokeng, the girls worked for money to buy their trousseaux.
30. Rebelliousness followed by later conformity is of course a common theme of studies on youth: see for example Bozzoli's description of how in the successful peasant economy of Phokeng it was boys who had the greatest desire to escape the strictures of society's patriarchal controls, but were later to gain more rewards than women out of 'accepting the system' – eventual independence and access to land (Bozzoli 1991: 81).
31. Mmagopine Khulwane and Mmagojane Kgalema, in recorded discussion with members of *Dithabaneng*, Nchabeleng, 19/7/91.

32. Comaroff suggests that 'headscarves are widely worn by black women in South Africa and express the canons of mission modesty, which overlaid the elaborate code of hairdressing' (1985: 224).
33. Members of *Dithabaneng*, recorded discussion with DJ and PM, Nchabeleng, 19/7/91.
34. *Ibid.*
35. Members of *Dithabaneng*, recorded discussion with DJ and PM, Nchabeleng, 19/7/91.
36. Mmagomotala Mofele, discussion with DJ and PM, Nchabeleng, 17/7/91.
37. Mmagoviolet Phakwago, recorded discussion with DJ and PM, Nchabeleng, 17/7/91.
38. Mmagojane Kgalema, recorded discussion with PM, Nchabeleng, 29/12/90.
39. Salome and Andronica Machaba, recorded discussion with DJ, Johannesburg, 19/10/91.
40. To separate *Dithabaneng*'s members out into those who have and those who have not married might seem to be a misguided exercise in static typologising, since as Murray has indicated most rural families undergo diverse temporal processes of change which may take them through several apparently discrete 'types' within a single generation (1981: 100–7, 155). In the area of Lesotho he studied, for example, many women after a period of virilocal residence as a wife in the absence of a husband might experience marital dissolution, work for some time as a migrant, and later return to rear children in a matrifocal household (*ibid.*: 155).
41. See James (1988) for an account of the contrasting ways in which married and unmarried women are affected by rules of inheritance.
42. See, for example, Murray (1981: 76–85); James (1987: 76–8). As in the Lesotho villages studied by Murray, landholders in *Sekhukhune* who have no money for ploughing frequently let out their land for sharecropping by people who have cash or own tractors (P. Delius, personal communication).
43. Lyrics from singers of *Mararankodi*, Nchabeleng.
44. See Colson and Scudder (1988) for an account of the declining ability of women to produce an income from home-brew as men began to favour bottled beer. In *Sekhukhune*, the rejection of sorghum brew in favour of the bottled variety was fuelled, as well, by fears that women might bewitch men by concealing some poisonous substance in their home-brew (Sam Nchabeleng, personal communication). See also the song *o tla loiwa ke batho* referred to in Chapter 4.
45. Mathabathe Mokwale, recorded discussion with PM, Nchabeleng, 29/12/90.
46. Raisibe Sebei, recorded discussion with PM, Nchabeleng, 29/12/90.
47. Mmagojane Kgalema, recorded discussion with PM, Nchabeleng, 29/12/90.
48. *Ibid.*

CHAPTER 6

1. See Chapters 1and 7.
2. Further evidence of this divide was provided by K. J. Nalane, recorded discussion with DJ and NP, Johannesburg, 27/10/89; discussion with Modderfontein dancers, Modderfontein Dynamite Factory, 11/11/91.
3. See Chapter 1.
4. NEC, evidence of Hunt, pp. 658, 706.
5. NEC, evidence of Hunt, pp. 658, 706, Kirsten, pp. 258–64, Urban location representatives, p. 90, Daneel, pp. 193–7.
6. NEC, evidence of Menne, p. 279, Kirsten, p. 268, Daneel, p. 193.

7. NEC, evidence of Motubatse, p. 740, Maserumule, p. 755, Thema, p. 317. See also Delius (1989: 595) for changing attitudes of communities in Sekhukhuneland to education during this era.

8. E TVL, evidence of Grobler, p. 59, Wedepohl, p. 94; NEC statement made on behalf of Chiefs Moloto, Ramakgopa, Matlala, Masasane and Mareli by Thema, and their evidence, pp. 316–40.

9. In both *Leboa* and *Sekhukhune*, girls of a given generation were educationally disadvantaged relative to their brothers, as will be further explored below.

10. This church, which has its headquarters at Moria near Pietersburg, has thousands of members in the Northern Province, and many more in the broader southern African region.

11. See Yawitch (1982: 31, 45–6, 95); James (1987: 66–7).

12. On state strategy in this era see Posel (1990, 1991: 227–55); on removals see Surplus People Project (1983), Maré (1980), Desmond (1971).

13. Rosina Seshothi, recorded discussion with DJ and MTN, Johannesburg, 21/4/90.

14. Joanna Maleaka, recorded discussion with DJ and MTN, Johannesburg, 24/3/90.

15. See Chapter 5.

16. See Morrell (1983: 181); James (1985, 1987: 128–9); Sharp and Spiegel (1990).

17. See James (1985: 182, 1987: 35) for similar cases among tenants in the Middelburg district, Transvaal.

18. E TVL, evidence of Stanford, p. 92; NEC, evidence of Senthumula and Khutama, p. 66, Lyle, p. 120.

19. Studies of relocated farm labourers in an area of south-western Lebowa and in Qwaqwa have shown that the longer families remained on farms, the greater the restrictions placed on the amount of land ploughed for themselves and on the number of cattle they could keep, and the more 'forced' their eventual relocation (James 1987: 22, 35–42; Sharp 1982).

20. Julia Lelahana, recorded discussion with DJ and PM, Johannesburg, 4/5/91.

21. *Ibid.*

22 James Makola, discussion with DJ and Philip Mbiba (hereafter PMb), Johannesburg, 8/9/91. Makola grew up on a farm near Pietersburg for a few years, and was later taken by his father to stay with Christian relatives at Mankweng in the *Molepo* reserve.

23. The exception was Thabia Makola, a Tswana-speaker who was later to be initiated by her co-singers in 1990, prior to her marriage to a Sotho man from *Molepo*.

24. Bozzoli, in the case of Tswana women of Phokeng, shows that a flight from or refusal to attend initiation may represent an escape from the old social order (Bozzoli 1991: 81).

25. Sarah Motswi, recorded discussion with DJ and MTN, Johannesburg, 19/10/90.

26. Andronica and Salome Machaba, recorded discussion with DJ and PM, 19/10/91.

27. *Ibid.* The format of visiting, competing with, and learning from one's hosts has much in common with certain non-mission forms of performance such as the *bepha* (musical expedition for young people) of the Venda (Blacking 1962), and also shows similarities to the process of visiting and imitating which characterised the spread of *kiba* described in Chapter 3.

28. The case of *makwaya* shows that people's use of cultural forms originating in the

mission does not necessarily have an 'overwhelmingly imitative character' as is claimed by the accounts which Ranger criticises (1975: 6), or signify 'the colonisation of consciousness' (Comaroff and Comaroff 1989). Even within the mission context and among converts, people may transform the religion of the colonisers into something significantly different, as Hofmeyr has shown in her excellent study of the oralisation of literate Christianity in an area which is part of *Leboa* (1994: 68–83). New and syncretic cultural forms which do arise among church-goers, as *makwaya* did, may spread through a variety of channels to reach – and to be actively sought out by – even those people who do not count themselves among the ranks of the converted.

29. Julia Lelahana, recorded discussion with DJ and PM, Johannesburg, 13/10/91.
30. The acquisition of such inheritances, including praising and divining, forms the theme of Chapter 7.
31. As has been mentioned above, most of these girls had the clothes of adolescence purchased for them by their fathers from the proceeds of farm labour or farm produce.
32. Surplus People Project (1983: I, 26–7). For an account of similar contrast between long-standing networks built up by *Sekhukhune* migrants and the lack of such networks among recently resettled labour tenants, see James (1987: 183), Sansom (1970: 71–4, 97–8).
33. Salome and Andronica Machaba, recorded discussion with DJ and MTN, Johannesburg, 13/5/90.
34. A fuller discussion of the marital careers of *kiba* women is given in Chapter 2, and a criticism of the literature which sees marital crisis as the major cause underpinning female migration.

CHAPTER 7

1. See Chapter 2.
2. In the northern Transvaal, one of the factors making for a less rigid distinction between mainstream and independent churches was that neither type of church, active in the area subsequent to the initial proselytising of the Lutherans, has insisted, as the Lutherans did, on non-attendance at initiation. In similar vein, none of these churches paralleled the Lutheran's requirement that Christians foreswear fealty to their chief in allying themselves in semi-feudal manner to the minister.
3. The *kiba* group to which she belongs: 'those of the royal leopard-skin clothing'. See Chapters 1–3.
4. Anna Dikotlo, recorded discussion with DJ and PM, Johannesburg, 17/8/91.
5. Joanna Maleaka, recorded discussion with DJ and PM, Johannesburg, 5/10/91.
6. Mary Kapa, discussion with DJ and PM, Johannesburg, 23/10/91.
7. Mmagoshower Debeila, recorded discussion with PM, Nchabeleng, 16/12/91; see also Mmagojane Kgalema, discussion with PM, Nchabeleng, 20/12/91.
8. Makgolo wa Pine Khulwane, recorded discussion with PM, Nchabeleng, 24/12/91.
9. Mmagoshower Debeila, recorded discussion with PM, Nchabeleng, 16/12/91.
10. Mr Makgaleng, discussion with DJ, Apel, 19/7/91.
11. Makgolo wa Pine Khulwane, recorded discussion with PM, Nchabeleng, 24/12/91.
12. *Ibid.*; Mmagoshower Debeila, recorded discussion with PM, Nchabeleng, 16/12/91; Ramogohlo Diphofa, discussion with PM, Mphanama, 23/12/91.
13. Helen Matjila, recorded discussion with DJ and PM, Johannesburg, 8/7/91.

14. Andronica Machaba, recorded discussion with DJ and PM, Johannesburg, 19/10/91.
15. *Ibid.*
16. See Chapters 2 and 4.
17. See Seeger (1987: 61–4) for an account of the way musical, spiritual and other 'gifts' are transmitted through genetic or other 'natural' means in three different societies.
18. See James (1988) for a fuller account of this process. Although I used the word 'inheritance' throughout this article to describe the transfer of residential and agricultural land, in retrospect I would have paid more attention to linguistic precision. The fact that the notion of 'inheritance' may be translated as a number of diverse concepts in *sesotho* was first brought to my attention by Patrick Pearson, whose help I gratefully acknowledge.
19. Lyrics and interpretation from *Dithabaneng*, recorded discussion with DJ and PM, Nchabeleng, 28/7/91. See Chapter 5, p. 120 for a previous citing of this song, and a discussion of its expression of the themes of womanly dependence.
20. This conception of *modimo* was explicitly spelt out by a number of informants; see also West (1975: 189, 200; Kuper 1987: 170).
21. Makgolo wa Pine Khulwane, recorded discussion with PM, Nchabeleng, 24/12/91.
22. Anna Dikotlo, recorded discussion with DJ and PM, Johannesburg, 17/8/91.
23. Flora Mohlomi, recorded discussion with DJ and PM, Johannesburg, 11/8/91.
24. *Ibid.*
25. Andronica Machaba, recorded discussion with DJ and PM, Johannesburg, 19/10/91.
26. This observation was made to me by numerous informants, and is also substantiated in the literature (Krige and Krige 1943: 76; Hammond-Tooke 1974b: 347–8; Kuper 1982: 60). See also Chapter 4.
27. See Chapter 4.
28. Salome and Andronica Machaba, recorded discussion with DJ and PM, Johannesburg, 19/10/91.
29. Salome and Andronica Machaba, recorded discussion with DJ and PM, Johannesburg, 19/10/91.
30. See Chapter 1, p. 28.
31. Andronica Machaba, recorded discussion with DJ and PM, Johannesburg, 19/10/91.
32. See Chapter 3 for a discussion of genre boundary blurring in oral forms of expression.
33. See Chapter 6.

CONCLUSION

1. My thanks to Jonathan Hyslop for bringing this source, and other sources on modernity, to my attention.
2. See, for example, Wilmsen (1993); Wilmsen and Vossen (1990); Goldin (1989). The concept of identity has previously been of concern more to psychologists or social psychologists than to anthropologists. See, for example, Brown (1985: 771).
3. It is Moore's suggestion that most cultures possess a male-dominated discourse in which the dominant image of appropriate male behaviour is valued more highly than that of the female. I have developed the argument in relation to ethnicity. Moore suggests that the insights of post-structuralism can be used to

suggest, as a substitute for the cohesive Western self, a self or subject involving a 'multiplicity of alternative subject positions' (1994: 8). Such a multiple subject is to be found positioning itself in the gap between the actual experience of individuals and the models of appropriate behaviour offered within a particular culture.

BIBLIOGRAPHY

1. ARTICLES, PAPERS, BOOKS AND DISSERTATIONS

Alnaes, K. 1969. 'Songs of the Rwenzururu rebellion' in P. Gulliver (ed.), *Tradition and Transition in East Africa*. London: Routledge and Kegan Paul.

—— 1989. 'Living with the past: the songs of the Herero in Botswana', *Africa* 59 (3), 267–99.

Alverson, H. 1978. *Mind in the Heart of Darkness: value and self-identity among the Tswana of Southern Africa*. New Haven: Yale University Press.

Andersson, M. 1981. *Music in the Mix: the story of South African popular music*. Johannesburg: Ravan Press.

Argyle, J. 1991. 'Kalela, Beni, Asafo, Ingoma and the rural–urban dichotomy' in A. D. Spiegel and P. A. McAllister (eds), *Tradition and Transition in Southern Africa: African Studies fiftieth anniversary volume* 50 (1 & 2), 65–86.

Ballantine, C. 1989. 'A brief history of South African popular music', *Popular Music* 8(3), 305–10.

Bank, L. 1991. 'Beyond the Bovine Mystique: entreneurship, class and identity in Qwaqwa', paper presented at the Anthropology Department, Witwatersrand University.

Banton, M. 1957. *West African City: a study of tribal life in Freetown*. London: Oxford University Press.

Barber, K. 1984. 'Yoruba *oriki* and deconstructive criticism', *Research in African Literatures* 15 (4), 497–518.

—— 1987. 'Popular arts in Africa', *African Studies Review*, 30 (3), 1–78.

—— 1991. *I Could Speak Until Tomorrow*: Oriki, *women and the past in a Yoruba town*. Edinburgh: Edinburgh University Press and Washington DC: Smithsonian Institution Press for the International African Institute.

Barber, K. and P. F. de Moraes Farias 1989. 'Introduction' in K. Barber and P. F. de Moraes Farias (eds), *Discourse and its Disguises: the interpretation of African oral texts*. Birmingham: Birmingham University Press.

Barth, F. 1969a. *Ethnic Groups and Boundaries*. London: Allen and Unwin.

—— 1969b. 'Introduction' in F. Barth (ed.), *Ethnic Groups and Boundaries*. London: Allen and Unwin.

Basso, E. B. 1985. *A Musical View of the Universe: Kalapalo myth and ritual performance*. Philadelphia: University of Pennsylvania Press.

Bauman, R. 1989. 'Performance' in E. Barnouw (ed.). *International Encyclopaedia of Communications*. Oxford: Oxford University Press.

Bauman, R. and C. L. Briggs 1990. 'Poetics and performance as critical perspectives on language and social life', *Annual Review of Anthropology* 19, 59–88.

Beinart, W. and P. Delius 1986. 'Introduction' in W. Beinart, P. Delius and S. Trapido (eds), *Putting a Plough to the Ground: accumulation and dispossession in rural South Africa 1850–1930*. Johannesburg: Ravan Press.

Beinart, W., P. Delius and S. Trapido (eds) 1986. *Putting a Plough to the Ground: accumulation and dispossession in rural South Africa 1850–1930*. Johannesburg: Ravan Press.

Berman, M. 1982. *All that is Solid Melts into Air: the experience of modernity*. Harmondsworth: Penguin.

Blacking, J. 1956. *The Role of Music among the Venda of the Northern Transvaal*. Roodepoort: International Library of African Music.

—— 1962. 'Musical expeditions of the Venda', *African Music* 3 (1), 54–78.

—— 1964. 'The Cultural Foundations of the Music of the Venda', unpublished PhD dissertation, Witwatersrand University.

—— 1967. *Venda Children's Songs*. Johannesburg: Witwatersrand University Press.

—— 1969. 'Songs, dances, mimes and symbolism of Venda girls' initiation schools', *African Studies* 28 (1), 3–36; 28 (2), 69–118; 28 (3), 149–200.

—— 1973. *How Musical is Man?*. Washington DC: Washington University Press.

—— 1977. 'Some problems of theory and method in the study of musical change', *Yearbook of the International Folk Music Council* 9, 1–26.

Boddy, J. 1994. 'Spirit possession revisited: beyond instrumentality', *Annual Review of Anthropology* 23, 407–34.

Bonner, P. 1990. '"Desirable or undesirable Basotho women?" Liquor, prostitution and the migration of Basotho women to the Rand, 1920–1945' in C. Walker (ed.), *Women and Gender in Southern Africa to 1945*. Cape Town, David Philip.

—— 1995. 'African urbanization on the Rand between the 1930s and 1960s: its social character and political consequences', *Journal of Southern African Studies* 21 (1), 115–45.

Bothma, C. V. 1962. *Ntshabeleng Social Structure*. Pretoria: Government Printer.

—— 1976. 'The political structure of the Pedi of Sekhukhuneland', *African Studies* 35 (3–4), 177–205.

Bourguinon, E. 1967. 'World distribution and patterns of possession states' in R. Prince (ed.), *Trance and Possession States*. Montreal: J. M. Buckle Foundation.

Bozzoli, B. (ed.) 1979. *Labour, Townships and Protest*. Johannesburg: Ravan Press.

—— 1983. 'Marxism, feminism and South African Studies', *Journal of Southern African Studies* 9 (2), 139–71.

Bozzoli, B. with M. Nkotsoe 1991. *Women of Phokeng: consciousness, life strategy and migrancy in South Africa 1900–1983*. Johannesburg: Ravan Press.

Brown, B. 1983. 'The impact of male labour migration on women in Botswana', *African Affairs* 82, 367–88.

Brown, R. 1985. 'Social identity' in A. Kuper and J. Kuper (eds), *The Social Science Encyclopaedia*. London: Routledge and Kegan Paul.

Brydon, L. 1987. 'Who moves? Women and migration in West Africa in the 1980s' in J. Eades (ed.), *Migrants, Workers and the Social Order*. London: Tavistock.

Cheater, A. 1986. *Anthropology: an alternative introduction*. Harare: Mambo Press.

Chernoff, J. M. 1979. *African Rhythm and African Sensibility: aesthetics and social action in African musical idioms*. Chicago: University of Chicago Press.

Clegg, J. 1981. 'The music of Zulu immigrant workers in Johannesburg' in *Papers Presented at the First Symposium on Ethnomusicology*. Grahamstown: ILAM.

—— 1982. 'Towards an understanding of African dance: the Zulu isishameni style' in *Papers Presented at the Second Symposium on Ethnomusicology*. Grahamstown: ILAM.

—— 1984. 'An examination of the umzansi dance style' in *Papers Presented at the Third and Fourth Symposia on Ethnomusicology*. Grahamstown: ILAM.

Clifford, J. 1988. *The Predicament of Culture*. Cambridge, MA: Harvard University Press.

Cock, J. 1980. *Maids and Madams*. Johannesburg: Ravan Press.

Cohen, A. 1969. *Custom and Politics in Urban Africa*. Berkeley CA: University of California Press.

Colson, E. and T. Scudder 1988. *For Prayer and Profit: the ritual, economic and social importance of beer in Gwambe district, Zambia*. Stanford: Stanford University Press.

Comaroff, J. 1985. *Body of Power, Spirit of Resistance: the culture and history of a South African people*. Chicago: University of Chicago Press.

Comaroff, J. L. 1987. 'Of totemism and ethnicity: consciousness, practice and the origin of inequality', *Ethnos* 52, 301–23

Comaroff, J. L. and J. Comaroff (eds) 1981. *The Management of Marriage in a Tswana Chiefdom*. Cape Town: Juta.

—— 1987. 'The madman and the migrant: work and labour in the historical consciousness of a South African people', *American Ethnologist* 14 (2), 191–209.

—— 1989. 'The colonisation of consciousness in South Africa', *Economy and Society* 18 (3), 267–95.

—— 1990. 'Goodly beasts, beastly goods: cattle and commodities in a South African context', *American Ethnologist* 17 (2), 195–216.

Cooper, F. (ed.) 1983a. *Struggle for the City: migrant labour, capital and the state in urban Africa*. Beverly Hills: Sage.

—— 1983b. 'Introduction' in F. Cooper (ed.), *Struggle for the City: migrant labour, capital and the state in urban Africa*. Beverly Hills: Sage.

Cope, T. 1968. *Izibongo: Zulu praise poetry*. Oxford: Oxford University Press.

Coplan, D. B. 1979. 'The African performer and the Johannesburg entertainment industry: the struggle for African culture on the Witwatersrand' in B. Bozzoli (ed.), *Labour, Townships and Protest*. Johannesburg: Ravan Press.

—— 1982. 'The emergence of an African working-class culture' in S. Marks and R. Rathbone (eds), *Industrialisation and Social Change in South Africa: African class formation, culture and consciousness 1870–1930*. London: Longman.

—— 1985. *In Township Tonight: South Africa's black city music and theatre*. Johannesburg: Ravan Press.

—— 1987. 'Eloquent knowledge: Lesotho migrants' songs and the anthropology of experience', in *American Ethnologist* 14 (3), 413–33.

—— 1988. 'Musical understanding: the ethnoaesthetics of migrant workers' poetic song in Lesotho', *Ethnomusicology* 32 (3), 337–68.

—— 1991. 'Fictions that save: migrants' performance and Basotho national culture', *Cultural Anthropology* 6 (2), 164–192.

Crapanzano, V. 1977. 'Introduction' in V. Crapanzano and V. Garrison (eds), *Case Studies in Spirit-Possession*. New York: John Wiley.

Crapanzano, V. and V. Garrison (eds) 1977. *Case Studies in Spirit-Possession*. New York: John Wiley.

Damane, M. and P. B. Sanders 1974. *Lithoko: Sotho praise-poems*. Oxford: Oxford University Press.

Delius, P. 1980. 'The Pedi polity under Sekwati and Sekhukhune, 1828–1889', unpublished PhD thesis, University of London.

—— 1983. *The Land Belongs to Us: the Pedi polity, the Boers and the British in the nineteenth-century Transvaal*. Johannesburg: Ravan Press.

—— 1986. 'Abel Erasmus: power and profit in the eastern Transvaal' in W. Beinart, P. Delius and S. Trapido (eds), *Putting a Plough to the Ground: accumulation and dispossession in rural South Africa 1850–1930*. Johannesburg: Ravan Press.

—— 1989. 'Sebatakgomo: migrant organisation, the ANC and the Sekhukhuneland revolt', *Journal of Southern African Studies*, 15 (4), 581–615.

—— 1990. 'Migrants, comrades and rural revolt: Sekhukhuneland 1950–1987', *Transformation* 13, 2–26.

Desmond, C. 1971. *The Discarded People*. Harmondsworth: Penguin.

Douglas, M. 1973. *Natural Symbols*. London: Barrie and Jenkins.

Drewal, M. 1991. 'The state of research on performance in Africa', *African Studies Review* 34 (3), 1–64.

Eades, J. (ed.) 1987. *Migrants, Workers and the Social Order*. ASA Monograph 26. London and New York: Tavistock.

Epstein, A. 1958. *Politics in an Urban African Community*. Manchester: Manchester University Press.

—— 1981. *Urbanisation and Kinship: the domestic domain of the Copperbelt 1950–1956*. London: Academic Press.

Erlmann, V. 1987. 'Singing brings Joy to the Distressed: the social history of Zulu migrant workers' competitions', mimeo, Witwatersrand University History Workshop.

—— 1991. *African Stars: studies in black South African performance*. Chicago: Chicago University Press.

Etienne, M. and E. Leacock 1980. *Women and Colonisation*. New York: Praeger.

Fabian, J. 1990. *Power and Performance*. Madison: University of Wisconsin Press.

Feld, S. 1982. *Sound and Sentiment: birds, weeping, poetics and song in Kaluli expression*. Philadelphia: University of Pennsylvania Press.

Ferguson, J. 1985. 'The bovine mystique: power, prosperity and livestock in rural Lesotho', *Man* 20 (4), 647–74.

—— 1990. 'Mobile workers, modernist narratives: a critique of the historiography of transition on the Zambian Copperbelt', *Journal of Southern African Studies* 16 (3 and 4), 385–412, 603–21.

—— 1992. 'The country and the city on the copperbelt', *Cultural Anthropology* 7 (1), 80–92.

Fernandez, J. 1973. 'The exposition and imposition of order: artistic expression in Fang culture' in W. d'Azevedo (ed.), *The Traditional Artist in African Society*. Bloomington: Indiana University Press.

Finnegan, R. 1989. *The Hidden Musicians*. Cambridge: Cambridge University Press.

Firth, R. 1969. 'Preface' in John Beattie and John Middleton (eds), *Spirit Mediumship and Society in Africa*. London: Routledge and Kegan Paul.

Freund, W. 1994. 'The art of writing history', *Southern African Review of Books* 33, 24.

Frith, S. 1978. *The Sociology of Rock*. London: Constable.

Gaitskell, D., J. Kimble, M. Maconachie and E. Unterhalter 1983. 'Class, race and gender: domestic workers in South Africa', *R.A.P.E.* 27/28, 86–108.

Gal, S. 1991. 'Between speech and silence: the problematics of research on language and gender' in M. di Leonardo (ed.), *Gender at the Crossroads of Knowledge: feminist anthropology in the postmodern era*. Berkeley CA: University of California Press.

Gay, J. S. 1980. 'Wage employment of rural Basotho women: a case study', *South African Labour Bulletin* 6 (4), 40–53.

Geertz, C. 1983. *Local Knowledge*. New York: Basic Books.

Gilmore, D. B. 1980. *The People of the Plain: class and community in lower Andalusia*. New York: Columbia University Press.

Gluckman, M. 1961. 'Anthropological problems arising from the African industrial revolution' in A. Southall (ed.), *Social Change in Modern Africa*. Oxford: Oxford University Press.

Goldin, I. 1989. 'Coloured identity and coloured politics in the Western Cape region of South Africa' in L. Vail (ed.), *The Creation of Tribalism in Southern Africa*. London: James Currey.

Gordon, E. 1981. 'An analysis of the impact of labour migration on the lives of women in Lesotho', *Journal of Development Studies* 17 (3), 59–76.

Gordon, R. and A. D. Spiegel 1993. 'Southern Africa revisited', *Annual Review of Anthropology* 22, 00 105.

Graves, N. and T. B. Graves 1974. 'Adaptive strategies in urban migration', in *Annual Review of Anthropology* 3, 117–151.

Gunner, E. 1989. 'Songs of innocence and experience: women as composers and performers of Izibongo, Zulu praise-poetry' in C. Clayton (ed.), *Women and Writing in South Africa: a critical anthology*. Cape Town: David Philip.

Gunner, E. and M. Gwala 1991. *Zulu Popular Praises*. East Lansing: Michigan State University Press.

Guy, J. 1990. 'Gender oppression in southern Africa's precapitalist societies' in C. Walker (ed.), *Women and Gender in Southern Africa to 1945*. Cape Town: David Philip.

Guy, J. and M. Thabane 1987. 'The Marashea: a participants' perspective' in B. Bozzoli (ed.), *Class, Community and Conflict: South African perspectives*. Johannesburg: Ravan Press.

—— 1991. 'Basotho miners, ethnicity and workers' strategies' in I. Brandell (ed.), *Workers in Third-World Industrialization*. London: Macmillan.

Halpenny, P. 1979. 'Three styles of ethnic migration in Kisengi, Kampala' in D. Parkin (ed.), *Town and Country in Central and Eastern Africa*. London: Oxford University Press for the International African Institute.

Hamm, C. 1987. Review of Coplan's *In Township Tonight*. *Popular Music* 6 (1), 353–5.

Hammond-Tooke, W. D. 1962. *Bhaca Society: a people of the Transkeian uplands*. Cape Town: Oxford University Press.

—— (ed.) 1974a. *The Bantu-Speaking Peoples of Southern Africa*. London: Routledge and Kegan Paul.

—— 1974b. 'World-view II: a system of action' in W. D. Hammond-Tooke (ed.), *The Bantu-Speaking Peoples of Southern Africa*. London: Routledge and Kegan Paul.

—— 1986. 'The aetiology of spirit in southern Africa', *African Studies* 45 (2), 157–70.

Hansen, K. T. 1986a. 'Domestic service in Zambia', *Journal of Southern African Studies* 13 (1), 57–81.

—— 1986b. 'Sex and gender among domestic servants in Zambia', *Anthropology Today* 2 (3), 18–23.

Harries, P. 1987. 'A forgotten corner of the Transvaal' in B. Bozzoli (ed.), *Class, Community and Conflict*. Johannesburg: Ravan Press.

—— 1989. 'Exclusion, classification and internal colonialism: the emergence of ethnicity among the Tsonga-speakers of South Africa' in L. Vail (ed.), *The Creation of Tribalism in Southern Africa*. London: James Currey.

Harries-Jones, P. 1969. 'Home-boy ties and political organisation in a copperbelt township' in J. C. Mitchell (ed.), *Social Networks in Urban Situations*. Manchester: Manchester University Press.

—— 1975. *Freedom and Labour*. Oxford: Blackwell.

Heath, D. 1992. 'Fashion, anti-fashion and heteroglossia in urban Senegal', *American Ethnologist* 19 (2), 19–33.

Hoernle, W. 1937. 'Social organisation' in I. Schapera (ed.), *The Bantu-Speaking Tribes of South Africa*. Cape Town: Maskew Miller.

Hofmeyr, I. 1994. '*We Spend Our Years as a Tale That is Told*': oral historical narrative in a South African chiefdom. Johannesburg: Witwatersrand University Press.

Hunter, M. 1936. *Reaction to Conquest: effects of contact with Europeans on the Pondo of South Africa*. London: Oxford University Press for the International African Institute.

Huskisson, Y. 1958. 'The Social and Ceremonial Music of the Pedi', unpublished PhD dissertation, Witwatersrand University.

Izzard, W. 1985. 'Migrants and mothers: case-studies from Botswana', *Journal of Southern African Studies* 11 (2), 258–80.

James, D. 1983. *The Road from Doornkop: a case study of removals and resistance*. Johannesburg: South African Institute of Race Relations.

—— 1985. 'Family and household in a Lebowa village', *African Studies* 44 (2), 159–87.

—— 1987. 'Kinship and Land in an Inter-ethnic Community', unpublished MA dissertation, Witwatersrand University.

—— 1988. 'Land shortage and inheritance in a Lebowa village', *Social Dynamics* 14 (2), 36–51.

—— 1990a. '*Mmino wa Setšo*: women's songs in a Lebowa village', mimeo, Witwatersrand University History Workshop Conference.

—— 1990b. 'A question of ethnicity: Ndzundza Ndebele in a Lebowa village', *Journal of Southern African Studies* 16 (1), 33–54.

—— 1990c. 'Musical form and social history: research perspectives on black South African music', *Radical History Review* 46/7, 309–19.

—— 1994. '*Mmino wa Setšo*: songs of town and country and the experience of migrancy by men and women from the northern Transvaal', PhD dissertation, University of Witwatersrand.

Johnston, T. 1971. 'The Music of the Shangana-Tsonga', unpublished PhD dissertation, Witwatersrand University.

—— 1973. 'Possession music of the Shangana-Tsonga', *African Music* 5.

—— 1974. 'Power and prestige through music in Tsongaland', *Human Relations* 27 (3), 235–46.

—— 1975. 'Tsonga music in cultural perspective', *Anthropos* 70, 761–99.

Junod, H. 1962. *The Life of a South African Tribe*. New York: University Books.

Keegan, T. 1988. *Facing the Storm: portraits of black lives in Rural South Africa*. Cape Town and Johannesburg: David Philip.

Kiernan, J. P. 1974. 'Where Zionists draw the line: a study of religious exclusiveness in an African township', *African Studies* 33 (2), 79–90.

—— 1977. 'Poor and Puritan: an attempt to view Zionism as a collective response to urban poverty', *African Studies* 36 (1), 31–43.

Kirby, P. 1934. *The Musical Instruments of the Native Races of South Africa*. Oxford: Oxford University Press.

—— 1959. 'The uses of European musical techniques by the non-European peoples of South Africa', *Journal of the International Folk Music Council*.

Koskoff, E. (ed.) 1989a. *Women and Music in Cross-Cultural Perspective*. Urbana: University of Illinois Press.

—— 1989b. 'An introduction to women, music and culture' in E. Koskoff (ed.), *Women and Music in Cross-Cultural Perspective*. Urbana: University of Illinois Press.

Kriel, T. J. 1976. *Popular Northern Sotho Dictionary*. Pretoria: Van Schaik.

Krige, E. J. 1975. 'Assymmetrical matrilateral cross-cousin marriage – the Lovedu case', *African Studies* 34 (4), 231–57.

Krige, E. J. and J. D. Krige 1943. *The Realm of a Rain Queen*. London: International African Institute.

Krige, J. D. 1937. 'Traditional origins and tribal relationships of the Sotho of the Northern Transvaal', *Bantu Studies* XI (4), 321–57.

Kuper, A. 1975. 'The social structure of the Sotho-speaking peoples of southern Africa', *Africa* 45 (1 and 2), 67–81; 139–49.

—— 1982. *Wives for Cattle: bridewealth and marriage in southern Africa.* London. Routledge and Kegan Paul.

—— 1987. *South Africa and the Anthropologist.* London: Routledge and Kegan Paul.

Kuper, A. and J. Kuper (eds) 1985. *The Social Science Encyclopaedia.* London: Routledge and Kegan Paul.

Kuper, H. 1973. 'Costume and identity', *Comparative Studies in Society and History* 15 (3), 348–67.

Kuper, H. and S. Kaplan 1944. 'Voluntary associations in an urban township', *African Studies* 3 (4), 178–86.

Kurtz, D. V. 1973. 'The rotating credit association: an adaption to poverty', *Human Organisation* 32, 49–58.

La Fontaine, J. 1969. 'Tribalism among the Gisu' in P. Gulliver (ed.), *Tradition and Transition in East Africa.* London: Routledge and Kegan Paul.

Lestrade, G. P. 1937. 'Traditional literature' in I. Schapera (ed.), *Bantu-Speaking Tribes of South Africa.* Cape Town: Maskew Miller.

Lewis, I. 1971. *Ecstatic Religion: an anthropological study of spirit possession and shamanism.* Harmondsworth: Penguin.

Little, K. 1967. 'Voluntary associations in urban life: a case study of differential adaptations' in M. Freedman (ed.), *Social Organisation: essays presented to Raymond Firth.* Chicago: Aldine.

—— 1972. 'Some aspects of African urbanisation south of the Sahara', *Current Topics in Anthropology* 5 (3), 5/1–32.

—— 1973. 'Urbanisation and regional associations: their paradoxical function' in A. Southall (ed.), *Urban Anthropology: cross-cultural studies of urbanisation.* New York: Oxford University Press.

Maddock, K. (ed.) 1991a. *Identity, Land and Liberty.* Nijmegen: Centre for Pacific Studies.

—— 1991b. 'Introduction' in K. Maddock (ed.), *Identity, Land and Liberty.* Nijmegen: Centre for Pacific Studies.

Manona, C. 1980. 'Marriage, family life and migrancy in a Ciskei village' in P. Mayer (ed.), *Black Villagers in an Industrial Society.* Cape Town: Oxford University Press.

Manuel, P. 1988. *Popular Musics of the Non-Western World: an introductory survey.* Oxford: Oxford University Press.

Maré, G. 1980. *African Population Relocation in South Africa.* Johannesburg: South African Institute of Race Relations.

Marks, S. and R. Rathbone (eds) 1982a. *Industrialisation and Social Change in South Africa.* London: Longmans.

—— 1982b. 'Introduction' in S. Marks and R. Rathbone (eds), *Industrialisation and Social Change in South Africa.* London: Longmans.

Mayer, P. 1978. 'Wives of migrant workers' in P. Mayer (ed.), 'Migrant Labour: some perspectives from Anthropology. Vol. 3', typescript, Rhodes University, Migrant Labour Project.

—— 1980. 'The origin and decline of two rural resistance ideologies' in P. Mayer (ed.), *Black Villagers in an Industrial Society.* Oxford: Oxford University Press.

Mayer, P. and Mayer, I. 1971. *Townsmen or Tribesmen.* Cape Town: Oxford University Press.

McAllister, P. 1980. 'Work, homestead and the shades: the ritual interpretation of labour migration among the Gcaleka' in P. Mayer (ed.), *Black Villagers in an Industrial Society*. Oxford: Oxford University Press.

—— 1985. 'Beasts to beer pots: migrant labour and ritual change in Willowvale district, Transkei', *African Studies* 44 (2), 121–36.

—— 1991. 'Using ritual to resist domination in the Transkei' in A. D. Spiegel and P. A. McAllister (eds), *Tradition and Transition in Southern Africa: African Studies fiftieth anniversary volume* 50 (1 and 2), 129–44.

McNamara, J. K. 1978. 'Social Life, Ethnicity and Conflict in a Gold Mine Hostel', unpublished MA dissertation, Witwatersrand University.

—— 1985. 'Black Worker Conflicts on South African Gold Mines: 1973–1982', unpublished PhD dissertation, Witwatersrand University.

Meintjies, S. 1991. 'Family and gender in the Christian community at Edendale, Natal, in colonial times' in C. Walker (ed.), *Women and Gender in Southern Africa to 1945*. Cape Town: David Philip.

Merriam, A. 1964. *The Anthropology of Music*. Evanston: Northwestern University Press.

Middleton, R. 1990. *Studying Popular Music*. Milton Keynes: Open University Press.

Mitchell, J. C. 1956. *The Kalela Dance*. Rhodes-Livingstone Institute, Occasional Paper No. 27. Manchester: Manchester University Press.

Molepo, M. M. 1983. 'Peasants and/or Proletariat: a case study of migrant workers at Haggie Rand Limited from Molepo Tribal Village', unpublished Honours dissertation, Industrial Sociology, Witwatersrand University.

—— 1984. 'The Changing Nature of Labour Migration from the Northern Transvaal with Particular Reference to Molepo village c.1900–1940', unpublished MA dissertation, University of London: SOAS.

Mönnig, H. O. 1967. *The Pedi*. Pretoria: J. L. van Schaik.

Moodie, D. 1983. 'Mine culture and miners' identity on the South African Gold Mines' in B. Bozzoli (ed.), *Town and Countryside in the Transvaal*. Johannesburg: Ravan Press.

—— 1991. 'Social existence and the practice of personal integrity: narratives of resistance on the South African Gold Mines' in A. D. Spiegel and P. A. McAllister (eds), *Tradition and Transition in Southern Africa: African Studies fiftieth anniversary volume* 50 (1 and 2), 39–64.

Moore, H. 1988. *Feminism and Anthropology*. Cambridge: Polity Press.

—— 1994. *A Passion for Difference: essays in anthropology and gender*. Cambridge: Polity Press.

Morrell, R. 1983. 'Rural Transformations in the Transvaal: the Middelburg district 1919–1930', unpublished MA dissertation, Witwatersrand University.

Morris, B. 1987. *Anthropological Studies of Religion: an introductory text*. Cambridge: Cambridge University Press.

Mphahlele, E. 1971. *Down Second Avenue*. Harmondsworth: Penguin.

Murray, C. 1981. *Families Divided*. Johannesburg: Ravan Press.

Niehaus, I. 1993. 'Witch-hunting and political legitimacy: continuity and change in Green Valley, Lebowa', *Africa* 63 (4), 137–60

—— 1994. 'Disharmonious spouses and harmonious siblings: conceptualising household formation among urban residents in Qwaqwa, South Africa', *African Studies* 53 (1), 115–36.

Nketia, J. H. K. 1975. *The Music of Africa*. London: Gollancz.

Ortner, S. 1974. 'Is female to male as nature is to culture?' in M. Z. Rosaldo and L. Lamphere (eds), *Woman, Culture and Society*. Stanford: Stanford University Press.

—— 1984. 'Theory in anthropology since the sixties', *Comparative Studies in Society and History* 19 (1), 127–66.

Ortner, S. and H. Whitehead 1981. 'Introduction: accounting for sexual meanings' in S. Ortner and H. Whitehead (eds), *Sexual Meanings: the cultural construction of gender and sexuality*. Cambridge: Cambridge University Press.

Parkin, D. 1966. 'Voluntary associations as institutions of adaption', *Man* (n.s.) 1 (1), 90–5.

—— 1969. *Neighbours and Nationals in an African City Ward*. London: Routledge and Kegan Paul.

——(ed.) 1975a. *Town and Country in Central and Eastern Africa*. London: Oxford University Press for the International African Institute.

—— 1975b. 'Introduction' in D. Parkin (ed.), *Town and Country in Central and Eastern Africa*. London: Oxford University Press for the International African Institute.

Parpart, J. 1991. 'Gender, Ideology and Power: marriage in the colonial Copperbelt towns of Zambia', mimeo, African Studies Institute, Witwatersrand University.

Parpart, J. and S. Stichter 1988. *Patriarchy and Class: African women in the home and workforce*. Boulder CT: Westview Press.

Pauw, B. 1974. 'The influence of Christianity' in W. D. Hammond-Tooke (ed.), *The Bantu-Speaking Peoples of Southern Africa*. London: Routledge and Kegan Paul.

Pearson, P. 1978. 'Authority and control in a South African goldmine compound' in *Papers Presented at the African Studies Seminar at the University of the Witwatersrand, Johannesburg During 1977*. Johannesburg: African Studies Institute, University of the Witwatersrand

Pitje, G. M. 1950. 'Traditional systems of male education among Pedi and cognate tribes', *African Studies* 9 (2), 53–75; 3, 105–24; 4, 194–201.

Posel, D. 1990. 'The state and policy-making in apartheid's second phase', unpublished paper, Witwatersrand University History Workshop Conference.

—— 1991. *The Making of Apartheid 1948–1961: conflict and compromise*. Oxford: Clarendon Press.

Preston-Whyte, E. 1974. 'Kinship and marriage' in W. D. Hammond-Tooke (ed.), *The Bantu-Speaking Peoples of Southern Africa*. London: Routledge and Kegan Paul.

—— 1978. 'Families without marriage: a Zulu case study' in J. Argyle and E. Preston-Whyte (eds), *Social System and Tradition in Southern Africa: essays in honour of Eileen Krige*. Cape Town: Oxford University Press.

—— 1981. 'Women migrants and marriage' in E. J. Krige and J. L. Comaroff (eds), *Essays on African Marriage in Southern Africa*. Cape Town: Juta.

Radcliffe-Brown, A. R. 1948. *The Andaman Islanders*. Glencoe: Free Press.

Ramphele, M. 1986. 'The male and female dynamic amongst migrant workers in the Western Cape', *Social Dynamics* 12 (1), 15–25.

Ranger, T. O. 1975. *Dance and Society in Eastern Africa, 1890–1970: the Beni Ngoma*. London: Heinemann.

—— 1983. 'The invention of tradition in colonial Africa' in E. Hobsbawm and T. O. Ranger (eds), *The Invention of Tradition*. Cambridge: Cambridge University Press.

Reader, D. H. 1966. *Zulu Tribe in Transition*. Manchester: Manchester University Press.

Robertson, C. 1984. 'Women in the urban economy' in S. Stichter and M. J. Hay (eds), *African Women South of the Sahara*. London: Longman.

Rogers, S. C. 1975. 'Female forms of power and the myth of male dominance: a model of female/male interaction in peasant society', *American Ethnologist* 2, 727–56.

—— 1978. 'Woman's place: a critical review of anthropological theory', *Comparative Studies in Society and History* 20, 123–62.

Roseberry, W. 1989. *Anthropologies and Histories: essays in culture, history and political economy*. New Brunswick NJ: Rutgers University Press.

Rycroft, D. 1958. 'The new 'town' music of Southern Africa', *Recorded Folk Music* 1.

—— 1977. 'Evidence of stylistic continuity in Zulu 'town' music' in K. P. Wachsmann (ed.), *Essays for a Humanist*. New York: Town House Press.

SAIRR Survey 1966, 1985, 1986, 1987–8. Johannesburg: South African Institute of Race Relations.

Sansom, B. 1970. 'Leadership and Authority in a Pedi Chiefdom', unpublished PhD dissertation, University of Manchester.

—— 1991–2. 'Song and political opposition in Sekhukhuneland, 1961-62', *Anthropological Forum* 6 (3), 393–427.

SAR (South African Review) 1983 (Vol. 1), 1984 (Vol. 2), 1986 (Vol. 3), 1987 (Vol. 4), 1989 (Vol. 5), 1992 (Vol. 6) G. Moss and I. Obery. South African Research Service. Johannesburg: Ravan Press.

Schapera, I. 1940. *Married Life in an African Tribe*. London: Faber and Faber.

—— 1957. 'Marriage of near kin among the Tswana', *Africa* 27 (1), 139–59.

—— 1965. *Praise-Poems of Tswana Chiefs*. Oxford: Oxford University Press.

Schapera, I. and S. Roberts 1975. 'Rampedi revisited: another look at a Kgatla ward', *Africa* 45 (3), 258–79.

Scheub H. 1975. *The Xhosa Ntsomi*. Oxford: Oxford University Press.

Schutte, A. G. 1972. 'Thapelo ya sephiri: a study of secret prayer groups in Soweto', *African Studies* 31 (4), 245–60.

—— 1974. 'Dual religious orientation in an urban African church', *African Studies* 33 (2), 113–20.

Seeger, A. 1987. *Why Suya Sing: a musical anthropology of an Amazonian people*. Cambridge: Cambridge University Press.

Sharma, U. 1986. *Women's Work, Class and the Urban Household: a study of Shimla, North India*. London: Tavistock.

Sharp, J. 1982. 'Relocation and the problem of survival in Qwaqwa: a report from the field', *Social Dynamics* 8 (2), 11–29.

Sharp, J. and A. D. Spiegel 1990. 'Women and wages: gender and the control of income in farm and bantustan households', *Journal of Southern African Studies* 10 (3), 527–49.

Sibisi, H. 1975. 'The place of spirit possession in Zulu cosmology' in M. G. Whisson and M. West (eds), *Religion and Social Change in Southern Africa: anthropological essays in honour of Monica Wilson*. Cape Town: David Philip.

Skinner, E. P. 1974. *African Urban Life: the transformation of Ouagadougou*. Princeton NJ: Princeton University Press.

Southall, A. (ed.) 1973. *Urban Anthropology: cross-cultural studies of urbanization*. New York: Oxford University Press.

—— 1975a. 'Forms of ethnic linkage between town and country' in D. Parkin (ed.), *Town and Country in Central and Eastern Africa*. London: Oxford University Press for the International African Institute.

—— 1975b. 'From segmentary lineage to ethnic association – Luo, Luyia and others', in M. Owusu (ed.), *Essays in honour of Lucy Mair*. Evanston: Northwestern University Press.

Spiegel, A. D. 1980. 'Rural differentiation and the diffusion of migrant labour remittances in Lesotho' in P. Mayer (ed.), *Black Villagers in an Industrial Society*. Cape Town: Oxford University Press.

—— 1987. 'Dispersing dependents: a response to the exigencies of labour migration in rural Transkei' in J. Eades (ed.), *Migrants, Workers and the Social Order*. ASA Monograph 26. London: Tavistock.

—— 1989. 'Towards an understanding of tradition: uses of tradition(al) in apartheid South Africa', *Critique of Anthropology* 9 (1), 49–74.

—— 1990. 'Cohesive cosmologies or pragmatic practices?', *Cahiers d'études africaines* 117 (XXX–XXXI), 45–72.

—— 1991. 'Changing Continuities: experiencing and interpreting history, population movement and material differentiation in Matatiele, Transkei', unpublished PhD dissertation, University of Cape Town.

Spiegel, A. D. and P. A. McAllister (eds) 1991. *Tradition and Transition in Southern Africa: African Studies fiftieth anniversary volume* 50 (1 and 2).

Stadler, J. 1996. 'Witches and witch-hunters: generational relations and the life-cycle in a lowveld village', *African Studies* 55 (1): 87–110.

Stichter, S. 1985. *Migrant Laborers*. Cambridge: Cambridge University Press.

Stichter, S. and M. J. Hay (eds) 1984. *African Women South of the Sahara*. London: Longman.

Sundkler, B. G. M. 1961. *Bantu Prophets in South Africa*. London: Oxford University Press for the International African Institute.

Surplus People Project 1983. *Forced Removals in South Africa. Vols 1 and 5*. 5 vols, Cape Town: Surplus People Project.

Thomas, H. J. 1988. 'Ingoma Dancers and their Response to Town: a study of Ingoma dance troupes among Zulu migrant workers in Durban', unpublished MA dissertation, University of Natal, Durban.

Thomas, N. 1992. 'The inversion of tradition', *American Ethnologist* 19 (2), 213–32.

Thompson, R. F. 1974. *African Art in Motion*. Los Angeles: California University Press.

Tracey, A. 1970a. 'Matepe mbira music', *African Music* 4 (4), 37–61.

—— 1970b. *How to Play the Mbira Dza Vadzimu*. Roodepoort: International Library of African Music.

—— 1971. 'The Nyanga panpipe dance', *African Music* 5 (1), 73–89.

Tracey, H. 1948. *Chopi Musicians: their music, poetry and instruments*. London: Oxford University Press for the International African Institute.

—— 1958. 'Towards an assessment of African scales', *African Music* 2 (1).

—— 1969. 'The Mbira class of instruments in Rhodesia', *African Music* 4 (3), 78–95.

Turino, T. 1988. 'The music of Andean migrants in Lima, Peru: demographics, social power and style', *Latin American Music Review* 9/2, 127–50.

Tyrrell, B. 1968. *Tribal Peoples of Southern Africa*. Cape Town: Books of Africa.

Vail, L. (ed.) 1989a. *The Creation of Tribalism in Southern Africa*. London: James Currey.

—— 1989b. 'Introduction: ethnicity in Southern African history' in L. Vail (ed.), *The Creation of Tribalism in Southern Africa*. London: James Currey.

Vail, L. and L. White 1978. 'Plantation protest: the history of a Mozambican song', *Journal of Southern African Studies* 5 (1), 1–25.

—— 1983. 'Forms of resistance: songs and perceptions of power in colonial Mozambique', *American Historical Review* 88 (4), 883–919.

—— 1991. *Power and the Praise Poem: southern African voices in history*. London: James Currey.

van der Hooft, G. A. 1979. *De Malopodans: een transcultureel-psychiatrische studie*. Leiden: Rodopi.

van Onselen, C. 1975. 'Black workers in central African industry', *Journal of Southern African Studies* 1 (2), 228–46.

—— 1982. 'The witches of suburbia' in *Studies in the Social and Economic History of the Witwatersrand, 1890–1914.* Johannesburg: Ravan Press.

van Warmelo N. J. 1935. *Preliminary Survey of the Bantu Tribes of South Africa.* Ethnological Publication No. 5. Pretoria: Government Printer.

—— 1952. *Language Map of South Africa.* Pretoria: Government Printer.

—— 1953. *Die Tlokwa en Birwa van Noord Transvaal.* Pretoria: Government Printer.

—— 1974. 'The classification of cultural groups' in W. D. Hammond-Tooke (ed.), *The Bantu-Speaking Peoples of Southern Africa.* London: Routledge and Kegan Paul.

van Zyl, H. J. 1941. 'Praises in northern Sotho', *Bantu Studies* 15 (2).

Walker, C. (ed.) 1990a. *Women and Gender in Southern Africa to 1945.* Cape Town: David Philip.

—— 1990b. 'Women and gender in southern Africa to 1945: an overview' in C. Walker (ed.), *Women and Gender in Southern Africa to 1945.* Cape Town: David Philip.

Wallerstein, I. 1963. 'The political role of voluntary associations in middle Africa' in J. S. Coleman and C. Roberg (eds), *Political Groups in Middle Africa.* Berkeley CA: California University Press.

Waterman, C. A. 1990. *Juju: a social history and ethnography of an African popular music.* Chicago: Chicago University Press.

Webster, D. 1991. 'Abafazi Bathonga Bafihlakala: ethnicity and gender in a Kwazulu border community' in A. D. Spiegel and P. A. McAllister (eds), *Tradition and Transition in Southern Africa: African Studies fiftieth anniversary* volume 50 (1 and 2).

West, M. 1975. 'The shades come to town: ancestors and urban independent churches' in M. G. Whisson and M. West (eds), *Religion and Social Change in Southern Africa: anthropological essays in honour of Monica Wilson.* Cape Town: David Philip.

Whisson, M. G. and M. West (eds) 1975. *Religion and Social Change in Southern Africa: anthropological essays in honour of Monica Wilson.* Cape Town: David Philip.

White, L. 1982. 'Power and the praise poem', *Journal of Southern African Studies* 9 (1), 8–32.

Wilmsen, E. 1993. 'Auxiliary Instruments of Labour: the homogenization of diversity in the discourse of ethnicity', mimeo, African Studies Institute Seminar, Witwatersrand University.

Wilmsen, E. and R. Vossen 1990. 'Labour, language and power in the construction of ethnicity in Botswana', *Critique of Anthropology* X (1), 7–37.

Wilson, F. 1972. *Migrant Labour in South Africa.* Johannesburg: SPROCAS/South African Council of Churches.

Wilson, M. 1982. 'The Nguni people' and 'The Sotho, Venda and Tsonga' in M. Wilson and L. Thompson (eds), *The Oxford History of South Africa.* Cape Town: David Philip.

Wilson, M. and L. Thompson (eds) 1982. *The Oxford History of South Africa.* Cape Town: David Philip.

Wolpe, H. 1972. 'Capitalism and cheap labour power in South Africa: from segregation to apartheid', *Economy and Society* 1 (4), 425–56.

Yawitch, J. 1982. *Betterment: the myth of homeland agriculture.* Johannesburg: South African Institute of Race Relations.

Zempleni, A. 1977. 'From symptom to sacrifice: the story of Khady Fall' in V. Crapanzano and V. Garrison (eds), *Case Studies in Spirit-Possession.* New York: John Wiley.

2. GOVERNMENT SOURCES

Informa November/December 1989, 36 (10).

Majority Report of the Eastern Transvaal Natives Land Committee, UG 31–1918. Cape Town: Government Printer.

Minutes of Evidence of the Eastern Transvaal Natives Land Committee, UG 32 1989. Cape Town: Government Printer.

Native Economic Commission, 1930–2, evidence, housed in the Church of the Province Library, Witwatersrand University.

RSA Population Census, 1970, 1985. Cape Town: Government Printer.

3. NEWSPAPERS

Rand Daily Mail 23 August 1984.

Sowetan 16 May 1984.

Weekly Mail 30 August to 5 September 1991.

INDEX